Alexander Del Mar

The Science of Money

Alexander Del Mar

The Science of Money

ISBN/EAN: 9783743317376

Manufactured in Europe, USA, Canada, Australia, Japa

Cover: Foto ©ninafisch / pixelio.de

Manufactured and distributed by brebook publishing software
(www.brebook.com)

Alexander Del Mar

The Science of Money

THE SCIENCE OF MONEY

Price 15s. net.

BY THE SAME AUTHOR.

A

HISTORY

OF

MONETARY SYSTEMS

IN

VARIOUS STATES.

THE
SCIENCE OF MONEY

BY

ALEXANDER DEL MAR, M.E.

FORMERLY DIRECTOR OF THE BUREAU OF STATISTICS OF THE UNITED STATES OF
AMERICA; MINING COMMISSIONER TO THE UNITED STATES MONETARY
COMMISSION OF 1876; AUTHOR OF A "HISTORY OF THE PRECIOUS
METALS," A "HISTORY OF MONEY," ETC., ETC.

SECOND EDITION—REVISED BY THE AUTHOR

LONDON
EFFINGHAM WILSON
ROYAL EXCHANGE
1896

All rights reserved

AMERICAN COPYRIGHT NOTICE.

The first Edition of this work was duly entered according to Act of Congress in the year 1885 by ALEXANDER DEL MAR in the Office of the Librarian of Congress at Washington, D.C.

INTRODUCTION.

ALTHOUGH the commercial world has not yet recovered from the disastrous consequences occasioned by the demonetisation of one of the precious metals, and the engrossment of the other by the money-lenders of the Continent, the recent increase of the gold product is awakening the attention of another class of money-dealers who are already discussing the means of avoiding what appears to them a grave peril to their interests. In other words, a section of Lombard Street is regarding South Africa precisely as La Haute Banque viewed Nevada thirty years ago; and the proposed remedy will probably be of similar character. The reply to Nevada was to close the mints to silver, and keep them open for gold; the reply to South Africa will be, to close them to gold, and reopen them to silver.

Apart from other considerations, the present vast consumption of gold in the arts renders it improbable that the vacuum caused by the demonetisation of silver will ever be filled with gold, whether from Africa or elsewhere. As to the note of alarm which has been sounded by the organs of usury, its sincerity may well be doubted. But assuming it to be both sincere and well-founded it is time to declare in the general interest that this huge see-saw between gold and silver money shall not be permitted to again disturb the affairs of commercial states. Agriculture, Manufactures, Trade, Professional services and Labour, all of which have suffered from the demonetisation of silver, will demand a clear understanding upon the subject, and the establishment of money in each

State upon such an equitable and permanent basis as will satisfy the requirements of justice and of an advancing civilisation. There is no desire to weaken the security of capital, nor to deprive it of its just reward; there is no desire to inflate, any more than there is to contract the currency; there is no desire to experiment with untried moneys or untried principles: but there is a resolve that the monetary mechanism shall no longer be subverted to the intrigues of a few avid men, whose gains have already been so enormous that their presence in a State has come to be regarded as a source of danger.

In short, the promotion of under-handed legislation concerning money can no longer be tolerated. There must be no more pompous Latin Unions, created to dupe the vain, trap the unwary, and enlist the treacherous; no more surreptitious suppressions of Royal Prerogatives; no more Mint Codes, to be read by title and enacted in secret; no more deceptively Revised Statutes, to be passed *en bloc;* and no more incumbents of high office betrayed or allured. These disgraceful devices and practices are of the past; in future, the noisy clamourers for "honest money" must bow to the decision of the State on this subject; or, like the Tarpeian woman, they will be left to perish beneath the objects of their own avidity. Although the gold of South Africa is being produced at the present time with labour which costs but £3 a month, the system has to be sustained by methods that are rapidly exploiting the labourers, and may render it necessary ere long to recruit them from the working classes of Europe;—an event that will entirely change the bearings of this industry.

If an equitable settlement of monetary systems can be brought about, the past thirty years of financial intrigue, and the industrial distress to which it has led, will not have been suffered by the community in vain. For two hundred and odd years the goldsmith and money-lending class have used a Public Measure—the coins of the realm

—as an instrument of their own enrichment and aggrandisement; in this design they have not scrupled at dissimulation, treachery, the employment of bribery, or the altering of ancient statutes. But this is all over now; South Africa has followed too closely upon the heels of the silver demonetisation. The present generation cannot again be inveigled into an alteration of the monetary laws, either in or out of an international convention, without scrutinising very closely the character and bearing of the proposed alteration. The anticipated plethora of gold, should it occur, will hoist the goldsmiths with their own petard, and in all future settlements of the currency question, they will have to come to terms with Industry, or else stay where the petard will leave them.

It is therefore timely to discuss these terms. Previous to the reign of the Stuarts, the entire institution of money was in the hands of the State. Said Malynes, writing in 1603: "Money being the Public Measure to maintain a certain equality in buying and selling, must therefore have his (its) standing valuation only by public authority of Princes, as a matter annexed to their crown and dignities; for they be the warrant of the money unto their subjects. And to the end that this Measure of Things, namely Money, should not be falsified, by making the same generally more or less (whereby the price of things would become incertain, if private men be suspected to have the handling thereof), therefore, are Princes so careful to observe a certainty and equality of the price of Money from time to time."

The decision rendered by the Privy Council in 1604, given at length in the present work, established the Public and Social character of money even more distinctly and emphatically. It recognised money as a Measure, whose equitable operation could only be secured by the State, which therefore was alone entrusted with the power to "make the same generally more or less" (as Malynes puts it), by increasing or diminishing its volume, or altering the composition of its symbols. The Council sustained these principles by an array of philosophical authority and legal precedents, which extended backwards to the remote æra of the Greek republics, and which is not without its echo in more recent opinion.[1]

But the plunder of India and America which occurred during the Stuart dynasty, overthrew both law and philosophy. It rendered abortive every attempt on the part of the Bench, even of the Crown, to retain for the State the time-honoured and necessary prerogative of Coinage. Scipio's plunder of Spain, his destruction of the nummulary system of Rome, and his intrigues and embezzlements of the *opima spolia*, were enacted all over again.

First at Goa, afterwards in Spanish America, and eventually in Holland and England, the avidity of the plunderers abroad and of the money-lenders with whom they were in league at home, broke down every safeguard of the law, destroyed every limitation of the monetary measure, and reduced money to the degraded position of metal, or *ponderata*. This was done by legally permitting individual or private coinage, subject to the stamp of the mint. Under this law the owners of bullion could increase the currency by having their metal coined, or diminish it by melting the coins, and so could alter the Measure of Value at pleasure without loss or expense; the State even consenting to perform gratuitously the mechanical work of coinage and the detective work of incriminating counterfeiters. Such was the practical outcome of the Act of 1666, and such is the law to this day. A more senseless and mischievous Act was never procured.

Upon the working of this law was erected an entirely new and fallacious theory concerning the Wealth of

[1] "To put this currency upon a proper footing it is indispensable that it should be issued by Government, and Government only."—Sir Archibald Alison's *History of Europe*, Vol. VIII., p. 119.

Nations, its origin and its mode of increase; a theory which was never heard of before, and will not be heard of again whenever the coinage and the melting down or exporting of the national Measure of Value shall cease to be prostituted to private cupidity. The name which has been given to this law and theory is the Mercantile System: its proper name is Metallism. It assumes among other things that value is an intrinsic attribute of matter, the expression "intrinsic value" occurring so early as the Dutch Mint Act of July 21st, 1622; that exchange, even in civilised States, is conducted upon the basis of the cost of production; and that money is and must necessarily be a commodity, valued as such, namely (so runs the theory) at the cost of the production of coins, which cost, in most cases, down to that time, was in point of fact chiefly rapine, slavery and murder. All of these assumptions are taught and widely entertained at the present day. Neither of them, as this work will endeavour to show, has any foundation whatever in fact.

Value is a numerical relation; it is not inherent, it is not intrinsic, it is not an attribute of matter, it does not exist in the isolated state, it only occurs in the social state, and is determined solely by exchange. Value is measured not by the circumstances of production, but by those of exchange. The value of a commodity is the number of other commodities it will fetch in exchange; it is not the efforts nor the things that the commodity cost to produce or may cost to reproduce.

The value or purchasing power of the gold produced by savage labour in South Africa or coolie labour in Asia does not and will not follow the cost of its production, but will be derived from its parity in the exchanges. The cost may (or it may not) affect the quantity produced, and the quantity may (or it may not) affect the value; but cost has no necessary nor direct influence upon value, which arises immediately from exchange. Go into the bourses of the world, and ask those dealers whose transactions embrace the principal exchanges in finance and commerce if they buy or sell upon the basis of the cost of production, and they will smile at the simplicity of the question. Yet these dealers, when, in some unprofessional movement, they air their own knowledge of political economy, will tire you out with this same cost-of-production theory which they have inherited from the schools, and which, though totally unknown to their practice, still lingers upon their lips.

Upon what basis, then, it may be asked, are commodities and services exchanged, not in the remote past, not among savage or semi-civilised communities, but now, and here, in the commercial States of Christendom? The answer is: Upon the basis of number, the relative numbers of commodities and services offered for exchange in a given time. And the just measure of this numerical relation?

Is Money. This, in each State, consists of a limited number of Denominations impressed upon ponderable symbols, which are legally receivable for public rates and taxes, and payable for private debts.

And Price?

Before going any further with this catechism, let it be observed that the principles conveyed in the answers are not drawn from the realms of dogma, but from the practical workings of monetary systems that cover a period not merely of two, but of twenty-five centuries, and from precepts which are embalmed in legal codes of great antiquity, which principles, therefore, constitute all that we have any right to regard as the Science of Money. They may appear unfamiliar to those who have been educated in the schools of the prevalent system; but the Bench continues to recognise them, and practical men employ them in their everyday transactions. In short, they are sanctified both by law and custom.

To say that Price is value expressed in money is to give a definition where an explanation is required. Such an explanation may best be afforded by means of an illustration. If, in a given community, it were necessary for the purposes of distribution to transact a thousand exchanges per diem, if the subjects of each exchange proved to be of equal value, and the money of such community consisted of a thousand "sovereigns" with a circulating velocity of once a day, the price of each commodity or service exchanged would necessarily be just one "sovereign," no matter whether the "sovereigns" cost much or little to produce, no matter whether they were made of gold or glass. A change in either of the factors would result in a change of price. If the exchanges were more or less rapid, prices would change; or if the money circulated more or less rapidly, prices would change. In a certain sense, therefore, price is a relation between two velocities.

A London bill-broker recently favoured the author with the following rough estimate of the exchanges and circulating money of the United Kingdom; exchanges, about 23,000,000,000 of pounds a year, say £23,400,000,000; circulation (including coins, notes, bills of exchange, promissory notes and open accounts, all reduced to a like velocity of use and re-use), £130,000,000, with a mean velocity of once in two days, or 180 times a year. Therefore $130 \times 180 = 23,400$ millions a year, identical with the annual sum of exchanges. The result of this equation is the present level of prices. It is evident that if either of these factors were changed, prices would change; and that this would occur, and would have to occur, without the slightest reference to cost of production. It is not denied that cost of production has an important relation to price; what is asserted is that after price and cost of production have mutually affected each other to the utmost extent, price has to undergo a further modification, one that has no relation to cost of production, but only to money and exchanges and to their relative velocities.

Whether *par pro pari* arose teleologically from the

desire of personal safety, or military ascendancy, or from equality of service or sacrifice, or from passion or caprice, it is not the province of this work to inquire. Practical Science knows nothing about *first causes*. The remote origins of customs may with advantage be left to the researches of antiquarians. The practical world wants a working theory or explanation of money as it now stands in law and fact; a theory which explains precisely what money does, and precisely how it does it. The explanation is, that money measures value by expressing it in price, and that price is a numerical relation expressed in the symbols of money, a relation between two sums and velocities, the sum of exchanges in time, and the sum of the circulation in time. The illustrious John Stuart Mill distinctly laid the foundation of this theory when he said that "the value of money is inversely as its quantity multiplied by what is called the rapidity of circulation". Our merchants tacitly recognise the theory when they consult the bank clearings and discounts, because these indicate the increase or diminution in the sum of exchanges which is to be measured by money; they act upon the theory when their transactions are guided by the shipments or movements of gold, because, as the law of money now stands, these movements rudely mark the shrinkage or augmentation of money in the State. If money ever ceases to be made of the precious metals, the merchants will have fewer of these distracting indications to watch; they will be enabled to concentrate their attention upon their own proper province, the movement of commodities, and to leave money, as they now leave the regulation of other public measures, to the custody and consideration of the State.

Since the enactment of the law of 1666, which destroyed Money as a Public Measure, and surrendered the regulation of its volume to private hands, those hands have, through its powerful agency, grasped control not only of all the metallic money, but also of a considerable portion of the other wealth of the kingdom. Among the various devices procured or employed by them have been: I. Frequent alterations of the ratio between gold and silver coins. These alterations have since been ascribed to the work of nature, the operation of the market, the caprice of princes, and a variety of other fanciful causes. The petitions, cahiers and plakkarts of the period to which they refer, prove that they often originated with the money-lenders themselves. II. Changing the material of full legal tender coins from gold to silver, or silver to gold. III. Issuing convertible notes upon an inconvertible basis. IV. Alternately swelling and shrinking the currencies of particular States, by monopolising the produce of mines, shipping bullion to and fro, transferring securities from one State to another, speculating in exchange, and other like practices. The colossal profits of these operations have been drawn from the channels of Industry, which now demands, not yet an indemnity, but such a settlement of the monetary laws as will cease to afford facilities for their repetition.

The basis of such a settlement must be the re-establishment of the Royal Prerogative of money, that complete restoration of its control by the State, without which experience has abundantly shown that the preservation of equitable relations between the various individuals and classes of society is utterly impossible. The time of this settlement should not be longer delayed. The real or fancied interests of money-lenders may deter *them* from urging any change in the coinage laws until the anticipated flow of gold from Africa and Russian Asia becomes more marked. But the requirements of justice and the welfare of the industrial classes demand reform at once. By such reform is not meant the abandonment of gold and silver coins, but an abandonment of the law of private or "free" coinage. The details of the settlement may safely be left to the wisdom of the Executive Government. They should embrace a provision that the banks may retain their existing privileges of issuing circulating notes, but subject always to the control of the State, so that such notes may form a fixed and definite portion of the whole Measure of Value. In short, the essential reform of Money which is suggested by the study of its history and principles, is the repeal of that clause of the Act 18 Chas. II., c. 5, which gave to "private men the handling thereof".

BIBLIOGRAPHY.

The following list of books is to be read in connection with the lists published in the Author's previous works on the Precious Metals and Money. The numbers at foot of each title are the press-marks of the British Museum Library.

AGUILERA Y VELASCO. Código Civil Italiano. Madrid. 1877. 8vo. 5373. h. 15.
ALI IBU HUSAIN. Ibu Ali (Abu al-Hasan). Al-Masudi. De rebus Indiæ loci. Arab. and Lat. 1838. 8vo. 14565. b. 15.
——— Hist. Encyclopedia, trans. by A. SPRENGER. 1841. 8vo. 752. g. 29.
——— Account of the . . Fatimite Dynasty in Africa. A.H. 290-300. Tübingen. 1840. 8vo. 14555. c. 5.
ARENDT (OTTO). Der Wahrungsstreit in Deutschland. Berlin. 1886. 8vo. 8226. b. 1.
BACHE (ALEX.). Report on Weights and Measures. Washington. 1857. 8vo.
BARBOUR (D.). Theory of Bimetallism. London. 1886. 8vo. 8226. eee. 28.
BARNARD (Prof. A. J.). Metric System. Washington. 1862. 8vo.
BAYLE (PETER). Historical and Critical Dictionary, trans. by DE MAIZEAUX. London. 1734-8. 5 vols., fol. 2037. f.
BÉDARRIDE. De la Lettre de Change.
BLANCHET (J. A.). Manuel Numismatique. 1890.
BOISTEL. Manuel de Droit Commercial. Paris. 1887. 8vo. 6825. b. 5.
BOSANQUET (CHARLES). Practical Observations on the Report of the Bullion Committee. 2nd ed., with Supplement. London. 1810. 8vo. 1028. e. 2. (1).
BRAVARD-VEYRIERES. Traité de Droit Commercial. Paris. 1862-5. 6 vols. 8vo.
BRIGHTLY (F. C.). Digest of the Laws of Pennsylvania: a Continuation of Purdon's Digest. Phila. 1873-8. 3 vols. 8vo. 6752. c.
——— Digest of Decisions. 1754 to 1877.
CACHARD (HENRY). The French Civil Code. London. 1895. 8vo. 5423. df. 7.
CARLI (G. R.). Dell' origine e del comercio, della moneta dell' instituzione delle zecche Italia della decadenza dell' Imperio sino al secolo decimo-settimo. All Haja. 1751. 4to. See *Magistris*. 664. c. 27 (4).
CASSATION (COUR DE). See *France*.
CHEVASSUS (H.). L'Etalon monetaire universel. London. 1883. 8vo. 8229. de. 30 (7).
CINAGLI (ANGELO). Monete de' Papi. Fermo. 1848. Folio. 603. l. 29.
COBBETT. See *State Trials*.
COLINET DE SANTERRE (E.). Manuel élémentaire de Droit Civil. Paris. 1844. 8vo. 5423. de. 8.
COUR DES MONNAIS. See *France*.
DALLAS (A. J.). Reports of Cases Ruled and Adjudged in the Courts of Pennsylvania. 6752. a.
DALLOZ (E.). Jurisprudence Générale. Paris. 1878. 3 vols. 8vo. 5406. ff. 9.
DALLOZ-VERGÉ (Edouard Dalloz; Charles Vergé). Les Codes Annotés. Code de Commerce. Paris. 1877. 4to.

b

DALSÈME (J.). La Monnaie. Illustrated. Paris. 1882. 8vo. 12205. ff.
DAVIES (Sir JOHN). Les Reports des Cases et Matters, en Ley, resolves
    et adjuges en les Courts del Rey en Ireland. London. 1674.
    Quarto.   510. k. 20 (1).
——— A Report of Cases Adjudged . . in Ireland. Dublin. 1762.
    Fol.   20. a. 19.
DESTUTT DE TRACY (A. L. C.). Economie Politique. Paris. 1825. 12mo.
                                                        08207. de. 1.
DU CHAILLU (PAUL). The Viking Age. London. 1889. 2 v. 8vo. 2259. c. 17.
ECKHEL (JOSEPH H. VON). Doctrina Numorum Veterum Conscripta.
    2 Pt. Vindobonæ. 1792-8. 4to.   674. g. 11.
ECKHEL (JOSEPH H. VON) and KOLB (G. J.). Traité Élémentaire de
    Numismatique. Paris. 1825. 8vo.   602. f. 25.
ENGLAND. Mint. Some Reasons humbly offered for the Speedy Opening
    of the Mint to the Coining of Silver. London. 1695. Fol.
                                                        816. m. 10-20.
——— Court of Star Chamber. The Stop and Refusal of Farthing
    Tokens. Order Restricting their Issue. London. 1634.
    Fol.   506. h. 12-39.
——— Star Chamber. Report of Cases in the Courts of Star Chamber
    and High Commission. (Star Chamber, Easter, 1631 to
    Trinity, 1632; High Com., October, 1631, to June, 1632.)
    London. 1886. 4to. (Camden Society.)   Ac. 8113-126.
——— Proclamations by the King (James I. and Charles I.) 1604-35
    relating to the Coinage.
FIORAVANTE (B.). Italian Numismatics. 1734. 4to.   602. c. 26 (6).
FRANCE. Coleccion de las Causas mas Celebres. Parte Francesca.
    Barcelona. 1855-60. 4 tom. 8vo.   6056. cc.
——— Annuaire de Legislation Etrangère. Paris. 1872, etc. In
    progress.   Ac. 2115. c. 3.
——— Journal du Palais. Recueil le plus complet de la Jurispru-
    dence Francaise. Paris. 8vo. 1750, annually to the present
    time.   PP. 1369.
——— Cour de Cassation. Bulletin des Arrêts de la Cour de Cassation
    rendus en matière civile. Années, 1860 à 1876.   PP. 1371.
——— Cour des Monnais. Ordonnance faicts par les Court des
    Monnoyers—1555—des Monoyer de Billon, etc. Paris. 1556.
    8vo.   7755. aa. 24.
——— Ordonnances des Monnoyers, 16me siècle.   7755. aa. 1-28.
——— Gazette des Tribunaux. Paris. In progress. Fol. Years
    1862-1876. (No index to this publication in the Br. Mu. Lib.
    since 1861.)   PP. 9466.
FULLARTON (JOHN), F.R.A.S. On the Regulation of Currencies.
    London. 1844. 8vo.   1390. f. 7.
FUZIER-HERMAN (EDOUARD). Repertoire Générale Alphabetique du
    Droit Francais. Paris. 1886, etc. 4to.   5424. ee. 6.
GALIANI (FERDINANDO), Abbate. Della Moneta. Libri Cinque. Napoli.
    1750. 4to.   278. i. 10.
GALLAND (ANTOINE). Touchant Quatre Médailles Antiques. Caen.
    1697. 8vo.   602. a. 35 (2).
GARDINER (SAMUEL RAWSON). See England. Star Chamber.
GARIEL (E.). Monnaies Royales de France. Strasbourg.   1883. Fol.
GNECCHI (FRANCESCO and ERCOLE). Saggio di Bibliografia Numis-
    matica delle Zecche Italiane Medicevale e Moderne. Pp. xxi.-
    468. Milano. 1889. 8vo.   011902. k. 36.
——— Le Monete di Milano. Milano. 1884. 8vo.   7757. i. 12.
——— Monnais de l'Empire Romaine, etc. 1894. 8vo.   7757. h. 13.
——— Guida Numismatica Universale . . Contenente 2322 nomi,
    etc. Pp. xxxii.-325. Milano. 1886. 8vo.   7756. b. 10.

GRIOLET-VERGÉ. Repertoire Alphabetique de Legislation de Doctrine et de Jurisprudence. Paris. 1894. 4to.
GROTIUS (HUGO). De Jure Belli ac Pacis, Libri tres, etc. Amstelaedami. 1720. 8vo. G. 19406.
—— Eng. trans., by J. Morrice. London. 1715. 3 vols. 8vo. 1127. d. 2-4.
—— An abridged trans., by W. Whewell. Cambridge. 1853. 8vo. 6955. d.
GIBBONS (RODMOND). Physics and Metaphysics of Money. Money in the Early History of California. New York. 1886. 8vo. 8223. aa. 6.
HARVEY (WILLIAM H.). See *Horr*.
HAZLITT (WM. C.). History of the Republic of Venice. London. 1858. 4 vols. 8vo.
—— Coinages and Mints of Europe. London. 1893. 8vo.
HORR (Hon. ROSWELL G.). The Great Debate between Hon. Roswell, G. Horr, and William H. Harvey. Chicago. 1895. 8vo.
HOWE (J. B.). Economy in the Use of Money. Boston. 1878. 8vo. 8206. ff. 9.
—— Common Sense and Metaphysics of Money. Boston. 1881. 8vo. 8229. c. 8.
HUGHES (THOMAS P.). Dictionary of Islam. Articles: Money, Quintar, Dinar, Dirhem, Mines, etc.
HUME (DAVID). Essays. London. 1764. 2 vols. 8vo. 8405. h. 23.
JOURNAL DU PALAIS. See *France*.
JUSTICE (ALEXANDER). A General Treatise of the Dominion and Laws of the Sea . . and Trade . . and Law of Insurances. London. 1705. Fol. 21. a. 12.
KEBLE (JOSEPH). The Statutes at Large in Paragraphs. London. 1676. Fol. 506. h. 2.
KITSON (ARTHUR). A Scientific Solution of the Money Question. Philadelphia. 1895. 8vo.
LANGLOIS (VICTOR). Numismatique de la Géorgie. Paris. 1852. 4to.
—— Numismatique de l'Armenie. Paris. 1855. 4to. 7756. e. 20
LEBER (M. C.). Essai sur l'Application de la Fortune Privée au Moyen Age. Paris. 2nd ed. 1847. 8vo. Pp. 340.
LEBER, SALGUES, and COHEN. Collection, etc., Relatif à l'Histoire de France. Paris. 1826. 8vo.
LOCKE (JOHN). Essays on Money, Interest and Trade. London. 1696. 12mo.
LOCRÉ (J. G.). Esprit du Code Napoleon. Paris. 1805. 5 vols. in 3. 4to. (The Commentary ends with Art. 515.) 5405. g. 2.
—— Legislation Etrangère. Paris. 8vo.
LOWNDES (WILLIAM). A Further Essay for the Amendment of the Gold and Silver Coins. London. 1695. 4to. 8223. a. 35.
LYON-CAEN and RENAULT. Traité de Droit Commercial. 2e ed. (The 1e ed. was crowned by the Institute: Prize Wolowski.) Paris. 1893. 5 vols. 8vo. See *Bravard-Veyrieres*. 6825. eee. 6.
The much vaunted, praised, and rewarded work of Lyon-Caen has no general index, nor no reference to the articles in the Civil Code relating to the Law of Money. Vol. IV., under *Lettres de Change*, commences with the archaism that money is a commodity; that the symbols have the same value before and after they are stamped; and that the stamp merely certifies the weight and fineness, which latter fix the value, irrespective of the stamp! Money is accordingly defined as follows : *un lingot dont le poids et le titre sont certifiés par l'autorité.*
MCCULLOCH (J. R.). Political Economy. London. 1854. 8vo.
MACLEOD (N.). Bimetallism. 2nd ed. London. 1894. 8vo.
MAGISTRIS (S. M. DE). Delle osservazionè sopra di un libro intitolato Dell' Origine e del Comercio, della-Moneta, etc. *A reply to Carli*. Roma. 1752. 4to. 8226. g. 4.
MALYNES (GERARD DE). England's View on the Unmasking of Two Paradoxes. London. 1603. 12mo. 712. c. 1 (1).
—— Consuetudo, vel Lex Mercatoria, or the Ancient Law Merchant. London. 1686. Fol. 509. h. 4.

MARTELLO (TULLIO). La Moneta. Firenze. 1883. 8vo. 8228. b. 25.
MARX (CARL). Capital: a Critical Analysis of Capitalist Production. Translated from the 3rd German ed. by S. Moore and E. Aveling. London. 1887. 2 vols. 8vo. 2240. bb. 10.
MASSÉ (GABRIEL). Le Droit Commercial. Paris. 1844-7. 6 v. 8vo. 822. g.
MASUDI. See *Ali Ibn Husain*.
MESSEDAGLIA (A.). La Moneta e il Sistema Monetario. Roma. 1882. 8vo. 8229. i. 12 (3).
MINT. See *England*.
MOLINAEUS (CAROLUS). De Mutatione Monetæ. Cologne. 1591. 4to.
MONTESQUIEU (CHAS. DE, SECONDAT, *Baron of*). Esprit des Lois. London. 1752. 2 vols. 8vo. 6281. cc. 20.
MORÉRI (LOUIS). Le Grand Dictionnaire Historique. Lyon-Paris. 1688-9. 3 tom. Fol. 610. m. 9-11.
MULLER (LUDWIG). Undersögelse af græske Mynter med Tegnet Tau til Typ. (Examen des monnais grecques ayant pour type le signe *tau*.) Kjöbenhavn. 1859. 8vo.
MUN (THOMAS). England's Treasure, by Forraign Trade. Written 1664, republished 1895. London. 12mo.
NICHOLAS (Sir EDWD.). See *Warner*.
NUMISMATIC CHRONICLE. London.
PACIFICI-MAZZONI (EMIDIO). Codice Civile Italiano Comentato. 3rd ed. Firenze. 1875. 6 vols. 8vo. (Incomplete.) 5322. bbb.
PARTINGTON (C. F.). *Scientific Gazette*. On the Ducat; on Scythian Origin of Money, etc. London. 1826-31. 5 vols. 4to. PP. 1680.
—— The British Encyclopedia. London. 1835. 2 vols. 4to.
PLEBANO (A.). Sulla Moneta e Sul Biglietto di Banco. Roma. 1884. 8vo. (Tipogr. dell' "Opiñione," pr. 4 lire.) 8226. eee. 20.
The keynote of this work is furnished in the following extract, from p. 19:—
"Un sistema monetario, qualunque esso sia organizzato a base di numerazione, deve anzitutto avere stabilita un' unità che la numerazione permetta. E poichè ciò che qui si tratta, per cosi dire, di disciplinare e l'uso del metallo, l'unità monetaria sarà costitua, scegliendo per essa una quantita di metallo esattamente determinata in ragione del suo peso. Poco importa se questa quantita sia grande o piccola; basta che essa sia stabilmente determinata, che tutti la conoscano e che sulla base di essa, ed attorno ad essa, tutto il sistema venga coordinato."
PUFFENDORF (SAMUEL DE). De Jure Nat. et Gentium.
PUTTER (JOHN S.). Institutiones Juris publici Germanici. Goettingae. 1770. 8vo. 502. c. 20. (2).
REVUE DE LA NUMISMATIQUE FRANCOISE. Blois (afterwards Paris). In progress. 8vo. PP. 1877 and 836.
ROUSSET (G.). Analyse Critique et Rédaction Nouvelle du Code Napoleon. (Incomplete.) Toulon. 1867. 8vo. 5405. d. 2.
SARRAZIN (T.). Le Tresor. Paris. 1865. 8vo. 5423 b.
SAVOT (LOUIS). De Raris et Communibus Imperatorum Romanorum Nummis Judicium. 1770. 8vo. 2072. a.
STATE TRACTS. For Darien Scheme and Spanish Cruelty to the American Indians, see Vol. III., p. 495.
STATE TRIALS. Cobbett's Complete Collection of. London. 1809. 8vo. See Vol. II., p. 114, for Case of the Mixt Moneys. 2019. d.
STATISTICAL SOCIETY. Journal of the. London. 1880-95. 2097. d.
STATUTES. See *Keble*.
TOOKE and NEWMARCH. History of Prices. London. 1857. 6 vols. 8vo.
VANDENPEEREBOOM. Numismatique Yproise. 1877. 8vo.
VATTEL (EMER DE). Les Droits des Gens. Leide. 1758. 2 vols. 4to.
VILLANI. History of Florence.
VOLTAIRE (F. M. A. DE). General History. London, 1754. 3 vols, 8vo,

WALLACE (JOHN WILLIAM). Cases Argued and Adjudged in the Supreme Court of the United States. 22 vols. 8vo.   6614. cc. & d.
WARNER (G. F.). Selections from the Papers of Sir Edward Nicholas, Secretary of State to Charles I. and Charles II. London. (Camden Soc.) 1886. 4to.   Ac. 8113-127.
WESTON (A.). Treatise on Money. New York. 1880. 8vo.
WHEATON (HENRY). Elements du Droit International. Leipzig. 2 v. 8vo.
WOOLHOUSE (W. S. B.). Measures and Moneys of all Nations. London. 1881. 6th ed. 12mo.   8548. bbb. 10.

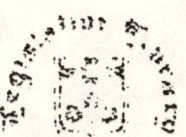

CONTENTS.

Chapter I.

EXCHANGE. Exchange is a social act—The Greek, Roman, and French philosophers deemed exchange and money as part of the structure of society—Barter—Distinction between barter and selling for money—Essential characteristics of money—It constitutes a public measure—Barter leads to slavery; money to freedom—Effigy of Liber Pater on ancient coins—Its significance—Enslavement of the Frisians—The dangers of metallism have given rise in modern times to an increasing proportion of paper promises to serve as money—Dangers arising from their assumed convertibility 1

Chapter II.

VALUE IS A NUMERICAL RELATION. Legal use of the words "unit of value"—Their importance—They are not defined in the law—Unit a synonym for measure—Evolution of the word "value"—Its classical meaning related to the power of numbers—During the Dark Ages it became associated with labour—In the Renaissance it acquired the meaning of an attribute of matter—Fallacy of this last view—The correct nature of value rediscovered by Montesquieu and Bastiat—Value shown to be a numerical ratio between all exchanged things—Value measurable by the whole numbers of money—The existing mint laws practically make the whole numbers of money (or the unit or measure of value) to consist of an indefinite sum, whose only limits fluctuate between illimitable demand and uncertain supply. . . 7

Chapter III.

PRICE. It is the expression of value in money—Price implies precision—It is intended to be a precise expression of value—But this it cannot be unless the whole sum of money is limited and known—Harris, Smith, Mill, Locke, Hume—Price cannot be definitely expressed in a single coin independently of others—Prices of commodities tend to fall; of services to rise—This tendency defeated by private coinage and the monopolisation of gold—Price not due to cost of production; it expresses a dynamical or kinetic relation between money and exchanges in time 20

Chapter IV.

MONEY IS A MECHANISM. Money is a mechanism designed to measure value with precision—The law alone can determine what is and what is not money—The function of money correctly understood by Aristotle—During, or shortly previous to, the æra of that philosopher, the volume of money in each country was limited, and it formed a definite measure of value therein—It is now everywhere unlimited, and has lost its character of an exact measure—Money at present is not defined in the laws. For this reason it is unlike all other measures—Money is intended, but not now fitted, for a measure—The size or weight of a dollar or pound sterling furnishes no guide to the whole number of dollars or pounds: yet it is this which constitutes the measure of value—The measuring function of money is altered with every change in the whole number of so-called units of value—Not so with the units of weight, length, volume or area . . 25

Chapter V.

CONSTITUENTS OF A MONETARY MECHANISM. Control over the precious metals—Mines royal—Treasure trove—Control of the coinage—Use of two or more metals for coins—Coins as numerical symbols—Size, weight, fineness and shape—Mark of authority—Denominations—Compulsory use—Legal-tender—Restrictions upon hoarding, melting, or exporting—Counterfeiting—Interdict of private coinage—Taxes on mining, etc.—Most of these regulations are now overthrown—Private coinage has degraded money to metal—The use of metal in place of money reduces all commerce to the basis of barter—Numerous States have avoided this by resorting to paper systems, and this tendency is increasing—The demonetisation of silver is promoting that of gold 57

Chapter VI.

HISTORY OF MONETARY MECHANISMS. Evolution of money—Barter—Valuing commodity—Baugs—Coins—Their defects—Nomisma—Its downfall—Coins subjected to legal and sacerdotal regulations—Monetary systems of the Roman Empire and of European States—Coinage Acts of the sixteenth century—Origin and progress of private coinage—Private money, or metallism—This is the present phase of monetary mechanisms—It is virtually a return to barter—Its consequences have been the enrichment of money-lenders and the impoverishment of States—The remedy adopted in many States has been paper systems 60

Chapter VII.

THE LAW OF MONEY. The Greek law—The Roman law—The Common law—Philip le Bel—Decision under English law—Corn rents—The Code Napoleon—The Court of Cassation—Decisions of the United States Supreme Court—Metallic theory—Black Laws of James III. of Scotland—Special Contract Law of 1878—Disastrous effects of this legislation—Imperative demand for its repeal—The Law of Nations relative to money 95

Chapter VIII.

THE UNIT OF MONEY IS ALL MONEY. Origin of the word "money"—Its employment with reference to any period before B.C. 273 an anachronism—Money, or *nomisma*, meant originally the whole numbers of money—This was its classical meaning—During the Empire and the Dark Ages money came to mean one or more coins—This is the meaning attached to it in the laws of modern nations, because these laws originated in the Dark Ages—During the Renaissance it meant the whole quantity, not numbers, of money—This is the meaning sometimes attached to it by the Economists, because their systems date from the Renaissance—Incongruous nature of this definition—In speaking with precision, money can only mean all the numbers of money of a given country—Teleologically, the unit of money is all money 109

CHAPTER IX.

MONEYS CONTRASTED WITH OTHER MEASURES. Differences between moneys and other measures, even when both are limited—1. Money is used to determine the value of numberless things at the same time; a yard-stick to determine the length of one thing at a time—2. Money determines a dynamical and variable relation; other measures, a statical and fixed one—3. Money determines a numerical and extrinsic relation; other measures determine quantitative or qualitative attributes—4. Money determines an equitable relation; other measures determine quantities which have no connection with equity—5. Moneys have a tendency to instantly amalgamate, and two or more moneys will merge into one money of the combined volume of both, which is not the case with other measures . . . 123

CHAPTER X.

LIMITATION IS THE ESSENCE OF MONEYS. Resemblances between money and other measures—All measures of precision are of artificial dimensions—To become a precise measure money must also be of artificial dimensions—All other measures are susceptible of exact numerical expression—To become a just measure money must be defined numerically—The efficiency of all measures, money included, depends upon the exactness of their limits, not the substance of which they may be composed—The limits of other measures are not left to be determined by supply or demand, nor should be those of money . 127

CHAPTER XI.

LIMITATION: A PREROGATIVE OF STATE. The limitation of the monetary measure was anciently a prerogative of State—Its surrender by the State in the sixteenth century—Since that period money has been in a chaotic condition—The "automatic system" is no system at all—Neither individuals nor corporations can regulate money—The State alone can do this—Nor may the State do it arbitrarily—Circumstances and considerations that should control State action on the subject 130

CHAPTER XII.

UNIVERSAL MONEY A CHIMERA. This project was born with the legislation which permitted private coinage—Its progress down to the present time—Its agency in elevating and enriching the moneyed class—Their advantages threatened by the growing use of government paper money—Universal money is a scheme to enable these advantages to be retained by the money-lenders—Its impracticable character—Universal money impossible without universal government—Evils and dangers of national metallism—These are now local—With universal metallism they would become general—It threatens the autonomy of the State—It tends to degrade Europe to the level of India—Absolute measures of value—The basis of "universal money" is the cupidity of the money-lenders 134

CHAPTER XIII.

CAUSES AND ANALYSIS OF A RATE OF INTEREST. Causes of a rate of interest—Temporary supply of money—Rate of profit in trade—Rate of profit in production—Rate at which animals, plants and minerals increase—Rate at which the means of subsistence increase—Subsistence ultimately governs the rate of interest—Subsistence also governs the growth of population; so that population and the rate of interest are related—When to the rate of interest, arising from increase of subsistence, there are added allowances for risk, taxes, and the cost of superintending loans, the market rate of interest follows—Present tendency of the market rate—Ignorance of American ministers of finance—Usury laws 142

CHAPTER XIV.

VELOCITY OF CIRCULATION. Opinions of Locke, Thornton, Mill, and Fawcett—Elements of the calculation—Money used for paying labour—Money and credits used for commerce—Transportation—Finance—Real estate transactions—Money used for insurance—Savings—Taxes—Summary—Comparison with actual circulation and reserves—Deduced rate of velocity—Unwarranted conclusions of Mr. Horr and others—Coincidence of the sum of exchanges with that of money and credits, when reduced to a like velocity 148

CHAPTER XV.

RELATION OF MONEY TO PRICES. Given the level of prices and the sum of exchanges in time, the sum and velocity of the circulation are deducible—Prices have nothing to do with the material of money—Nor value with the names of coins—Blunder of striving to maintain metallic systems with private coinage—Voice of authority—Logic of events—Nearly every modern State has been obliged to abandon such systems—Example of Russia—False principles deduced from metallism—Different influences on prices and trade, of metallism and numerical money 164

CHAPTER XVI.

INCREASING AND DIMINISHING MONEYS. The fallacy that value flows from labour—Dr. Smith and Bastiat—Error of supposing that the currency of a State cannot be artificially increased—Historical examples to the contrary—Milan—Spanish America—The United States during the Civil War—Crescendo and diminuendo moneys . 170

CHAPTER XVII.

EFFECTS OF EXPANSION AND CONTRACTION. Consequences of increasing and decreasing moneys—Their influence upon trade, upon social and domestic relations, upon character, upon genius and invention, upon morality, upon crime, upon political affairs—Opinion of the Monetary Commission—Social consequences of contraction—Opinion of Mr. Tooke—Influence of expansion upon enterprise and art—Money and civilisation—The halcyon age of Europe 177

Chapter XVIII.

THE PRECESSION OF PRICES. Explanation of price—It cannot be expressed in a given coin or sum of coins independent of other coins—It varies directly with the whole numbers of money—Logically a doubling of money will instantly effect a doubling of all prices—In point of fact, this doubling occurs in time, and the time varies in various States and with different commodities—This variance subject to natural law—Such law called the Precession of Prices, or Movement of Prices in Time—Results of practical observations on the working of this law—Danger of employing a money without fixed limits—Other practical observations concerning moneys . . . 184

Chapter XIX.

REVULSIONS OF PRICES. Coins are made of gold and silver not because of the intrinsic qualities of these metals—The practice arose from the superior constancy of their quantity as compared with other substances, and during æras when artificial moneys of fixed quantity were politically impracticable—Historical examples—The precious metals were never permanently used for coins until the conquest of Spain by Rome—When the first effects of this conquest subsided, the precious metals were less used as materials for coins, until the Spanish conquest of America—The effects of the conquest of America and its great supplies of gold and silver to Europe upon prices have been sustained by means of convertible paper notes—This system incapable of further safe extension—Necessity for reform in money—Fluctuations of prices which have resulted from the failure of "convertible" note systems—Their disastrous and baneful effects 190

Chapter XX.

REGULATION OF MONEYS. Fluctuations of price which do not belong to the domain of science—Variations which do—Practical considerations for the regulation of money—Effect in the United States of an absolutely fixed sum—Influence of a fixed sum per capita of population—Actual movement of population and money during the past century—Had money been regulated instead of being left to commerce, chance, and political contention, the great panics of 1815, 1821, 1837, 1861, 1873, and 1893 might have been averted 197

THE SCIENCE OF MONEY.

CHAPTER I.

EXCHANGE.

Exchange is a social act—The Greek, Roman, and French philosophers deemed exchange and money as part of the structure of society—Barter—Distinction between barter and selling for money—Essential characteristics of money—It constitutes a public measure—Barter leads to slavery; money to freedom—Effigy of Liber Pater on ancient coins—Its significance—Enslavement of the Frisians—The dangers of metallism have given rise in modern times to an increasing proportion of paper promises to serve as money—Dangers arising from their assumed convertibility.

EXCHANGE is a social act: no man can exchange with himself. Exchange therefore implies society. That "it takes two to make a bargain" is axiomatic. We shall presently see that value, which is the basis of exchange, has also a social origin; and that money, when it is designed to be a correct measure of value, is, and must of necessity be, a social instrument. The Greek philosophers regarded exchange and society as inseparable. Said Aristotle: "There would be no society if there were no exchange, and no exchange if there were no money".[1] The writings of Paulus and other Roman jurisconsults prove that they also were imbued with the same conviction. The modern French philosophers were of a similar opinion. Said Destutt Tracy: "Society is in fact held together by a series of exchanges".[2] Said Frederic Bastiat: "Exchange is political economy—it is society itself; for it is impossible

[1] Book V., on *Justice*. [2] *Economie Politique*, p. 78.

to conceive society as existing without exchange, or exchange without society".[1] The reason given for this opinion is, that "in the isolated state our wants exceed our powers, whilst in the social state our powers exceed our wants"; and this they are enabled to do by the operation of exchange, which is a union of powers, the sum of which is more effective than that of our several powers applied separately or successively.[2] Exchange is based upon value, not upon cost. Alfred, the cowherd, can spare one of his animals, and prefers a gold bracelet instead. Balder, the shepherd, knows Canute, the miner, who will give him twenty pennyweights of gold for three sheep. Having need of a cow he exchanges three of his sheep for the gold, and the latter for a cow. In these transactions the parities of exchange, or equivalents of value, are 1 cow = 3 sheep = 20 dwts. of gold.

This kind of exchange is called barter. No matter how intricate or involved it may be, it is only barter. It is the voluntary exchange of one specified commodity or service for another specified commodity or service, neither of which commodities is limited in supply, nor prohibited from being monopolised or engrossed by individuals, nor necessarily related to other commodities or exchanges. The fact that one of the commodities exchanged is gold, does not alter the nature of the transaction. Nor would it be altered if the gold were authoritatively stamped with its weight and fineness. It is still barter: it is commodity against commodity, or give and take.[3] The valuation is rude and inexact. It has no regard for precision: it does not consider other parities of value made at the same time and place: it takes no heed of the parities made at other

[1] *Harmonics*, Chap. IV.

[2] Yet there is a class of Socialists (the Idealists) who would forbid the use of money altogether.—Blatchford's *Merrie England*.

[3] "What must be remarked at the very outset of the science is that exchanges, which are effected by means of an intermediate commodity, do not lose the nature, the essence, the quality, of barter."—Bastiat, *Har. Polit. Econ.*, p. 83.

times and places: it ignores both the past and the future: it cannot be applied to the parities of a deferred exchange; it is not related to exchanges in general, but only to one exchange; it begins and ends with an isolated transaction.

Such is not the case with money. This is designed to measure the value of all things with equity or precision. Money measures not merely the value of certain commodities and services at one time and place, as barter does; money measures all commodities at all times and places. Barter can only measure present exchanges, each one by itself; money can measure all exchanges, both present, deferred, and involved. Barter is a measure for the use of individuals, or a petty tribe; money is the measure demanded for the exchanges of a nation.

It is essential that the radical distinction between exchanges by barter and exchanges by means of money should be clearly understood, and always borne in mind. In the example above cited, Alfred has obtained twenty dwts. of gold for his cow. Should he next desire to exchange his gold for something else, he would be obliged to find somebody who wanted gold, and was willing to give for it some other commodity or service acceptable to Alfred. This might not be easy; perhaps not practicable. But if the twenty dwts. of gold were declared by his tribe to be money, the case would be entirely altered; for then there would be created a universal demand for it, and it could readily be exchanged for any other commodity or service which Alfred might desire, and which the vendor might wish to exchange for something else purchasable with Alfred's money, whether now or at any other time. To give practicable and equitable effect to such monetary declaration it would be necessary for the tribe to control and regulate the supply of gold to the mint, in order that such gold might measure value with precision and equity; divide it into small pieces suitable for transference from hand to hand; stamp these with some mark of public authority, in order to distinguish them from gold pieces not monetised; monopolise their coinage; permit the substitution of silver or some other material for the gold, in case the supplies of the latter to the mint proved inadequate; give the pieces some denomination; impose a penalty on individuals for coining, hoarding, secreting, engrossing, defacing, melting down, or exporting such gold pieces, in order to prevent the public measure of value from being altered; and provide that all public revenues and expenditures shall be paid in such pieces, that all contracts shall be expressed in them, and that no man shall refuse them without incurring a penalty. Sweep away these regulations, and the pieces will sink to the rank of a commodity, which no man is obliged to accept or pay, which has no stability of quantity or numbers, and which therefore may rise or fall in value to a ruinous extent; so that prices, if couched in such commodity, may differ enormously, even in adjacent places, and contracts based upon pieces current in a past generation may serve to enslave the present one. Such are the disadvantages, the inequities, and the dangers of barter, which money was designed to remove or remedy. The logical outcome of barter is slavery; that of money is freedom. The ancients, well aware of this fact, made the god of freedom likewise the god of money. He was called Liber Pater; and either his name, or synonym, his effigy, or his symbols, will be found stamped upon a large proportion of their mint issues.

Says Tacitus (*Annales*, IV., 72): "In the course of this year the Frisians, a people dwelling beyond the Rhine, broke out into open acts of hostility. The cause of the insurrection was not the restless spirit of a nation impatient of the yoke; they were driven to despair by Roman avarice. A moderate tribute, such as suited the poverty of the people, consisting of raw hides for the use of the legions, had been formerly imposed by Drusus. To specify the exact size and quality of the hides was an idea that never entered into the head of any man until Olennius, the first centurion of a legion, being appointed governor over the Frisians, collected a quantity of the hides of wild forest bulls and made these the standard both of weight and dimension. To any other nation this would have been a grievous burden: to this one it was unbearable, because the cattle (called 'Uri'), which run wild in the forest, are of prodigious size, whilst the domestic breed is small. At first the Frisians groaned under this oppressive demand. Next, they surrendered their property and lands. Finally, they were obliged to sell their wives and children into slavery."

Here is an instance where payment in kind, or barter, without control over the substance contracted for, led to the enslavement of the imprudent contractors, or, what is almost the same thing, the enslavement of their wives and children. It is not the only example of the kind which history affords us. We are incurring the dangers of a barter system at the present time. Private coinage of the precious metals has almost reduced the monetary systems of the Western world to one of barter, which in many States is now little more than a system of barter for gold metal.

The regulation of metallic money was formerly secured by means of mines-royal, coinage, seigniorage, and other prerogatives reserved by the State. Since the plunder of America and India, notably since the surrender of the coinage into private hands, which in England dates from 1666, the limits of money have been, on the one hand, the produce of metals from the gold and silver mines, minus the absorption of these metals into the arts; and, on the other hand, the substitution of paper notes.

The increase of commerce, which gave rise to open mints and private coinage, has so vastly outstripped the supplies of metal to the mints, that whereas in 1666 almost the only paper moneys in Europe were the "transport notes" of the Bank of Sweden, the proportion of paper notes in 1829 was 25 per cent. This rose in 1873 and 1876 to 39 per cent., and at the present time it amounts to over 55 per cent. of the total circulation of the European world, as shown in the following comparison :—

Table showing the population, stock of coined money, paper money, total money, money per capita and percentage of paper to total money in circulation in the European world (including America and the Colonies) at intervals since 1829. (Population in millions; stocks of money in millions of pounds sterling.)

Year.	Pop.	Coin.	Paper.	Total.	Per Cap.	Paper %
1829	240	345	115	460	38/-	25
1850	300	400	169	469	38/-	30
1876	400	700	462	1162	58/-	39
1883	430	600	600	1200	56/-	50
1893	470	550	665	1215	52/-	54½
1896	480	600[1]	744	1344	56/-	55½

Apart from the incongruity of adding together sums of money belonging to various systems, in each of which a similar coin or note has a different ratio of velocity and therefore a different purchasing power, all the systems embraced in this table consist in part of so-called convertible notes, whose convertibility fails every few years and brings on bankruptcy and commercial disaster.

The doctrine that money consists merely of pieces of metal stamped by the State in order to certify their weight and fineness, and that their value is derived from the cost of producing such metallic contents, was unknown to antiquity, and took its rise in the Mercantile system of the sixteenth and seventeenth centuries. Its emptiness can easily be demonstrated. Erase that line from the law which gives names and legal-tender to these pieces (almost the sole remaining relic of the ancient institution of money); and money would cease to exist.

[1] The stock of gold and silver coins is about 800 millions sterling; of which about one-fourth is held as reserve, leaving about 600 millions in circulation.

CHAPTER II.

VALUE IS A NUMERICAL RELATION.

Legal use of the words "unit of value"—Their importance—They are not defined in the law—Unit a synonym for measure—Evolution of the word "value"—Its classical meaning related to the power of numbers—During the Dark Ages it became associated with labour—In the Renaissance it acquired the meaning of an attribute of matter—Fallacy of this last view—The correct nature of value rediscovered by Montesquieu and Bastiat—Value shown to be a numerical ratio between all exchanged things—Value measurable by the whole numbers of money—The existing mint laws practically make the whole numbers of money (or the unit or measure of value) to consist of an indefinite sum, whose only limits fluctuate between illimitable demand and uncertain supply.

THE laws of certain States ordain that either one of several different coins weighing so many grains, or of pieces of paper of such a size, each called a pound, a dollar or franc, shall be "the unit of value". Important as they are, neither of these words, "unit," or "value," is defined in the law. Reasoning from its use in analogous cases, "unit" is a synonym for measure; but the meaning of "value" is not to be determined by analogy, for there is no analogous use of it in the statutes.

When it is remembered that the ablest logicians of all countries, from Aristotle to Mill, have vainly endeavoured to give it form, it will begin to be seen how complex and obscure the nature of value must be, and therefore in what great uncertainty the statutes have involved all commercial relations, by using, without defining, this intricate term.

Nor is its use a mere matter of speech, of interest alone to pedants or grammarians. The existing law treats value as a thing, and measures our affairs and fortunes by means of assumed relations to this thing, which, we shall see as we go on, is not a thing at all.

The law ordains that each one of its plural and numberless units of value called dollars, etc., shall be the measure of value in every exchange; and it compels these so-called units of value to be accepted in lieu of commodities and services, and for taxes, fines, and judicial awards. The law says, practically, " You shall pay a unit of something which Aristotle never discovered; you shall be taxed ten units of something which Mill could not define; you shall be awarded a hundred units of something which is not described in the present law, and of which everybody at the present time has a different conception ".

Words are subject to an evolution which marks the course of ideas, just as—going a step further back—ideas follow the material progress of man. Thus, with the growth of the social organism words are created, refined, and specialised. With its decay they lose their special meanings and refinement; they become attached to grosser and grosser conceptions, and finally are absorbed into other words, and lost. If a societary revival occurs, and the old word is resuscitated to grow anew, the new growth may be of quite a different character from the old.

Bearing in mind the numerical character of the ancient Greek and Roman monetary systems, the word "value," whose root is " valeo," or " power," appears to have originally become attached to the power of numbers employed as a common denominator for services and commodities. This, again, by metonym, came to mean purchasing power. In later times, when money of limited numbers had been supplanted by a coinage whose limits were controlled by the sovereign-pontiff, when the Roman commonwealth had become an empire, and the public weal was supplanted by the interests of favoured classes, the original refined meaning of value was lost, and the term became associated with grosser conceptions, until, in the Dark Ages, it was attached only to individual services, and their produce; it became a thing;

and it is in this erroneous sense that it is used in some existing laws.

With the Renaissance—the revival of commerce and the study of commercial facts and phenomena—the term " value " revived and acquired a new growth. From being a thing, or the associate of things, it rose to be classed with the attributes of things. It is in this sense that it is viewed by the Economists, who successively imagined that they had discovered value in the attributes of materiality, durability, difficulty or cost of production or of reproduction, utility, desirability, scarcity, etc.

Upon applying certain crucial facts to these last named views, they are seen to be erroneous. Services have neither materiality nor durability; yet the fact that they are paid for proves that they are valuable. Ideas that are not difficult to evolve often fetch a valuable consideration. Neither buyer nor seller consults the cost of production or reproduction, else there would be no great variance of value, no sudden and widespread rise or fall of prices. It would be difficult to find more than the merest traces of utility in those works of art and luxury which possess the highest value. If we look for value in desirability, both land and water, and a myriad of other things which form the first objects of man's desires, but which nature has supplied to him gratuitously, arise in view to defeat the search. As for scarcity, nothing is scarcer than a correct definition of value; but who is willing to pay for one, and how much is he willing to pay?

Unable to resolve value as a whole, the Economists attempted to manage it in parts.[1] They split it into pieces, calling them variously temporary, permanent, positive,

[1] " When the Turks had conquered Greece and occupied Athens, after demolishing it, they attempted to rebuild it; but the stones of which the public buildings were made, and which the ancients had handled with ease, this (then) half-civilised race found too large to lift back to their places. They were therefore compelled to break them up; and thus perished most of the beautiful and symmetrical architectural triumphs of antiquity."—Leake's *Topography of Athens*, p. cvii. London, 1821. 8vo.

negative, relative, intrinsic, market, monopoly, natural, exchange, cost, and speculative, value, until each fragment was small enough for their purpose. But in vain; there always remained an element of value which neither their mechanics nor their alchemy could dispose of, and which constituted the enigma of the science.[1] Such was the importance of this element that Bastiat afterwards said of it: "Every truth or error which this word 'value' introduces into men's minds is a social one".

Some approach was made to the solution of value when its normal variations were observed to coincide with rarity or scarcity; these conditions being merely the rude forms of a numerical relation.

That the nature of value was, indeed, numerical, was somewhat confusedly indicated by the illustrious Montesquieu, whose familiarity with both the monetary history of Rome and John Law's recent experiments in France enabled him to declare that, "fundamentally, price depends entirely upon the numerical proportion of commodities to monetary symbols"; and "as the total sum of money is to the total sum of commodities in trade, so is a fraction of the one to a like fraction of the other". This does not explain value, but price; nevertheless, an attempt to explain value through the medium of price indirectly points to the numerical character of the former.[2]

To the gifted Bastiat was left the task of successfully demonstrating that value did not reside in any object, and therefore could not be an intrinsic attribute of matter; that it was a relation between different objects; and that this relation only appeared during the act of exchange. Hence followed his definition that "Value is the relation of two services exchanged".[3]

---

[1] Bastiat has a chapter on this subject in his *Harmonies of Political Economy*.

[2] See, on this subject, Wallace and Smith, in Chap. XIV.

[3] *Harmonies*, p. 108. Jevons appears to have approached equally near to the true solution of value when he regards it as a "proportion". *Primer of Political Economy* and *Money*.

But, as Jean Baptiste Say very truly remarked: "It is not given to any one to reach the confines of science: philosophers mount on each other's shoulders to explore a more and more extended horizon". When Bastiat discovered the general nature of value, he stopped. He found that it was a relation, and that it only appeared in exchange. Beyond this point he did not venture.

Yet no man was ever nearer to the whole discoverable truth without discovering it. He proved that "value does not reside in matter"; "nature has nothing to do with value"; "value is a relation"; "value implies measure"; and "value is to political economy what enumeration is to arithmetic".[1] Had he taken another step forward he could scarcely have failed to perceive that value was itself an arithmetical relation; for it can only be expressed in numbers. But death took him away before his immortal treatise was completed.

Not only is his explanation of value incomplete, it is not broad enough. Why should value be restricted to an exchange between two services? Why does it not exist—as Montesquieu suspected—between all services (and commodities) which are being exchanged, or liable to be exchanged?

The edifice which shelters us, for example, is not exchanged, nor being exchanged: yet it is valuable; and although that value cannot be definitely ascertained without offering to exchange the edifice for something else, it may be determined in a rude way by referring to the value of similar edifices which have been exchanged at the same place and at nearly the same time. Value, therefore, exists not merely between two commodities or services, but between all of such; it exists not only between things which are being exchanged, but, by analogy, between all things exchangeable.

The opinion that money measures the value of only

---

[1] Bastiat, *Harmonies of Political Economy*, pp. 104, 107, 125, 127, 133.

those things which are in market, up for sale, or being exchanged, is evidently derived from contemplating the disparity between the number or magnitude of all commodities and available services and the littleness of the measure—the sum of money—which marks their nominal equivalent. But the sum of money is of its present magnitude simply because it was so chosen to be, or so left to become; it can be made larger or smaller at man's pleasure, whenever he chooses to exercise over it the same dominion that he has chosen to exercise over yard-sticks and pint-pots; that is, whenever he chooses to define and limit by law the magnitude of the measuring unit, which, in the case of money, is, and can only be, from the nature of things, the whole sum in use. Such increase or diminution of the sum of money will not change the value of other things one to the other;[1] it will only change the expression of it in the fractions of money, such expression being called price. Nevertheless, this price, or value expressed in money, can only be determined by the act of exchange.

In the same manner, the pint-pot is of its present size because it was so chosen to be; it would answer the same purposes and prove equally efficient, no matter what its size was made; only in case of alteration, the expression of liquid measure in total pints would be different. The numerical relations between all other things would remain the same as before.

Whatever may be the origin of the notion that value only exists between things that are being exchanged, it is evidently erroneous. The fact is that nothing is *being* exchanged. It never can be truly said to be twelve o'clock, for time passes eternally, and whilst we speak, nay, whilst we observe the clock, time has elapsed and escaped fixture. The act of exchange, indeed all actions, are equally unfixable; and if value pertained to objects only during the act of exchange, it would practically not pertain to them at all.

---

[1] Mill's *Political Economy*, III., 7, 2, p. 298, says: "Causes which affect all commodities alike do not act upon values".

Value must, therefore, relate to things exchangeable as well as to those which are regarded as being exchanged; in other words, to all commodities and services.

The soundness of this conclusion is proved by the fact that when an exchange is being made, the value of all things is held in view through the medium of price. No man will sell a horse, for example, until after he ascertains not merely what the intended buyer but what all other men, within reach, will give for it. This, the latter determine, not with direct reference to the cost of production of horses, nor to the degree of their utility, nor to their lastingness nor desirability, nor to the prices of the corn, land, and labour which have contributed toward their cost, nor even to the supply and demand for horses; but simply to their price, which means their value in money. This price connects the horse, in a rude way, with all other exchangeable things at hand, and, by means of commerce and intercourse, with all exchangeable things in the commercial world. It does not follow from these premises that the price of a similar horse would be the same everywhere, because the money of each country consists of a sum by itself, a sum which is only remotely connected (if at all) with somewhat similarly constituted sums in other countries, and also because the relation between the local supply and demand for horses may not be the same in any two places.

Thus far we have seen that value is a term of the highest commercial and political importance, yet one whose definition is nowhere to be found in the law; that the term has passed through many meanings, due to its long-time use and the vicissitudes of European civilisation; that the economists of the Renaissance regarded it as an attribute of matter; that Bastiat proved it to be a relation between two services exchanged; and that further reasoning shows it to be a numerical relation, which in a rude way exists between all exchangeable things, as well as services, appears with precision during the act of exchange, and is to be measured most readily by means of money.

If it be asked: What is the essential character of this numerical relation called value? the reply must be, that although it depends upon many uncertain and incalculable elements, as human necessity, desire, passion, speculation, and caprice; yet that, as shown in another part of this work, it is essentially an equitable relation, or one that between equal parties has a tendency to become equitable; that it is extremely variable;[1] that it is extrinsic to and not connected with the physical properties of, nor difficulty of producing, commodities; and that it is susceptible of precise expression in numbers; and in numbers only.

Being thus susceptible of expression, it is sufficient for the purpose of dealing with it practically if value be for the present regarded as a numerical relation which involves the unknown ratio between the demand and supply of a service or commodity at a given place and time, as opposed to the unknown ratio between the demand and supply of another service or commodity at the same place and time; and that by comparison and analogy it extends to and between all services and all commodities.

In other words, value, though difficult to define, is not immeasurable. In this respect it resembles time, space, gravity, and the other primordial conditions or relations of matter. The human measure each of time, of space, of gravity, is an arbitrary standard, adopted by human law; and so must be the measure of value. It is physically

---

[1] During the American Civil War a member of the New York Stock Exchange made a profit of several thousand dollars by accepting both of two offers which were made by different persons at almost the same instant of time, the one offering to sell certain railway shares at a lower price than the other offered to buy them at. This variation of value and double bargain must all have taken place within a half-second of time. The writer has known mining shares in San Francisco in 1878 to double and at other times to diminish one-half in value within a few hours. He has heard of an instance in the "early days" of California when the price of a common hay-scythe rose in value from 25 cents (one shilling) to 100 dollars (£20) in the course of a few days; and of another instance when plug-tobacco fell from a dollar (4s.) a pound to nothing, and was cast into the street-hollows as valueless.

impossible to correctly measure value with gold, silver, or any other substance, as such. Value is not matter, but a condition or relation of matter: like distance. The distance between two objects is not intrinsic to either of them: it is not a thing nor an attribute of things; it is merely a relation between things, a relation measured by miles. So value is not intrinsic to services or commodities; it does not inhere in matter, it is not a thing nor an attribute of things; it is merely a relation between things—to wit, a relation which can only be precisely measured by money, and which cannot be so measured by gold or any other commodity as such.

There is no source of value, any more than there is a source of distance. There is no cause of value, any more than there is a cause of distance. The only way in which distance can be perceived and correctly measured is by means of comparison,—not a comparison between two or more objects, but between two or more distances. It is the same with value: the only way in which value can be perceived and correctly measured is by means of comparison,—not a comparison between two or more objects, but between two or more values. An attempt to measure one distance without reference to another distance could only end in failure: the thing is physically impossible. Yet an analogous attempt to accomplish a physical impossibility has ruled the world ever since 1666, when the numerical limits of money were sold by Charles II. to the goldsmiths of England and Flanders. This attempt consists of endeavouring to measure value with precision by means of metal as metal. It cannot be done.

Value is not merely a relation between services; it occurs between commodities. If it related only to services, or to the services employed in producing or reproducing commodities, then the cost of production or of reproduction would be a correct measure of value: but this is not true, *e.g.*, of silver at present. Of this metal there is a superfluous stock on hand, and its present value must be below that of reproduction. So with the tobacco thrown into the street-hollows of San Francisco. If, instead of the cost of reproduction, we say the cost of obtaining a like service or commodity, this only shifts the inquiry without answering it. What determines the value of a service or commodity? Answer: a like service or commodity; and so on *ad infinitum*. The truth is that there is no source of value. It does not arise from labour, any more than it does from crime or delusion. Several years ago a swindler imposed upon the British Museum a forged MS., for which it paid a high price. Upon what basis was this price paid? Labour? There are a million of books in the British Museum which cost more labour, but far less price. Scarcity? There are even scarcer books. Crime? Had the crime been known, the price would certainly not have been paid. The Museum authorities paid this price while labouring under a delusion,—the delusion of supposing that it was a very ancient copy of an "inspired" book. So Louis IX. paid to the Latin "emperor" Baldwin £100,000 for what he believed was the true Cross; so the Mormon Church recently offered 100,000 dollars for what they believed was the original Book of Mormon; so tens of thousands of deluded votaries annually pay sums of money to see or touch the Holy Coat of Treves. Is delusion, then, to be taken as the source of value? To state the proposition is to negative it.

Although the law at present declares that the measure of value shall consist of one single coin, it really and in point of fact consists of all coins and notes circulating within scope of the law. The law can, indeed, render one single coin the measure of value; but it can only do so by prohibiting and banishing all other coins. This it does not do. On the contrary, after declaring a single coin of a certain description to be the measure of value, it orders several hundred millions of similar coins to be fabricated; it makes them each and all payable for taxes and fines, and exchangeable for commodities, services, and each other, and thus renders them altogether, in lump, one measure of value; because, as money relates to all things, and value is usually expressed in money, so value relates to all things, and not to any one thing by itself. In other words, such is the nature of value, such the law, and such the operation of the system of exchange, that the pieces of money cannot be used separately; they must be, and in fact always are, used collectively; so that the actual unit or measure of value is the whole legal or tale sum of circulating money, of whatever material or materials it may be composed.

We know already that the law has not specifically limited this measure. But has it no limits whatever? Is the measure of value a mere abstraction? No. Under existing laws it has certain rude and indefinite limits, which have been left to chance, commerce, caprice, war, intrigue, legislation, etc. These limits are roughly known as the supply of money. By rendering so much money as may be found by experiment to express the value of any object of man's desire an effective offer in exchange for such object, the law has made the demand for money illimitable. On the other hand, the supply of money in existing monetary systems is left to be determined by the march of conquest, the progress of slavery, the vicissitudes of mining discovery, the development of mining economy, the social affairs of distant nations, the happening of war, the currents of trade, the progress of the arts, the course of legislation in various countries, the plots of financiers and speculators, the melting of coins, the wear, tear, and loss of coins, the profits of banking, the emissions of State and bank notes, and numerous other events and conditions, both uncertain and unstable.

Hence we have for value a complex numerical ratio of exchange, but precisely measurable by money; and for money, a measure susceptible of precise limitation, but, as the case now stands, actually left to vary between illimitable demand and more or less uncertain supply.

Value, being a definite relation, cannot with propriety

be coupled with an indefinite article. "A value," for example, is erroneous. So are the expressions "great value," "marvellous value," etc., so commonly used by tradesmen. The substitution of "value" for "price," and the use of "value" as a noun or substantive, are other forms of error in the use of this term. Graham, in his excellent work on "Synonyms," also notices its confusion with the term "worth". "Value," he says, has an active; "worth," a passive meaning. The quality "worth" is what a thing has in itself; its "value" is determined by what it does for you. Worth is intrinsic; value depends on circumstances. It may be added that these circumstances relate exclusively to exchange.

Says a recent commentator on this subject: "A relation existing between two things cannot be an 'intrinsic' quality of either. Value is such a relation, just as is marriage. There is no such thing as 'intrinsic' marriage, or 'intrinsic' value, because both value and marriage refer to the relation between two or more persons or things, and not to a thing by itself. There can be no marriage without bride and groom. There can be no value unless one thing or one service is compared, or considered in relation to other things. Were value an 'intrinsic' characteristic of gold, or diamonds, or anything else, there would have to be a new word coined to express the connection between the article so endowed by nature, and the other articles for which it is exchanged or exchangeable. Marriage is that which shows the relation of husband to wife. Value is that which shows the exchange relation of one or more things or services to others. Both marriage and value are by virtue of this fact 'extrinsic,' not 'intrinsic,' characteristics. A man is not endowed by nature with the relation of marriage, as he is with the 'intrinsic' qualities which form his personal being; and neither is any product endowed with value, as it is with the 'intrinsic' characteristics of its composition. Value being 'extrinsic' may fall or rise without affecting the valued substance. Were the value of a metal 'intrinsic' it could not be altered without the application to the metal itself, of fire, or water, or a hammer, or some other physical agent. Being 'extrinsic,' being simply the relation in which the metal in question stands in relation to other exchangeable commodities, it may be altered and modified without the application of any of these physical agencies. 'Intrinsic' value is the same contradiction in terms as 'intrinsic' marriage. It is an absurdity, a misleading phrase, a finger-post pointing to economic error."[1]

Value only appears in the social state, and merely applies to exchangeable things. When used with respect to health, religion, etc., or anything connected with man in an isolated state, it is a metonym for worth, as when we say a man keeps a good table, meaning that he keeps good viands. The value of money is also used to mean the rate of interest thereon at a given time and place; but this is a merely technical expression, into the merits of which it is not necessary to enter in this place.

[1] *Peoria Journal*, editorial, 1895.

CHAPTER III.

PRICE.

It is the expression of value in money—Price implies precision— It is intended to be a precise expression of value—But this it cannot be unless the whole sum of money is limited and known—Harris, Smith, Mill, Locke, Hume—Price cannot be definitely expressed in a single coin independently of others—Prices of commodities tend to fall; of services to rise—This tendency defeated by private coinage and the monopolisation of gold—Price not due to cost of production; it expresses a dynamical or kinetic relation between money and exchanges in time.

PRICE is the expression of value in money. Value may be stated in numbers of oxen, sheep, ounces of metal, or any other objects susceptible of numerical expression; but owing to the fact that the total number of these objects is not limited or not subject to limitation, such valuation can only be rude or approximative. Price implies precision: it is, or is intended to be, a precise expression of value; and it approaches actual precision in proportion as the whole number is limited and known of the pricing symbols or denominators; because the whole number of such symbols is the only steady, stable, permanent, immovable point from which such precise measure of value can be made.

Price being the expression of value in money (meaning the whole sum of money), and value being the relation between two or more services or commodities, when exchanged or viewed as exchangeable, it follows that price is the relation between the whole sum (not number) of exchanges when expressed in money and the whole sum of money itself.

The very moneyers and economists, who in other parts of their books inconsistently argued that value could be precisely measured with a single coin irrespective of its cogeners, were forced to admit the stability of the whole sum of money as a measure of value. Joseph Harris (pp. 66-72), Adam Smith (I., ii., p. 178), John Stuart Mill (III., viii., 2, p. 299), and in fact the entire school of Economists, admit that "the total sum of money will always have the same value". Here the word "sum" is used as a synonym for numbers; and "value" as a synonym for measuring function, or measuring capacity, or measuring power. Stated with less ambiguity, the principle is that "the total numbers of the symbols of money of equal denomination will always have the same measuring power". If the sum is changed then the value of each constituent of the sum must vary; if the whole sum be composed of a greater or less sum of constituents than previously, the value of each separate constituent must vary inversely with the whole sum. The illustrious Mill observed this deduction, and laid it down in these words: "The value of money varies inversely as its quantity"; but the lesson has been wholly lost upon his degenerate successors.

Both Locke and Hume asserted the principle that the measuring capacity of money was governed by the total number of coins or other moneys in trade, or in circulation: it was left for Joseph Harris and Adam Smith to bury this basic principle of political economy and subvert it to the fallacious and inequitable doctrine of Metallism.[1] Mill subsequently resurrected it; but his teachings on this head were not entirely free from ambiguity, and they have lost the influence to which many of them were justly entitled. To-day some people doubt the soundness of the "quantitative principle" of money, who would perhaps have hardly ventured to question it had it been dubbed with its proper name of "numerical principle". Value is not merely a quantitative relation, it is a numerical one;

[1] See *Black Laws* of James III., further on.

and when expressed in price, the expression is not merely quantitative, but numerical; which is far more exact.

Price cannot be definitely expressed in a single coin, or a sum of coins, independent of other coins; because coins are legally interchangeable one for the other. When circulating notes are legally interchangeable for coins and coins for notes, or when bullion, coins, and notes are all interchangeable, as is the case at present in the foremost States of the world, then price can only be expressed in the total sum of such composite money, or the definite fractions thereof.[1]

Owing to improvements in the arts, the tendency of the value of commodities as compared with that of services is to fall.[2] In other words, the tendency of capital is to fall and of services to rise in value. This is the compensation with which Nature seeks to rectify the inequalities of fortune and the defects of distribution. There is but one way to defeat this benign process; and that way has been discovered and employed by the money-lenders. It is to alter the ancient law of money, to wrest it from the hands of the State, to acquire for themselves the privilege of private coinage, to turn money into a commodity (some commodity of limited supply and easily subject to control), and to require that all taxes, contracts, and debts shall be paid in specified quantities of such commodity,—for example, gold. By monopolising this commodity the moneyed classes have got Nature by the throat and the community under their heels. They could not prevent services from rising in *value* as compared with commodities; that was impossible; but they have prevented services from rising in *price*, such price being expressed in their monopolised commodity, gold. Hence they can purchase services, and, through them, commodities, at an always falling equivalent. Compared with this process, usury is mere child's play.

It is a common fallacy to suppose that price is derived

---

[1] See Chapter XVIII. herein.   [2] Bastiat, *Har. Polit. Econ.*, p. 150.

from cost of production. The fact is that price is due to an entirely different source,—to wit, the numerical relation between exchanges and money. If price were due to cost of production, the English farmer would be able to sell his wheat at a profit, which, as the case stands, he is wholly unable to do. Nor is the price of wheat in England due to the cost of producing it in America, or India, or anywhere else. It is due to the relation of exchanges and money. Instead of production governing price, it is precisely the reverse; price governs production. The price of wheat being fixed by the relation between exchanges and money, those who can produce wheat below this price will go on: those who cannot, will stop; and this is precisely what the English agriculturist has been forced to do ever since the present system of money was established. Put an end to Metallism, and England will again produce her own breadstuffs; continue it, and not merely agriculture but all the industrial arts will gradually flee the country.

There is a further peculiarity of price which appears to have entirely escaped the Economists. This is its relation to time. Price is not merely the relation between money and exchanges; we shall presently see that it is the relation between money and exchanges *in time*. Given a whole sum of money with a given velocity of circulation on the one side, and a whole sum of exchanges in a given time, on the other, a given level of prices will be the result. But if either of these factors is changed, if the velocity of money is altered, or if the number of exchanges in time is altered, then the level of prices,—in other words, all prices,—will change, until they conform to the new relation between exchanges and money.

For example, in Chapter XIV. it is shown that the total money and credits used in place of money, employed for payments in the United States at the present time, when both are reduced to a like circulating velocity of once a week, is about 1460 million dollars. This is equal to 75,920 millions a year: thus, $1460 \times 52 = 75,920$. It is shown that this is also the total annual sum of the exchanges, that is to say, the sales and transfers of services, merchandise, and property, for money, or credit, in that country. The result is the present level of prices, including the price of wheat. Increase the amount or velocity of the money, and these prices will rise; diminish its amount or velocity, and the prices will fall. Similarly, if the period during which these exchanges are effected is extended, prices will rise; if the period is contracted, prices will fall. Price is therefore seen to be an equation between two velocities: the velocity of money on the one hand, and of exchanges on the other; and that, directly, it has nothing to do with cost of production.

Yet it is the working of this complex mechanism and system of numerical relations, this profound kinetic problem, that every huckster in goods and amateur in science deems himself fully competent to discuss!

CHAPTER IV.

MONEY IS A MECHANISM.

Money is a mechanism designed to measure value with precision—The law alone can determine what is and what is not money—The function of money correctly understood by Aristotle—During, or shortly previous to, the æra of that philosopher, the volume of money in each country was limited, and it formed a definite measure of value therein—It is now everywhere unlimited, and has lost its character of an exact measure—Money at present is not defined in the laws. For this reason it is unlike all other measures—Money is intended, but not now fitted, for a measure—The size or weight of a dollar or pound sterling furnishes no guide to the whole number of dollars or pounds; yet it is this which constitutes the measure of value—The measuring function of money is altered with every change in the whole number of so-called units of value—Not so with the units of weight, length, volume or area.

MONEY is a mechanism of societary life designed to measure and determine value. It is what the law or custom makes receivable for payments, taxes and debts. Therefore its precision, efficiency, stability and equitable operation depend primarily upon the strength and virtue of Government. Such is the case even when the measure is made concretely of metallic symbols, or when the latter are susceptible of conversion into other objects; for it is Government alone that can establish and maintain the purity, weight, and uniformity of coins, regulate their numbers, sizes, names, and employment in the payment of taxes, fines, and dues, or fix the value between them when the symbols are made of different materials, as gold, silver, bronze, and paper. A curious instance of the dependence of money upon law is furnished by Du Chaillu, the African traveller. He says that on certain parts of the African coasts which Europeans have long frequented, the natives are very reluctant to accept coins in payment, whilst a few miles further inland coins are refused altogether.[1] The reason for this refusal is that the people know nothing of the laws which establish the value of these coins. They do not use coins themselves, and they prefer other commodities to the materials of which the coins are made.

As for the definition given by Mr. Francis Walker that "money is as money does," it is no more applicable to money than to steam engines, or cartwheels, and it does not enable us to distinguish money from either of these objects. What is it that "is as it does," is a puzzle to which a thousand answers might be given, without either of them leading to "money". It is a definition without any definitive idea behind it.

Another economist, Mr. John Henry Norman, believing that he has discovered the true nature of money, has embodied it in a pamphlet, of which he says he has sent "2000 copies to the rulers and finance ministers of the empires, kingdoms, and states of the world, to political economists, learned societies, senates, universities, etc.". His view is that money must consist of a substance of "unlimited quantities," and "possessing value" derived from "cost of production" from labour, in order that it may measure the thing or attribute called value, which is likewise the result of labour. The State is to make this substance unlimited legal-tender, coin it for its owners for nothing, and make good their losses from the wear and tear of coins. "The other school," he loftily continues, teach that "money is what money does". To this the scientific school (that is, Mr. Norman's school) would reply, that "to favour any commodity by the interposition of legislation, disqualifies the substance from becoming money". This learned man was actually permitted to give "a lecture on Prices and Monetary and Currency Exchanges, when Mr. J. R. Diggle, of the London

[1] *Viking Age*, I., 261.

School Board, was good enough to occupy the chair". Between the "schools" of Mr. Francis Walker and Mr. John Henry Norman there does not seem to be any such difference as the latter supposes. I should say it was chiefly one of degree.

More than twenty centuries ago the nature and characteristics of money were so correctly laid down by Aristotle as to leave but little room for improvement. "Money (*nomisma*) by itself is but a mere device. It has value only by law (*nomos*) and not by nature, so that a change of convention between those who use it is sufficient to deprive it of its value and of its power to purchase our requirements."[1] "By virtue of voluntary convention, money (*nomisma*) has become the medium of exchange. We call it '*nomisma*' because its efficiency is due not to nature but to law (*nomos*), and because it is in our power to regulate it."[2]

The function of money was described with equal brevity and clearness. "The function of money" (*nomisma*), said the Stagyrite, "is to measure value." If we add "with precision," the definition appears to satisfy all requirements. When Aristotle wrote, no such addition was necessary. The volume of money in several of the Greek States was, or had been, limited by law; and in each one it formed a definite and precise measure of value.[3]

But such is no longer the case. In each and nearly all of the various States of the world the whole numbers or

---

[1] *Politica*.   [2] *Ethica*.
[3] A full account of these moneys will be found in the author's *History of Monetary Systems*—chapter on Greece. The following principles of money are from the *Pandects* of Justinian, and are said to have been introduced into that code of laws from the works of Julius Paulus, a Roman lawyer of the third century A.D. In the author's opinion, they are much older. "As it seldom happened that what one (man) possessed (to sell) the other (man) wanted (to buy)—and conversely—a thing was fixed upon whose legal and perpetual value remedied, by its homogeneity, the difficulties of barter. This thing, being officially fabricated, circulates and maintains its value not so much from its substance as from its quantity."

volume of money is at present unlimited, and money has lost its character of a precise measure. It is a measure, but one whose dimensions are fluctuating; so that its function is practically impaired. It does its work badly.

When we say that the function of gallon measures is to measure the volume of liquids, we mean by gallon measures certain concrete things of prescribed sizes or limits; contrariwise, when moneys are mentioned there is, under existing circumstances, no precise meaning to be attached to them. The laws of modern States do not define the sizes nor limits of moneys; nor does custom establish them.

Let us state this proposition more at length.

To measure is to number; all measurements are ascertainments of numerical relations; numerical relations can only be stated in numbers.

But in point of fact, certain measurements are made with yard-sticks, pound-weights, and the like.

What is the reason for such a practice? If to measure is to number, why will not numbers alone, without yard-sticks or pound-weights, serve to measure length, weight, etc.?

Because numbers are abstract and illimitable, whilst the relations or attributes to be measured are concrete and limited; and in order to measure them with precision it is necessary to employ concrete and limited measures. To say that the length of a building is 100 means nothing; to say that it is equal to that of 100 yards, meaning 100 yardsticks, has a precise significance, and one which everybody comprehends.

In order to measure value, it would certainly seem that just as concrete and limited a money is required as yardsticks for distances, or gallon measures for volumes. But whilst the law defines the dimensions of a yard, a pound, and a gallon, with great precision, it wholly fails and omits to define the dimensions of money.

It follows that money, until it be precisely defined and

limited, is an inexact measure; and to say that its function is to measure value is to say a thing that, however true in principle, can have, as matters now stand, no precise signification. The money we now use is a very poor measure.

Remembering the present position of money in the law, unnamed, unrecognised, undefined, unlimited, there exists between it and other quantitative measures not a similarity; but, on the contrary, the most important difference. The efficiency of other measures runs no risk of being impaired, either by alterations in the law, disturbances of the peace, the currents of trade, the conspiracies of designing men, or the caprices of fashion. The efficiency of money as it now stands is liable to be affected by all these causes, and many others.

Under the same legal jurisdiction there is but one— an unalterable—measure of weight, one of length, one of volume, etc. These measures, carefully described and identified in the law, are kept by the Government in some safe place—for example, the Treasury building at Washington, or the Tower of London. All other weights and measures under the same law are copies or duplicates. By the aid of these copies a vast number of measurements can be made at different times, or at the same time at different places, without disturbing, changing, or wearing out the originals; and as, when a measure is once fixed and publicly defined, it is plainly the interest of society to keep it so, and it would be a flagrant violation of equity to alter it, there is little or no danger that these measures will be changed by either edict or legislation.

But such is not the case with money as it now stands. It is not recognised, not defined, not limited in the law; there is no description of it to be found in the statutes of any country; there is none, for example, in the laws of the United States or Great Britain; no prototype of money is kept in any safe place by the Government; money has no peculiar size, shape, dimensions, volume; it is not a precise measure, nor is it essentially like precise measures; and to draw conclusions from its apparent resemblance to such measures is to do violence to the facts.

Those who would clothe money with the attributes of a precise measure do indeed accord it the function for which it was intended, but for which it is not at present fitted. They forget that all other measures enjoy legal recognition; that they are defined in the law with all the precision that modern scientific observation and refinement can effect; and that, on the contrary, money—as we have unthinkingly adopted it from the law of 1666 — is an undefined and shapeless thing, whose dimensions and fitness as a measure of value are whatever the chances of war, trade or fashion, or the caprices or intrigues of the rich, the powerful, or the indifferent, may choose to make it.

If it be argued that whilst money is not recognised nor described in the law, the undetermined fractions of money, as coins, bank notes, etc., are both recognised and described, the answer is that since the quantitative relations of such coins or bank notes to the whole money are unknown, they fail to resemble the fractions of other measures, and they cannot and do not precisely measure anything.

Nobody has ever ventured to deliberately maintain that any one coin was the measure of value, nor that any number of coins less than the whole number in use constituted such a measure. To do so would have been to maintain a palpable absurdity. As the whole number of coins, notes, etc., is what really constitutes the measure of value, and as, at the present time, no precise limit is assigned to the whole number, it follows that there is no precise limit to the measure of value. If a mile were nowhere described in the law, but instead, some indeterminable fraction of a mile were stated to be exactly so many inches and barleycorns long, then the legal position of miles and moneys would be alike. But in such case, who would be able to determine the length of such a mile? and who can now determine the measuring function, or, as it is called, the value of such a money?

MONEY IS A MECHANISM. 31

If it be answered that the "value" of money is determined by the cost of producing the material of which it is made, the reply to this is that all the political economists, without exception, have admitted that to double the number of pieces of money of the same denomination—no matter of what material made—would be to diminish the measuring capacity of each piece by one-half, and *vice versâ*.[1] Hence it follows that the so-called value of money is determined by numbers, and not by material. But there is a reply whose cogency to some will perhaps appear more evident than this one. That reply is that the value of the material (gold, for example) is itself determined not by the cost of production, but (chiefly) by the quantity of the stock on hand, and the extent of its use as money; and that neither the stock on hand nor the cost of production regulates the quantity produced from time to time. The quantity produced is often all that *can* be produced, whether it pays or not.[2]

Let us endeavour to comprehend the subtle function of money by looking at the subject from another point of view.

In the laws of the United States, for example, the American gallon is described as "a vessel containing 58372·2 grains (8·3389 pounds avoirdupois) of the standard pound of distilled water, at the temperature of maximum density of water, the vessel being weighed in air in which the barometer is 30 inches at 62° Fahrenheit".[3]

The vessel thus described is kept in the United States

---

[1] "If the whole money in circulation were doubled, prices would be doubled."—John Stuart Mill, *Polit. Econ.*, III., 8, 2, p. 299.

[2] Consult my *History of the Precious Metals*, where this subject is dealt with inductively, and at great length.

[3] Executive Document No. 27, 34th Congress, 3rd Session: consisting of Professor Bache's Report on Weights and Measures. Washington, 1857. "The relation of this gallon measure to weight is said to disagree slightly with that accorded by the same authority to the bushel."—Barnard's *Metric System*, p. 39.

Treasury building at Washington, and copies or duplicates are furnished, on application, to such persons as may desire them. It matters not how many copies of this vessel are made, nor whether they are made of brass, tin, wood, glass, or other substances; nor whether the copies are cheap, dear, stamped, unstamped, in use, or out of use, the original gallon or standard, and its functional power as a measure, remain wholly unaffected; and, for the reasons already stated, it is likely to so remain indefinitely.

Is this the case at present with the measure called Money? Not at all. It is nowhere mentioned in the law; its volume, its dimensions, the number of its pieces or constituent parts are entirely ignored. They have no place whatever in the legal institutions of the United States, nor, indeed, of any other country. It may again be argued that although money is not defined in the statutes, coins are. But this does not help the case, because there is no legal requirement concerning the number of such coins as shall constitute the volume or whole of money. Moreover, by a confusion of language which could only have arisen out of the grossness of the conception upon which these statutes are founded, and the loose language in which they are couched, these coins are termed "units of value". Says one statute: "The gold coins of the United States shall be a dollar piece, which at the standard (*i.e.*, nine-tenths fine) weight of twenty-five and eight-tenths grains shall be the unit of value,"[1] and then it goes on to mention other gold coins. Another statute confers a similar character upon the silver dollar piece of 412½ grains, nine-tenths fine. The statutes do not say that either of these pieces shall be the unit of value in preference to the other, but make

[1] Act of 12th February, 1873, section 14, included in the Revised Statutes of the United States, section 3511. The blunder of calling the dollar a "unit" appears in the Act of 1792, section 9, where it is applied to the silver dollar. On the edge of the coins themselves appear the words "dollar or unit". To this blunder was added in 1873 the crime (for it was little less than a crime) of calling the gold dollar (any other dollar would have been as bad) the "unit of value".

them both equally units; which, as the law in this respect is not inoperative, should have suggested the truth that neither of them are units. The same statutes and the decisions of the Supreme Court of the United States also make several other pieces of money, some composed of metal, others of paper, equally units of value; so that there are at the present time no less than twenty odd different kinds of units of value recognised by the laws of that country, and with a number of each of which a debt can lawfully be paid. Is not this defiance of reason, this violation and confusion of language, which the law commits, in itself a sufficient proof that the theory from which it arises is false, and that neither of these pieces is in fact the unit of value, but that all of them together compose such unit?

If we disregard both fact and reason, and, following the law, accept either of these pieces of money as the unit of value, we immediately become involved in practical difficulties.

It is a well-known fact that every time an additional one of the coins called dollars or pounds, and miscalled units of value, is put into circulation, the measuring value of the original one becomes impaired. More than this, the function of this coin is certain to be modified by the emission of every promise of a "dollar" or "pound" coin which the law may authorise to be tendered for payments, or which custom may sanction for the same purpose. Even a shipment of uncoined bullion, either into or out of a given country, will, as the laws now stand, affect the measuring power of money in such country.[1] From these circum-

---

[1] The affairs of the New England colonies were often thrown into disorder by the arrival of plate-ships from the West Indies. Sir Isaac Newton records similar results in England which followed the arrival of plate-ships from America; and other instances are mentioned in Mavor's *Voyages*, II., 223, *et seq.* This subject is fully treated, and numerous instances given relating to it, in the author's *History of Money*. At the present time (1895) Wall Street trembles whenever it is announced that shipments of gold are being made to Europe.

stances it appears that what the law calls a unit of value in fact is not a unit at all. The law views it and defines it as though it were distinct and separable from all other things; but nature instantly merges it with all like and many unlike things, and makes the whole number of these things the real measure or "unit". As this whole number is not specified nor defined in the law and remains unknown, it follows that the real "unit" has no definite limits nor dimensions, and therefore that it has no determinable relation to value.

In substance the law says: "Such a thing shall be the unit of value; there shall be a blank number of such things made; they are of such a nature and shall have such legal attributes that they can only be used collectively and therefore in point of fact the real unit of value must be the whole number of them combined; but I decline to state what that number shall be; I decline to place any limit to it; I decline to fill up the blank".

The essential difference between money as it now stands in the law and other measures, whether of length, weight, volume, or area, is thus rendered evident. The units of these are concrete and defined; they are not liable to be changed by edict or legislation, and cannot be modified by duplication; whilst money remains abstract and undefined, and coins, bank notes, and other so-called "units of value," are in fact modified in functional power and efficiency with every increase or decrease of their combined number.[1] The unit of money is not one coin, but all coins or moneys combined; whilst, on the contrary, the unit of length or measure is not all yard-sticks or pint-pots collectively, but only one of them. An increase or diminution of the whole numbers of yard-sticks will not affect the relation of length between any one yard-stick and any other object. An increase or diminution of the whole numbers of coins or notes clothed with

[1] This distinction was pointed out by the gifted Bastiat. See his *Harmonies of Political Economy*, London ed., p. 125.

MONEY IS A MECHANISM.

the functions of money will instantly begin to change the relation of value between any one such coin or note and any other object. And such increase or diminution—as the law now stands—is within the power of every man to make in direct proportion as he is rich and powerful. When money shall be recognised in the law, when it is defined, when its volume, magnitude, dimensions, limits, are set forth as precisely, fixed as unchangeably, and protected as securely from alteration, as are now the dimensions of the yard-stick, the pint-pot, and the pound-weight, then, and then only, will money perfectly resemble other measures; for then only will it become a concrete thing of known dimensions. When this comes to pass, Aristotle's definition of its function will resume its original correctness, and money will be as fit in fact, as it is now only in theory, to measure the relation called value. Some writers on the subject have insisted upon the propriety of including in money the sum of private bills of exchange and promissory notes in use, though not payable to bearer on demand; others, the sum of the discounts and loans of banks, which loans are usually made upon such bills and notes; others, the sum of bank cheques drawn, etc. I shall endeavour to show in another part of this work the precise relation which these instruments of credit bear to money. For the present it will suffice to say that the theories which mistake them for money, though not destitute of plausibility, are unsound. Money is a mechanism of society; possessing an universal incessant and uniform function or currency. Private bills, cheques, and notes are devices or instruments of credit, with a restricted, spasmodic, and varying function or currency. Money is what the law or custom makes receivable for payments, taxes, and debts; which is not the case with the instruments, or agencies, mentioned. Rather are they quickeners of money, or devices, which, so long as they last, or continue in use, render it more efficient or rapid; whilst sum for sum, they are of vastly less efficiency than money, and cannot properly be included in money without great reduction.

Said Sir Robert Peel, in his speech of May 6, 1844: "In using the word 'money,' I mean to designate by that word the coin of the realm and promissory notes payable to bearer on demand.[1] In using the words 'paper currency,' I mean only such promissory notes. I do not include in these terms bills of exchange, or drafts on bankers, or other forms of paper credit. There is a natural distinction, in my opinion, between the character of a promissory note payable to bearer on demand and other forms of paper credit, and between the effects which they respectively produce upon the prices of commodities and upon the exchanges. The one answers all the purposes of money, passes from hand to hand without endorsement, and without examination—if there be no suspicion of forgery; and it is in fact, what its designation implies it to be, currency, or circulating medium."

Said the Chief Justice of the United States, Mr. Salmon P. Chase, previously the Secretary of the Treasury, and author of the "Greenback" and "National Bank" systems, in a letter to the writer dated 6th December, 1869: "I notice in your table of currency (this table was afterwards printed in my *History of the Precious Metals*, p. 214) that you put the amount in 1862-63 and afterwards considerably higher than I do. My idea is that no interest-bearing paper can properly be called currency. No doubt such paper, and many other things, and especially bank cheques, private cheques on banks, and sight bills, largely fulfil the functions of currency; but they cannot properly be so denominated. Whilst I was Secretary of the Treasury the amount of United States notes and National Bank notes did not exceed four hundred and eighty million dollars; besides which, there were about sixty million dollars of 'State Bank' notes afloat. Of the United States notes fifty million dollars were a 'reserve' for the 'Temporary Loan,' and rose and fell with the amount of it inversely."

[1] This restricts such notes to bank notes, because private individuals are not allowed to issue notes payable to bearer on demand, and intended to circulate as money.

The table referred to did not include "bank cheques, private cheques on banks, sight bills," promissory notes, nor indeed any other kind of currency, or so-called currency, except the following: gold and silver coins, demand notes, greenbacks, interest-bearing greenbacks, National Bank notes and State Bank notes; all of which, except the State Bank notes (then reduced to a comparatively small sum), were legal-tender moneys. With all respect for the opinion of his illustrious correspondent, the writer was unable to agree with him concerning the monetary character of interest-bearing legal-tender demand notes. When not held in the place of other classes of greenbacks, and so long as they circulated from hand to hand, they exercised precisely the same influences upon prices and exchanges. Under such circumstances they were, undoubtedly, money.

However, there is no need for being absolute on the subject. Interest-bearing notes, in common with many other monetary devices, are designedly of hermaphroditic character, and it is not always easy to determine whether they are money or not. Devices of this sort should never find place in the monetary system of an honest State. There should never be room to doubt what is or what is not money.

There are still other distinctions to be drawn between money and instruments of credit. Money has a limit. Such limit may be a rude, uncertain, and occasionally varying one; yet it may be nevertheless a limit. Credit has no limit. It does not merely vary in volume from time to time; it fluctuates continuously, rapidly, and to an enormous extent. Money is a self-contained mechanism, and its sum can be expressed and employed with or without reference to credit instruments; whilst instruments of credit cannot be expressed or used without reference to money. In short, money is national; credit is individual.

With regard to the origin of the term "money," this is of little practical importance. The Greeks of the republican period called it *nomisma*, from *nomos*, or law. The Romans of the republican period called it *numerato*, from the same root. Hence we still have in use the terms nummulary, numismatics, numbers, numerals, numeration, numeraire, and others, all having the same origin, and all pointing to law or convention as the essential and necessary foundation of arithmetical and monetary systems. The word *moneta* is usually traced to the name of the temple, that of Juno Moneta, which was the mint of Rome; and this is probably correct. The reason why Juno was so called is given by Suidas as follows: During their war with the Tarentines, the Romans, being in want of money, prayed to Juno, and were assured by the goddess that "so long as they observed the principles of equity, money would always be within their reach". The significance of this advice is lost unless we recall the circumstances of the period. In A.U. 369 the Romans adopted a nummulary system copied from the Greeks, and based on "principles of equity": in A.U. 406 they first began to allow pay to their troops; and as the latter had often to purchase their supplies, luxuries, or favours, in districts or from peoples among whom the nummularies had no currency, it was deemed necessary to pay them in silver coins. The rate of pay was two obols, equal in subsequent moneys to one sesterce, or two and a half aces, or uncia (nine-tenths of the full weight) per day; which at thirty-six days to the month equalled 90, called 100 aces per month, and at ten months to the year, 1000 aces, or one talent per annum.[1] This practice, and other circumstances, led, in A.U. 437, to the supersession of the nummulary system, by a gold, silver, and copper coin system, somewhat similar to the European systems of modern days. This coin system was not forty years old before its evil consequences manifested themselves. The supplies of material wherewith to make the coins fell short or became irregular. It was then that the Romans, "being

---

[1] Niebuhr assures us that at this period the Roman year was divided into ten months. Livy, Ovid, and other authorities, confirm the assurance. The gold coin equivalent of the silver talent in subsequent ages was called the "libra".

in want of money, prayed to Juno," who answered them that "so long as they observed the principles of equity," or, in other words, if they returned to their nummulary system, which was based on those principles, "money would always be within their reach". But it was too late. Having adopted a policy of aggression, which means, among other things, the pursuit of war upon foreign soil, having determined to pay the troops in silver obols, it became absolutely necessary to acquire the material with which to make such coins. Hence the war against Pyrrhus, A.U. 479, and the capture of Tarentum, A.U. 482, the period from which Pliny dates (A.U. 485) that extensive coinage of silver denarii which formed the basis for the subsequent money systems of Rome.

The following address, which the author delivered at Peoria, Illinois, in 1895, though it contains some repetition of what has already been said on this subject, presents it from a different point of view, and for that reason may throw some further light upon the nature of the monetary mechanism.

"Money is perhaps the mightiest engine to which man can lend an intelligent guidance. Unheard, unfelt, unseen, it has the power to so distribute the burdens, gratifications, and opportunities of life, that each individual shall enjoy that share of them to which his merits or good fortune may fairly entitle him; or, contrariwise, to dispense them with so partial a hand, as to violate every principle of justice, and perpetuate a succession of social slaveries to the end of time. Such a subject does not lend itself to rhetoric. It demands the full force of the intellect. There are no flowers on this Parnassus.

"The development of astronomy has always been deemed man's highest achievement. This is a mistake. Astronomy is a science that observes, interprets, and explains a department of Nature, which already exists, in wondrous beauty and perfection, and is open to the study of all. Money relates to an institution of man, a development, an imperfect engine of social life, whose evolution necessarily waits upon the tardy progress of its designer, and whose varied phases are enveloped in obscurity and sophistry. The sciences of astronomy and money are coeval. There was no science of astronomy previous to the time ascribed to the second advent of Budha, that is to say, the sixth or seventh century before our æra; because, until that time, the priesthood, both of Asia and the West, monopolised its study and forbade it to all others. This was likewise the period of the earliest monetary systems of which we have any clear, positive, and actual remains. The staters of Lydia and Persia, now in the British Museum, are not the oldest coins extant, but the oldest whose place and function we are able to locate in a well-defined monetary system. Yet, from Thales to Newton, to Leverrier, to Herschell, observe what prodigious strides astronomy has made; and contrariwise, since the age of Plato and Aristotle, how little progress has been made in the science of money.

"Aristotle, who lived during the fourth century before our æra, defined money as the measure of value—but he did not define value. From that time, indeed, from the time of Lycurgus, to the present, that is to say, for a period of nearly thirty centuries, the vaults of the earth have echoed this question; but have vouchsafed no reply. The priests of Egypt, if they knew the answer, preserved it among their numerous mysteries of statecraft, to be sold to tyrants, or employed in the service of the gods. The seers of Chaldea and Greece, who disclosed to the Western world the majestic movements of the heavenly bodies, failed to recognise the nature of value, or else kept it an unwritten secret, that it might not be employed in the subversion of civil liberty. 'The function of money is to measure value,' declared the school of Lycurgus; but neither the Spartan sages, nor Plato, nor the great Stagyrite, who, in a still later age, voiced their philosophical maxims, ever registered a definition of value. Its nature was left to be discovered by the gifted Bastiat, who died but a few years ago.

'Every truth or error which the word "value" introduces into men's minds,' wrote this lamented author, 'is a social one.'

"You will smile when I tell you what value is; it is so simple. But the simple truths of sociology, like the mite within the oaken gall, are so deeply embedded in rubbish, that they baffle the profoundest investigations. Like Columbus' puzzle of the egg, they are obvious enough when you are shown them, but are not so easy to discover without a guide.

"Value is simply an arithmetical relation. It is the relation of numbers between two or more commodities or services, when exchanged, or viewed as exchangeable. It cannot be expressed without the use of numbers. Thus, if one ox will exchange for three sheep, the value of oxen in sheep is one to three. In short, the value of a thing is the number of other things it will fetch. This seems obvious enough. It appeals at once to your experience and your common sense, which among the various senses ascribed to man, is, probably, the least misleading. It obtains your assent. But, but, but, there are a thousand volumes of sophistry wound upon this simple stick, and a thousand regulations which obscure it. The popular writers are full of delusions on this subject. Some of them have so entirely lost sight of the stick, that they angrily defame those who point it out to them. Alas, we are all terribly mortal!

"If value is an arithmetical relation, it can neither be a thing, nor an attribute of things; yet half of the books which treat this subject either commence with the assertion that value is a thing, or the attribute of a thing, or else they shirk the inquiry altogether, and begin by telling you from what source value is derived, which, according to their turgid phraseology, is 'demand and supply,' 'cost of production,' 'utility,' 'beauty,' or some other fanciful or confusing circumstance. The subject of the inquiry is not the cause of value, but the nature of it. The cause may be many causes, so many as to force you to the study of every element that composes the life and work of man and his complex relations to society. What we want to know at the outset is, what *is* value, so that we may be able to distinguish it from that which is not value. To begin by inquiring into the *cause* of it may beg the whole question. Should we begin the study of arithmetic by inquiring why four is greater than two, why the cube is greater than the root, it is safe to say that we would never make any progress in that science.

"Value is an arithmetical relation between two or more commodities or services, which makes its appearance during the act of exchange. When you have that great truth firmly fixed in mind, you will have laid a solid foundation for your knowledge of money. Without it, you will build upon quicksand. There is but one truth, the rest is vanity, perversion, and madness. Observe that the relation of value between commodities does not belong to either of them by itself. It is not an attribute of matter; it is not intrinsic, such as weight, bulk, colour. It is fundamentally the arithmetical relation of one thing to another, when the two things are exchanged. Therefore it is extrinsic to both. Yet we hear every day of 'intrinsic' value; some people referring to it as confidently as though they had seen it. Such a thing, or such an attribute, as 'intrinsic' value does not exist. You may as well speak of an intrinsic bargain or an intrinsic marriage as of intrinsic value. A bargain or a marriage takes two persons to make it. Value is a relation between two or more things when exchanged by man. It does not pertain to either of the things by itself. In a state of human isolation it does not exist at all. Robinson Crusoe found this out when he was wrecked on Juan Fernandez. His gold possessed no value at all, because he could buy nothing with it. There was nobody from whom he could buy.

"If value is an arithmetical relation, it can, evidently, only be measured, as between all things, by a set of numbers concretely limited. You can measure the present relation of value between oxen and sheep by means either of the oxen or the sheep; but when you extend the measurement to other things, and especially to all things, such simple measures will not suffice. Some measurements of value are confined, like the oxen and the sheep, to rough equivalents and to immediate exchanges between two commodities, where the thing sold is held in one hand whilst the other is stretched out for the thing bought. But most measurements of value, in these days, are very much more complex and involved; for example, the value of one hundred shares of Western Union, or Illinois Central stock. These could not be accurately measured with oxen or sheep, even if the animals were all alike and could be frozen solid or cut up into little bits, to be used when wanted. Take a still more complex case; the value of a cargo of wheat deliverable next winter—this depends in part upon the production, past and prospective, of wheat, and of substitutes for wheat, in this and other countries, and the endless circumstances that surround these considerations. Oxen and sheep cannot measure such a relation of value. Neither can metal, as such; for the only essential superiority of metal over oxen and sheep is its divisibility, convenience in handling, and capacity to resist decay. In respect of natural limitation, which is of more importance than divisibility, durability, or convenience of handling, metal has no essential superiority over cattle. Finally, let us take a very complex, and yet a very common case of exchange. Let us say that during my life I have produced more than I have consumed. I possess a little wealth. I wish to bequeath to my children that superabundance which I have garnered and which their health, strength, industry, merits, opportunities or good fortune may deny them. A thousand fields of investment are open to me. I may purchase land in Peoria; I may invest in the Chinese loan; I may buy a gold mine in California, or a silver one in Mexico; I may acquire shares in Edison's patents, the

Suez Canal, or the Trans-Siberian railway. It is obvious that in order to conjecture, even approximately, the future value of any of these investments, I must hold a great many parities or equivalents in view at once. Such parities cannot be measured with cattle. Neither can they be measured with unlimited ounces of metal, as proposed by Adolf Soetbeer, and seconded by Prof. E. C. Hegeler, of Chicago. This gentleman, in a recent number of the *Open Court* newspaper, denounces the law of legal-tender, and demands its abrogation. I am not surprised at this. It is the only logical outcome of Soetbeer's metallism. You start with an untruth, and you end in Bedlam. You are taught that value is a thing or an intrinsic attribute of things; hence it can only be measured by similar things, or by things with similar attributes. Of these things, the best, you are told, are the precious metals. Presently you notice that there exist certain ancient laws on this subject. But why retain human laws, if natural ones suffice? Reasoning thus, you are tempted to repeal these laws. You demonetise silver. A profound depression seizes the commercial world; but this you attribute to other causes, and persist in your work of demolition. You are next advised by the logician, Prof. Hegeler, to demonetise gold, and to buy and sell no longer for dollars, but for ounces of metal, without legal limit as to the number of ounces which may be thus employed. But logic is inexorable; you will not stop here. The ounce itself is an institute of law. The ounce is a limitation. Follow Hegeler's advice, and the monetary disputes of the future will divide upon the weight of the ounce. Some will want the ounce lighter—others will clamour for a heavier ounce. You will, therefore, abolish the limitation to the weight of ounces; you will next abolish the laws which regulate mining, the import, export and assay of the precious metals, beside a thousand other regulations which govern the production and use of gold and silver. You will then have destroyed the entire edifice of metallic money. But what will there be left? The logic of a false premiss and its inevitable result—chaos.

"Do not make the mistake of supposing that I am drawing an imaginative picture. Let me quote from the first chapter of *Money and Civilization*.

"'By the fifth century of our æra money had fallen to the degraded position of ponderata, when it was customary to weigh and assay each price, a custom which I am assured prevails to this day in Burmah. Before the eighth century, when those events (the rise of Islam) took place which led to the Renaissance, the weights themselves had been so frequently degraded that it was no longer safe to make a specific bargain for money. There was a law to define the weight of pounds and ounces, but no power to enforce the law beyond the immediate limits of the capital at Byzantium. Under these circumstances money, toward the confines of the Empire, became practically extinct. Nor was this the only societary institution that perished; all such institutions perished. There was no government except the sword; there was no law; there were no certain weights nor measures. Exchanges were made in kind, or for slaves, or for bags of corn which men could count to one another; holding the thing to be sold in one hand and extending the other for the purchased commodity. From the fifth to the eighth centuries coined money in Northern Europe was almost unknown; it was the period of baugs.'

"If value is a numerical relation it evidently cannot be measured with quantity, nor with weight, nor with bulk, nor with area; but only with numbers. We do not try to measure length with weight, nor bulk with heat, nor time with the expansion of mercury. Yet we continually essay the impossible task (at least, we do so in politico-economical books) of measuring value with quantities, or weights, of gold and silver. Vain attempt, doomed to endless disappointment! Vain attempt, already tried in a hundred different ways, and always frustrated! Vain attempt, born of heedlessness of the nature of value! Vain attempt, due to distrust in our fellow-men, or to craven fears that Governments will prove reckless or unjust! Exchange is a social act. No man can exchange with himself; and even when you offer with one hand the thing sold, and you hold out the other hand for the thing bought, there is a moment of time when you must trust your fellow-man. Value is in one sense the produce of this social act. There can be no value where there is no exchange. There may be worth, but not value. Worth comprises a number of attributes; value comprises none. Worth appears in the isolated state; value only in the social. Worth cannot be measured by money—value can. Were we to repeal the remainder of our monetary laws as we have repealed some of them, commerce would be impossible. Follow Hegeler, repeal the law of legal-tender; in other words, demolish the last vestige of money, and the whole social fabric would tumble upon your heads. The fact is that money is purely a legal institution; it is impossible without law; and, theoretically, it is perfect in direct proportion as it depends upon law. But man himself is imperfect, his laws are imperfect; his weakness, passions, vagaries, or necessities may induce him to alter the best of laws. The monetary systems of the day reflect this imperfection of human nature. They are a compromise between a perfect money, which must depend entirely upon the law, and barter, which places the least dependence upon it. A perfect money will correctly measure the present and future value of any or all things; barter can only measure, and very rudely at that, the present value of two things, namely the things actually bartered, one for the other. Our present money is a compromise between these two systems; and it is a very vicious compromise at that.

"There is scarcely any form of society now in existence which has not existed before; there is scarcely any form of exchange which has not been effected before; there is scarcely any example of value which has not been measured before; there is scarcely any kind of money or monetary system which has not been tried before.

MONEY IS A MECHANISM.

"In a work upon which I have been engaged for many years past, a work of some 500 or 600 pages of print, I have endeavoured to describe the various experiments which have been made with MONETARY SYSTEMS from very ancient times to the present. There is material enough to be had for twenty books; but although I have tried to be brief, yet I could not avoid producing a bulky volume. The demonetisation of the precious metals, the adoption of purely nummulary systems, with clay, porcelain, bronze, and paper symbols, indeed, every conceivable variety of money symbols, has been tried. Why need we waste further time and effort in experiment, when we may have recourse to experience? The true guide to monetary problems is to be found in history, and the basis of that history is the nature of value. What I have been endeavouring to make plain to you is not a theory hewn out of the imagination; it is not a hypothesis which involves a doubtful admission; it is not a postulate built upon ambiguous words; it is a plain, simple, scientific truth. If, as history and philosophy teach us, value is the relation which appears between two or more commodities or services when exchanged or exchangeable, then that relation is numerical; and it can only be expressed by numbers. When those numbers are symbolised by legal-tender coins or notes, the essential point is not what the coins are made of, nor what the notes promise, but how many of them there are, and what assurance is there that this number will remain constant.

"Numbers by themselves are illimitable. To measure value with them you must limit them. But how? By embodying them in a set of symbols or counters, suitable for transference from hand to hand. Made of what substance? Theoretically, anything you like, so long as they cannot be multiplied by counterfeiters, nor lessened by monopolists and hoarders; the essence of the mechanism, for it is only a mechanism, being limitation, resulting in stability of prices. These considerations have compelled us to avoid irredeemable paper notes, the material of which, being itself valueless, would best subserve the purposes of a measure of value. They compelled us, in view of history, experience and human frailty, to make our counters of gold and silver; and here is where all the trouble came in, for men soon lose sight of the fact that it is the number of coins which measures value, and they only think of the material of which the coins are made. This confusion is largely due to that licence of private coinage which the nations of antiquity never permitted, which was first attempted by the Saracens and grew out of the loose wording of Mahomet's Koran, and which we directly owe to the military operations of the British East India Company and specifically to the Act 18 Charles II., c. 5. It would take too much time to go into these matters. They are very interesting; they are also very long. No, we must not stop to seek for flowers. The work is heavy, and you will presently grow tired. We must go on with it.

"I say that the relation, which, for example, one metallic dollar bears to the whole number of dollars, in a given monetary system, is totally different from the relation which the metal of which that dollar may be composed, bears to all the like metal for which it is practically exchangeable.[1] Take the gold dollar of to-day. As a dollar, it is one of, say, 1500 millions of dollars of various kinds in this country, practically within your reach, and with which you may pay your debts. As a piece of metal, it is one of only, let us say, 200 or 300 millions of similar

[1] "The legal value of money cannot be regulated by the commercial value of the material out of which it is made. The commercial value of the material is influenced by the supply and demand of such material. As supply and demand fluctuate, this value fluctuates. Therefore money receives all its value as such from the law creating it. It is wholly a creature of law. The legal value, which is the only money value, remains the same so long as the law remains unchanged, though the commercial value of the material may fluctuate ever so often and ever so much."— *Chicago Record*, 12th June, 1895.

pieces of metal practically within your reach, with which you may pay your debts. It is this difference which constitutes the advantage of the cosmopolitan financiers, the power with which they alternately raise and lower the tide of commerce in this or that part of the world.

"Before the Act of 1666 the measure of value in England consisted of all the pounds, shillings and pence in the Kingdom, no matter of what material made, plus all the pounds, shillings and pence which the king, as advised by his Privy Council, might choose to decree. After that Act it consisted of all the pounds, shillings and pence in the kingdom and some others presently to be mentioned, only when such pounds, shillings and pence were made of gold and silver and of a fixed weight and fineness. As this Act threw open the mint to private coinage, so that bullion could be manufactured at the bidding of private individuals, into legal-tender coins, and as legal-tender coins could be melted down by anybody to bullion without hindrance or expense, the coins of the realm could be, and, in fact, were frequently augmented by fresh accessions of metal, or lessened by exportation or melting. The measure of value was previously of uncertain dimensions, because, as it has been alleged, the king chose to frequently alter it. It now became of still more uncertain dimensions, because the goldsmiths and merchants had discovered how to alternately swell and shrink it, so as to make it subserve their own interests. From this moment there grew up that class of universal bankers and cosmopolitan financiers who now govern the markets of the world. Macaulay has described the advent of this class, but he has omitted to mention the mischief they wrought upon the monetary system of England.

"To remedy this mischief arose the great Bank; out of the great Bank grew numerous smaller banks, and at length an irredeemable paper money system, during which silver was demonetised, but as yet without dangerous consequences, because the French, the American and other mints were still open to coin the discarded metal into money. During the American Civil War of 1861-5 these universal financiers got hold of 1000 to 1500 million American bonds at half price, and they at once started a movement or intrigue, which had for its object the raising of these bonds to par in gold. The obstacles in their path were the mint laws of France, England and the United States. Those of France they procured to be altered in 1867, England 1870, and the United States 1873. These alterations deprived the debtor of his previous option to pay in either gold or silver coins, and confined him to gold ones alone. They moreover prescribed and endeavoured to prescribe for all time the weight and fineness of such gold coins. By these means they claim to have converted a debt of francs, dollars or 'pounds' into a debt of gold metal. More than this. They not only altered the conditions, incidence and weight of the debt; they pinned down all the great States of Europe and the Western World to the future use of gold coins of a given weight and fineness, and thus mortgaged posterity to conditions so onerous that they may either refuse to be bound by them, or be obliged to suffer what may prove to be a ruinous alternative.

"The name of my adopted State, California, was derived from a romance which was very popular at the time of the Spanish discovery of that country. In a like manner, the term 'unit of value,' employed in the early mint laws, was derived, if my memory does not mislead me, from an essay printed in 1757, by one Joseph Harris, Master of the Mint at London. Somebody has said that history is composed of myths, and political economy of delusions. Well, this is one of the delusions. There is no such thing as a 'unit of value'; this phantom arises from the blunder of mistaking value for a thing, or an attribute of things; whereas, it is merely a numerical relation, which is seen in exchange, and therefore it has no unit.

"Because Mr. Harris knew how to manufacture coins, he

was indulgently accorded the merit of understanding the principles of money. The expressions he used found currency everywhere. They not only appeared in the earlier mint laws; they were adopted by Lord Liverpool in his famous Letter to the King, and in many other documents of the same historical period. But the inference about Mr. Harris was erroneous; what he knew about money was in fact very little. A man may know how to manufacture playing cards without being a Cavendish, or trumpets and kettledrums without being a Wagner. Mr. Harris wrote an admirable treatise on coins. The moment he ascended into the region of money, he was lost. It was Jack on the Beanstalk climbing into an unknown world. Of the history of money, even in his own country, Mr. Harris does not disclose any familiarity whatever; its principles, he evolved from the coin manufactory, just as some of the politicians deduce theirs—from the brewery.

"When, in process of time, the term 'unit of value' was seen to be objectionable, it was changed by monetary writers to 'integer of money,' or 'unit of money,' or 'monetary unit,' and it became attached to the principal coin used in each State, as the franc in France, the sovereign in England, and the dollar in America. This blunder was worse than the other, because it assumed that the value of money is determined by the quantity of metal contained in the so-called 'unit'; whereas, it is in point of fact determined by the arithmetical denominations and aggregate numbers, or volume, of all the 'units,' including legal-tender paper notes; no matter how much or how little metal the former may contain, or whether the latter are redeemable or not. In short, the unit of money, if we *must* use the misleading expression, cannot consist of one coin, unless that coin be the only one in existence; for the moment you add another coin to the circulation, you alter the value or purchasing power of the first one and destroy its integrity. Value is a social phenomenon: money is a social institution or mechanism which measures it; and of like social character, must necessarily be the terminology of money. There is no 'unit' to it, because there is no social unit, less than the whole nation; the unit of money cannot be one coin, but must necessarily be all the coins within a given legal jurisdiction. It is in this respect that money differs from all other measures. The measuring value of a pint-pot or a yard-stick is not affected by the multiplication or diminution of pint-pots or yard-sticks. Such is not the case with money. When the whole volume is increased, each coin, note, or other concrete symbol of numerical denomination, loses a portion of its arithmetical relation to the whole number of coins and notes; therefore, of a portion of its capacity to measure value. When the volume is diminished, each symbol gains in value or purchasing power. While, in neither case, does the whole sum either gain or lose. The whole sum of money is therefore the true and the only unit of value. This is not a mere theory; it is a physical fact.

"The Rev. Henry Thompson, in his *Dissertation on the Sources and Formation of the Latin Language*, says that the German *ein*, the English *one* and *unit*, and the Latin *unus*, are all derived from the Greek εἰς and ἕενς, meaning totality. The Tarentines had a similar term, with a similar meaning; so had the Goths, and many other nations of antiquity. It was derived from the name of Ies, the Sun-god. In this sense, that is to say, in the sense of totality, the phrase 'unit of money' is allowable; although I think the 'circulation' or the 'volume of money' is better. In the sense in which it is used by Mr. Harris and copied into the mint laws, it is worse than rubbish. It is a delusion and a snare.

"I have now to direct your attention to a very remarkable opinion; remarkable because, although repeatedly asserted by experts and susceptible of ample proof, it runs counter to popular belief. The opinion is that both gold and silver are produced, on the average, at a loss. The mint and market value of fine gold is $20.67 the ounce troy; the mint value of fine silver is $1.29 the ounce; the market value of the latter at the present moment is little more than half this sum. It is asserted that neither of these metals can be produced on the whole at these prices, nor at double nor treble these prices. Such is the testimony of Prof. John D. Hague; Superintendent Taylor, of the Comstock mines; Mr. Louis Garnett, formerly of the San Francisco mint; Prof. Wm. Newmarch in Tooke's *History of Prices*, ed. 1857, VI., 226; and numerous experts practically connected with mining and minting. You will find a great mass of testimony on this subject in my *History of the Precious Metals*. So long ago as the time of Adam Smith, it was observed that the mining States were the poorest in the world; that Mexico, Peru, La Plata, Brazil and Spain were always in a state of comparative indigence, whilst the agricultural and manufacturing States of Europe and America were every year growing richer. Take it to-day: California was settled two centuries ago; its vast treasures of gold were opened nearly half a century ago; yet it has little more than a million of population; whilst Kansas, Iowa, Minnesota, and other agricultural States, settled since the California rush, exceed it in population, and therefore, as the case stands, also in wealth. If you take the gold fields of California before machinery was used on them, you will find that the then current rate of wages multiplied by the number of men at work on the mines, was equal to the entire product of gold several times over. If you take the cost of land, machinery and labour on the Comstock Lode, you will find that they come to about 1500 millions; whilst the product, from first to last, fetched less than 350 millions. If you take the entire gold product of Australia and compare it merely with the amount paid to the miners for wages, you will find, as the Government Commissioners found, that the gold cost more than it fetched.

"Assuming this overwhelming mass of evidence to be true, how can the fact be accounted for? Easy enough. There has always been on hand in the world, a vast mass of the precious metals which was obtained by its present owners for (substantially) nothing. It was the fruit of conquest and slavery. The spoil of Darius, of Alexander, of Cæsar, of Mahomet, of Cortes, of Pizarro, of Albuquerque, of Drake, Morgan, Nadir Shah, Clive, Hastings, and Napoleon Buonaparte, cost substantially nothing to the States which acquired it through their depredations. The vast treasures which were wrung from the blood and tears of thirty millions of American natives, and as many Africans, brought hither to fill their empty places, cost comparatively little to the Spaniards. Twenty-five dollars a head was the price of a newly-landed slave in Brazil, during the seventeenth century, and ten cents a day the cost of maintaining him. This policy, that is to say, conquest and slavery, piled up in the world before mining began to be conducted as a free industry (namely about the year 1850) some $2,000,000,000 in gold and silver, which had cost little or nothing. This amounted to about thirty years' supply at the rate of production then current.

"It was against this stock on hand that the California miner had to contend. Suppose that there was at the present time a stock on hand equal to thirty years' growth of wheat throughout the world, do you think that any new wheat you might produce would fetch the cost of its production? Take it with coal or iron. If there were thirty years' supply on hand of these commodities, do you think it would pay to produce fresh iron or fresh coal? Of course not. Then why should we give heed to those purveyors of false statements and false theories, who go about with tales of silver which cost but 30 cents per ounce, and silver dollars that are worth but half a dollar? Silver metal is depressed at the present time when measured in gold metal, because you suddenly deprived the former of one of its employments. So would gold be depressed when valued in silver if you had treated it in the same way. But if it be true that neither of these metals can be produced on the average at their present value, then such depression of silver is only temporary, and it must sooner or later terminate.

"Time forbids my entering at length into the various causes that induce men to produce gold and silver at what is, on the average, unquestionably a loss. Free mines, private or 'free' coinage, the love of adventure, the excitement of mining, which while it beggars the community, enriches the exceptionally lucky prospector and miner,— these and other causes account for this singular phenomenon whose happening you now perceive is not merely an opinion, but a well-determined fact. Here is a comprehensive piece of information on the subject which you will find in my *History of the Precious Metals*. Since the year 1675, when the world's stock of gold and silver coins was about 1250 million dollars, there have been produced nearly 15,000 million dollars of the precious metals. Of this vast sum there only remain on hand to-day in the world about 3750 million dollars; so that 11,250 millions have gone into the arts, or been lost, destroyed, or shipped to Asia. Notwithstanding the inflated figures published by the Director of the Mint, there is in fact little or no gold or silver used or available for money in China. That State strikes neither gold nor silver coins. Its currency, except at a few treaty ports, is entirely of bronze and paper. The metallic currency of India is about 115 crores of rupees, or, nominally, 575 million dollars. If we allow 175 million dollars more for the metallic currency of Japan and of the other Asiatic States, it follows that of the whole production of the world during the past two and a quarter centuries more than two-thirds have gone into the arts, or been lost, or destroyed, and that less than one-third exists to-day in the form of money, or practically available for money. If gold and silver, when turned into money, were profitable, is it conceivable that over two-thirds of the entire product during more than two centuries would have declined the companionship of coins, and preferred to be absorbed in the arts? I should say not.

"This brings us to the question of the day. Why do so many citizens, fully aware of the evils of private coinage, join the ranks of the Silverites in this country? Because, owing to their high cost of production and low market value, the precious metals have an overwhelming tendency to seek the arts, transformed by which they fetch a far higher price than as bullion; because this leaves but a small available supply for coinage; because the stock of gold and silver coins is so small and so appropriated or devoted as to place the still smaller stock of gold coins and available gold bullion under the thumb of the cosmopolitan financiers; and because under anybody's thumb is no place for freemen.

"That's why. When these facts and principles are disproved, not by the writers of illiterate pamphlets, not by the editors of subsidised newspapers, not by paid orators, or hired buffoons; but by honourable men, competent to treat this subject, you may witness some accessions to the other party; but not till then.

"I have travelled from the Atlantic Ocean to the Mississippi River without having seen a single gold coin in circulation in this country. The gold of the world is, in fact, concentrated by money-lenders living chiefly in three States,—England, France, and Germany; in most other countries it is not in circulation, and in many of them it bears a premium. As for the public debt of this country, which it is claimed is payable in gold, let it be so paid; even though the claim be invalid. That is at present a comparatively small matter. The important matter is that gold has been 'cornered'; that commerce trembles when a million of yellow pieces are shipped abroad; and that your present monetary policy is pinning down the future to wholly impossible and ruinous conditions, opposed to prosperity and fatal to liberty!"

CHAPTER V.

CONSTITUENTS OF A MONETARY MECHANISM.

Control over the precious metals—Mines royal—Treasure trove—Control of the coinage—Use of two or more metals for coins—Coins as numerical symbols—Size, weight, fineness, and shape—Mark of authority—Denominations—Compulsory use—Legal-tender—Restrictions upon hoarding, melting, or exporting—Counterfeiting—Interdict of private coinage—Taxes on mining, etc.—Most of these regulations are now overthrown—Private coinage has degraded money to metal—The use of metal in place of money reduces all commerce to the basis of barter—Numerous States have avoided this by resorting to paper systems, and this tendency is increasing—The demonetisation of silver is promoting that of gold.

THE constituents of a monetary mechanism are not always the same. In the infancy of metallic money they were few; in its maturity they became sufficiently numerous to occasion dissatisfaction to all classes except those who were especially benefited by the confusion they promoted. With the invention of nummulary systems the mechanism was reduced to the simplest constituents: with the decay of these systems, the mechanism again became complex and cumbrous. This is the condition in which it remained down to a very recent period; and it is this phase of the monetary mechanism whose principal constituents will now be set forth. They embrace: (1) Governmental control over the supplies of the precious metals. This included the institutes of Mines royal and Treasure trove. (2) Control over the coinage. (3) The use of two or three different metals for the various denominations of coins. (4) Subdivision of the metal or metals into numerical symbols. (5) Shape, size, weight, and fineness of the symbols. (6) Mark of public authority. (7) Denominations, or relative measuring capacity, of the symbols. (8) Their compulsory use. Law of legal-tender. (9) Restrictions upon hoarding, melting, or exporting. (10) Punishment for counterfeiting. (11) Interdiction of private coinage. (12) Taxes on mining, amalgamation, coinage, and exportation. Besides these there were other constituents of the mechanism which appear in all mining codes and mint laws.

At the present time the most important of these regulations are swept away; so that money, as a societary mechanism, is virtually destroyed; and in its place stands a private system of "metallism," which amounts in many States to little more than barter. There is no public control over the supplies of the precious metals. The doctrine of Mines royal is still maintained in England, where there are no productive mines of the precious metals; but discarded in Australia, South Africa, California, and elsewhere, where such mines do exist. The Government has no control over the coinage of gold, which is made into full legal-tender coins; it only reserves control over silver and copper, which are made into coins of limited tender. The gold coinage is entirely subject to private individuals, who may increase or diminish its volume at pleasure. The Government merely executes their orders by turning their bullion, when requested, into coins, putting the mark of public authority upon them, and declaring them to be legal tenders for taxes, contracts, and debts: all of which it does gratuitously. There are no restrictions upon hoarding, or exporting; and practically none upon melting. There is no interdict which restrains private individuals from having their gold bullion coined whenever they wish. There are practically no taxes upon the production, coinage, or movement of gold.

Under these circumstances, gold coins have become a mere commodity; trade has degenerated to a barter of services, or commodities, for gold metal. The latter has fallen into the hands of, and been engrossed by, powerful syndicates, who alternately inflate prices when they sell for gold, plus an expanding private credit (their own); and depress prices when they buy for gold, plus a contracting credit. The vast and progressive populations of Great Britain, France, Germany, and the United States of America, who, every ten or fifteen years, are permitted to float upon the full tide of commercial activity, are compelled at alternate intervals to yield up a large portion of their profits in trade to a body of cosmopolitan financiers, "who toil not, neither do they spin," but who are enabled to control the markets of the world and turn its activities largely to their own advantage. These "squeezes" are fatuously termed commercial crises, and their periods commercial cycles. Some learned Economists have even connected them with the spots on the sun!

The remaining States of the European world, tired of this thimble-rigging, and anxious to guard the welfare of their people, have sought refuge from it in the use of governmental paper money. Such is the state of affairs in Russia, Austria, Italy, Spain, the Scandinavian, and other States. Should gold coins go to a premium in the United States, an event which is regarded by many writers as not improbable, an important foothold of the barter system will be lost. When this occurs in so important a country as the United States, it will very likely be followed by the abandonment of the gold barter system elsewhere. It is becoming more and more evident that the exchanges of the world have grown too numerous and important to be conducted on the basis of gold barter. Time was when barter led to slavery: but that time is past. Its practical outcome at the present time is leading us back to the system of Plato and of the Greek and Roman republics. The demonetisation of silver is rapidly promoting the demonetisation of gold.

CHAPTER VI.

HISTORY OF MONETARY MECHANISMS.

Evolution of money—Barter—Valuing commodity—Baugs—Coins—Their defects—Nomisma—Its downfall—Coins subjected to legal and sacerdotal regulations—Monetary systems of the Roman Empire and of European States—Coinage Acts of the sixteenth century—Origin and progress of private coinage—Private money, or metallism—This is the present phase of monetary mechanisms—It is virtually a return to barter—Its consequences have been the enrichment of money-lenders and the impoverishment of States—The remedy adopted in many States has been paper systems.

THE history of monetary systems or mechanisms has been treated at length in the author's previous works. It may here be conveniently summarised under four heads: (1) The general evolution of money; (2) The monetary systems of Europe; (3) Private coinage; and (4) Private money.

I. *The general evolution of money.*—The earliest form of exchange, that which is peculiar to rudimentary or savage communities, was barter. To remedy those inconveniences of barter which were disclosed by the progress of civilisation, some given commodity of common necessity and production was selected in each community as a rude measure of the value of other commodities. Such measure, whether it consisted of a number of beans, cloth, shells, or lumps of metal, enabled any given exchange to be effected upon a more equitable basis than before, simply by its operation in holding several rude parities in view at once. With the further growth of civilisation this measure was also found to be defective: it lacked precision. The beans, shells, gold, silver, etc., being useful for other purposes besides a measure of value, the slightest difference in the size or quality of beans, etc., became matters of consideration during the act of effecting exchanges; and thus their effectiveness as such measure of value was impaired. A further improvement was thereupon devised by reducing the pieces of the valuing commodity to like sizes and weights, and to a like quality or fineness. This could best be done with the precious metals, and thus a number of metallic pellets, sometimes rings (baugs), came to compose a measure of value, which, nevertheless, was still a very rude one.

The experience of the Norse traders assures us that the use of baugs promoted commerce, whilst increased commerce exposed the defectiveness of baugs. It was discovered that no matter what amount of labour was involved in the production or acquisition of the precious metals or of baugs, and no matter how carefully the latter were weighed or refined, their value, or power to purchase other commodities, was liable to enormous variation. The arrival or departure of a few ingots of metal, the discovery or exhaustion of a mine, and many other circumstances had the effect to rapidly alter the local value of baugs, and upset all calculations based upon their anticipated power to purchase other commodities.

The remedy adopted for this defect was to localise the emissions and currency of baugs. Each city, colony, and trading post made its own baugs, and stamped its seal or corporate mark on the emissions. The stamping of the baugs converted them into coins.[1] To complete the effectiveness of the new device, it was deemed necessary to forbid the use of all other coins. It is at this phase of money, namely, that of placing a stamp upon the pieces, that nummulary history usually begins.

[1] The origin of this term is usually traced to *cuneus*, the punch or die from which coins are struck; but this attribution is doubtful.

The device of stamped and localised moneys disclosed other ills, and gave rise to other remedies, all tending toward the solution of what in the end proved to be merely a mechanical problem. The ill that now developed itself was when one mint melted down and recoined the issues of another, and by this means resuscitated that defect of the measure of value which arose from suddenly increased or diminished supplies of the "valuing" commodity. To discourage such recoinages, seigniorage was introduced, and this gave rise to numerous other legal regulations, the character and intricacy of which can best be appreciated by attempting to master any of the extant mint codes, ancient or modern.

So long ago as the æra of Lycurgus it was perceived that the monetary problem was indeed a mechanical one; that, unlike length, weight, capacity, etc., value was not an intrinsic or inalienable attribute of matter, and therefore that it could not be measured by means of any commodity as a commodity, but only as symbols representing numbers, in short, by means of a nummulary system. Such a monetary device was employed not only in Sparta, but during some portions of the sixth and fifth centuries B.C., also in the Greek Republics of Ionia, Byzantium, and Athens. The device consisted of a limited and publicly known number of named counters belonging to and issued by the State (commonly discs of purposely rotted sheet iron or of bevelled bronze), having little or no value as pieces of metal, but (when regarded as a whole) possessing great and definite value as a public measure. Value (*valeo*), or purchasing power, was conferred at the outset upon these counters by the law of the State, which gave them the names of coins previously in use; it endowed them with the function of legal-tender for the payment of all debts, claims, purchases, and taxes; and it rendered these ordinances effective and permanent by limiting the issue of the counters, and taking means to protect them from being counterfeited. In a word, money became a public instrument, owned and controlled by the State.

From the employment of this device it is evident that the Lycurgan conception of value was that of an arithmetical relation. Each commodity or service was valued as an exchange. Each exchange was valued in relation to the whole number of exchanges, and these were valued at the whole number of counters. The system was complete in itself. Its practical outcome was that each commodity or service was valued in the market at so many counters, with the knowledge and certainty of what the latter would exchange for at a future time. This assurance was derived at first from experimental observation, and afterwards from the operation of the legal-tender law and the limitation of the currency. Whatever the relation between the commodity or service sold and the other one purchased, it was arithmetical; and, being so, it was probably found to be susceptible of exact expression only by means of named counters issued by the State, the total number of which was limited and definitely known: these last being absolutely fundamental and essential conditions to the working of the mechanism.

The success of this device is attested by its longevity: it lasted in Greece for centuries, and afterwards in Rome during the best days of the Republic. Not that it constituted a perfect measure of value, but the best that had yet been devised. Of the three principal defects which its working disclosed, two were inseparable from all measures, whether of weight, capacity, or value. Depending entirely upon the power of the law, its efficiency necessarily ended with the autonomy of the State. Besides this, it was unable without the aid of private credit to accommodate itself rapidly to expansions and contractions of commerce. Finally, it was exposed to the nefarious trade of the forger. The first defect was balanced by the reflection that it was hardly worth while to seek for a measure of value which should survive the downfall of the State; since all that such measure might be employed to value, would necessarily fall into the hands of the conqueror of the State.[1] The second defect is common to all moneys, especially metallic systems, and is probably irremediable. The third defect could only have been successfully met by so improving the mechanical fabrication of nomisma as to increase the difficulty of forgery.

The Persian wars and the discovery or practical opening of the silver mines of Laurium about the fifth century B.C., put an end to these nummulary systems.[2] The necessities of Athens now foisted upon her Colonies, and eventually upon all the States of Greece, coinage systems similar to those which they had found it expedient to discard centuries before. To remedy the well-known and ineradicable defects of coins, new devices were adopted. The State sought to prevent sudden variations of the measure of value by monopolising the fabrication, and especially by limiting the number of coins, at issue. Variations in the relative value of the coining metals were attempted to be remedied at first by coining both metals together (electrum coins),[3] and afterwards by reducing the coins of one metal or the other to limited tender or function. In short, the aid of the law was invoked to confer upon coins a different and more stable value than that of the commodities of which they were composed; and, to a certain extent, this effort succeeded.

In spite of these and other improvements the measure of value (when it came to consist of coins whose total number was apt to be irregularly lessened by loss, wear and tear, or melting, or increased by secret issues or

---

[1] In 1379, when the independence of the Venetian Republic was endangered, the rich Michael Mocenigo lent all his money to the State, saying: "If this land comes to ill, money is nothing to me".—Hazlitt's *Venice*, ed. 1860, Vol. III., p. 333.

[2] These mines are mentioned by Æschylus, Herodotus, Thucydides, Xenophon, Cornelius Nepos, and Pausanias.

[3] Artificial electrum is described by Pliny. The coins of Sardis, some of which are still extant, were made of this material.

counterfeiting, and therefore which could not be definitely and permanently fixed), consisted essentially and teleologically of a commodity. From this circumstance arose the custom of calling money *argyros* or *argentum*.

Again it went its round of experiment. Again was it noticed that as a commodity it was but ill fitted to measure the intricate and involved series of exchanges which are implied in the financial relations, contracts, speculations, inheritances, and property arrangements of commercial communities. It was also observed that the coins, though made of but a single metal, failed to retain a more permanent value than that of the material of which they were composed; and that this value rose and fell with every vicissitude of war, mining, mintage, commerce, and even fashion. Such a means of valuation might have answered well enough for archaic communities and for simple and immediate exchanges; but it was clearly unsuited for the determination of future and involved ones, such as the sale of growing crops, the rental of houses or farms, the repayment of loans, or the disposal of incomes by grant or testament. Consequently, it was deemed necessary to subject the valuing commodity to further restraints of law.[1]

The type, design, inscriptions, metal, alloy, weight, size, and tale-relations of coins; the charges for coinage, the tax of seigniorage, and the degree, kind, and territorial extent of the legal-tender functions of coins, had already been regulated by law. Mining for the money metals was now added to these regulations. Taxation and State monopolisation of the coinage, etc., were also resorted to. The number of slaves permitted to work the mines was regulated. The importation and exportation of the money metals were regu-

[1] The discerning reader will at once detect that this rapid sketch of the evolution of money is drawn from its history in the Western world. Nevertheless, money is very much more ancient than the Greek writers pretended or some modern ones suppose. It undoubtedly had a previous history in the Eastern world: but this is a subject into which it is not necessary to enter in this place.

lated. The right to strike coins was limited to sacerdotal authority and confined to the temples. The highest resources of art were bestowed upon the designs. Foreign coins were sometimes monetised, at others decried. The individual or private fabrication, counterfeiting, defacement, melting down or hoarding of coins was prohibited. The use of the money metals in the arts was restricted or forbidden. Gold and silver are twin metals which are frequently found together in the same matrix. Their production cannot be regulated at man's will, but is subject to great vicissitudes from chance discoveries, military conquest, and other causes. Therefore, their relative value or the ratio between them cannot be determined, like that of other commodities; but if these metals are used for coins, it must be regulated empirically. To secure permanency in this ratio, it also was subjected to sacerdotal sanction, and we shall find that as the result of this regulation, the ratio remained fixed for centuries; so that among the numerous guides to historical research afforded by the regulations of money, this is one of the most conspicuous and reliable. There is even reason to suspect that the Roman State, by means of the sacred devices impressed upon its coins, sought to convey to the holder of them that he was not their absolute possessor, but was only entitled to their use so long as the State refrained from employing its taxing power to confiscate or call them in.

Notwithstanding these various regulations, the stability of coins as a measure of value was still exposed to so much disturbance that further legal measures of greater and greater complexity were adopted to secure the important object of stability. The principal disturbance was now created by the wear and tear, and subterranean concealmeant, or "hoarding" or burial of coins, and the failure of slave-mining or foreign conquest to make good the continued loss of gold and silver metal.

New and higher denominations of value were given by law to the same coins, and frequent recoinages had to be made at great expense to the State, and great risk of public disorder. The evil and expense of recoinage were attempted to be avoided by still further legislation. The weight and standard of the new issues of coins were lowered, as in the denarii of Livius Drusus. Emissions were made of still more highly overvalued coins, like the plated denarii of Claudius, Trajan and Hadrian. Finally, as related in a previous work, moneys of account were created, or revived, by law, called libras, sicilici and denarii (£ s. d.). This was essentially merely an arithmetical scale of proportions which could be applied, without the necessity of recoinage, to the perplexing variety of existing coins which had now obtained currency, and which scale of proportions, as a matter of fact, was applied not only to these, but also to measurements of land, of bread, and of other things.

It will thus be seen that money, whatever it consisted of originally, grew in time to be a complex instrument of societary life, in short, an Institution of Law, designed to measure and determine value; and that its efficiency, precision, stability, and equitable operation depended largely, if not entirely, upon the strength, wisdom, and virtue of the governments by whose laws it was created and regulated. Instead of the simple and easy subject which some modern writers have airily supposed it to be, its proper understanding involves, as has been shown in *Money and Civilization*, the mastery of more than seventy separate legal institutes. These constitute what may be termed the Grammar of Money.[1]

II. With respect to the monetary systems of Europe, that is to say, of the Roman Empire and of the numerous States that grew up from its ruins, much of this is contained in my reply to Mr. MacLeod, published in the *Fortnightly Review* for April, 1895.

Mr. Henry Dunning MacLeod's argument against any proposal to return to the coinage of full legal-tender silver pieces was, that several centuries of history, statesmanship,

[1] From the Introduction to *Hist. Mon. Systems.*

and philosophical authority are against it; that it is impracticable for Government to maintain a fixed ratio of value between coins of the precious metals; and that, being impracticable, it is useless to discuss the advantages or policy of such a proposal.[1] His historical evidences begin with Charlemagne, of whom he says that he established that system of coinage which was afterwards adopted throughout the whole of Western Europe; that is to say, "he made the pound weight of silver the standard, and divided it into 240 pieces, called pennies. For some centuries these silver pennies were the only coins in circulation." His instances of statesmanship begin with Sir Thomas Gresham, of whom he says that (being in Antwerp in 1552, to borrow money for the Crown of England) he declared that when good and bad money circulated at the like value, people would prefer to hoard the good and pass away the bad; so that the former would disappear from, and the latter remain in, the circulation. Mr. MacLeod's philosophical authorities consist of two mediæval tracts rescued from oblivion some thirty odd years ago by Wolowski, of Paris, who took part in discussing the monetary contraction of 1867-73, of the claims of which to the approval of mankind, Mr. MacLeod is proud to be the champion. One of these mediæval tracts is by the good Bishop Oresme. It begins with Adam and Eve and the dispersion of the twelve tribes of Israel, cites the mythology of Ovid and Virgil, traces some connection between these latter flights of fancy and the coinage system of Charles the Wise, King of France, 1364-80, and, according to Mr. MacLeod, deduces the philosophical conclusion that the legal valuation between one coin and another should strictly conform to the "market value" of the metals of which they may be composed; otherwise the coins of one class will be undervalued, and will disappear from the circulation. It may as well be stated here that Oresme says nothing about "market value," and makes no such deduction as is claimed;

[1] *Bimetallism*, 2nd ed. 1894. Longmans.

moreover, that there was no "market value," other than the mint value, at the time that Oresme wrote, and for two centuries afterwards. However, this unwarrantable use of Oresme's tract is a small matter compared with what we shall presently have to say concerning Mr. MacLeod's argument. On account of the similarity of the supposd deduction of Oresme to that made by Gresham, Mr. MacLeod, who regards it as the great fundamental principle of coinage, gratefully proposes to call it the Oresme-Copernicus-Gresham law, and offers it as a complete objection to any present movement having for its object the rehabilitation of silver, as a material of full legal-tender coins.

Had Mr. MacLeod, in his search for the fundamental principles of money, studied the coins in the great national collections, the circumstances of their discovery, the legal codes of Theodosius and Justinian, the rolls containing the accounts of the English Exchequer collated by Madox, the Papal registers edited by Bliss, and other evidences of an authentic character, instead of wasting his time in paraphrasing the lucubrations of the pious bishop of Lisieux, he might have made a discovery more worthy of the admiration which his works on Credit have recently extorted from Lord Farrer. He might also have discovered that his conception of the Carlovingian coinage was totally erroneous and inadequate, and that this theory is contradicted, both by the coins, the texts of the period, and the Civil law. With regard to the £ s. d. system, this, in fact, is traceable to the earliest days of the Roman Empire, and was carried into all its provinces, so that to-day its remains will be found in the laws of Spain and Turkey, quite as distinctly as in those of France and England. The "standard," by which misapplied term Mr. MacLeod evidently means the monetary system, or measure of value, employed in the Carlovingian Empire, was not prescribed by Charlemagne, as he supposes, nor by his successors; but by the Basileus or Sovereign-Pontiff, of the Roman Empire, residing at Constantinople. It did not consist, as he imagines, solely of Carlovingian silver deniers, struck 240 to the pound weight of silver; it consisted largely of gold coins, variously called aurei, solidi, or besants, struck by the Basileus at Constantinople, of which, according to the Civil law, five went to the libra of account. This gold libra of five solidi was valued at 240 denarii, containing twelve times its weight in silver; in other words, the system was what would be called, in the monetary jargon of to-day, a "bimetallic standard". The gold coins were full legal-tender, having a forced, at all events an accepted, circulation, in all parts of the Empire. The Basileus (in his civil capacity) also struck silver coins; so also did the proconsuls, subject-kings, nobles, ecclesiastical dignitaries, and even municipalities of the Empire; but as these coins had only a local course, or legal-tender function, and as the taxes, tributes, fines, reliefs, aids, or other dues from the proconsuls to the Basileus were payable in Imperial gold coins, or else in twelve times their weight in silver coins—purity for purity—it mattered but little to the fisc what variation took place in the weight or fineness of the latter. There are not known to have been any legal limits to the coinage of gold by the Basileus, or to that of silver by the princes, proconsuls, and nobles. This system, a system which Mr. MacLeod and his admirer, Lord Farrer, have declared to be unknown to history, and commercially or financially impracticable, I say that this "bimetallic" system of money, at the ratio of twelve silver for one gold, lasted, within the Roman pale, without any variation of the ratio, except on the frontiers of the Empire, from B.C. 48 to A.D. 1204, a period of nearly thirteen centuries; and this, too, while the ratio in the coinages of India, Persia, Arabia, Moslem Spain, the English Heptarchy, Friesland, Saxony, and Esthonia, was based upon entirely different principles, and widely different ratios of value between the same precious metals.

Nor need Mr. MacLeod's monetary researches have

stopped at this point; he might have carried them much further and made discoveries that would have earned him the gratitude, not merely of Lord Farrer, but of all students of history. He might have recalled the fact, familiar to all ages and all governments, that the right of coinage, especially the right to coin gold, was regarded as the most essential and significant mark and proclamation of independent sovereignty; more essential than wearing a crown on the head, more significant than holding a sceptre in the hand. Tigranes, Tiriadates, Herod, Agrippa, Deiotaurus, Amyntas, and a host of other kings of antiquity, wore both crowns and sceptres, but they were not independent sovereigns; they did not strike gold coins. When, during the decline of the Empire, a Gothic king, who exercised the proconsular authority of Rome, rashly struck a gold coin, he was promptly checked by Justinian, who reminded him that he had dared what the great King of Persia would not have presumed to do. Ten centuries later, when the Portuguese reached India by sea, they found there the same significance attached to the prerogative of coinage. Says Duarte Barbosa, "There are many other lords in Malabar who wish to call themselves kings, but they are not so, because they are unable to coin money". From the moment that Pepin brought the truant provinces of the West again within the pale of Rome, until Constantinople, and with it the Empire, fell in 1204, no Christian prince, except the Basileus, ventured to strike a gold coin.[1] Yet compared with silver and copper coins, gold ones were as commonly in circulation then as they are now. In all the transactions and accounts of the Middle Ages the gold solidus or besant appears as frequently as does the gold sovereign to-day. The fines, escheats, and benevolences of royalty, the Roman exaction of Peter's pence, the Byzantine imperial price-lists of proconsular and other dignities are all couched in besants,

---

[1] The Norse Kings of Lombardy, Apulia and Sicily form no exceptions to this rule. Within the meaning of the Church they were not "Christian" princes; they were heretics.

or in libras of five besants each. Not only was this sort of gold coin in circulation : the Arabian gold dinar, as shown by the finds of recent years, was the principal coin employed in the trade of the Baltic; it was even struck in England by one of the then Pagan princes of Mercia; the Moorish maravedi was current at two-thirds of a besant, or seven and a half to the libra, in almost every State of the West. The Rhine, Garonne, Minho, Tagus, Guadalquivir, Rhone, and other auriferous rivers of the Continent, were successfully washed for gold; and both alluvial and quartz gold mines were worked in every country of Europe from Pannonia to Wales. For the diminished population and shrunken or extinguished industries of the Empire, the supplies of gold during the Middle Ages were ample. Although they all used gold coins, why is it that for 500 years, that is to say from the third year of Pepin to Frederick II., none of the Christian princes, except the Basileus, ever struck such coins? France, at one time, had fifty-odd Christian princes, each with a crown, a sceptre, a palace, a court, a royal pedigree, and a train of vassal knights, squires and serfs; yet not one of them struck a gold coin. England had at one time seven or eight Christian princes, some of whom announced themselves on their silver coins as Bretwealdas, others as sole kings of Britain, and one of them as of still loftier pretensions; yet none of them struck gold coins. Germany rejoiced in Christian princes by the score; aye, and in "emperors," too, some of them most puissant and redoubtable princes, as Pepin, who succoured the Pope; Charlemagne, who governed the Pope; Louis, who obeyed the Pope; Henry, who defied, and then did homage to the Pope; and Frederick Barbarossa, who fought the Pope; yet none of them struck a gold coin.[1] Finally, there were the Popes

[1] Blanchet, I., 101, mentions a triens, with "Carl. Fr. X.," which he attributes to Charlemagne. The Paris collection has two admittedly forged solidi of Louis Debonnaire, and one which is believed to be genuine, but which after personal inspection, I have no hesitation in declaring to be also a forgery. One has only to place it alongside of any genuine contemporaneous coins to perceive the cheat. Another so-called solidus of Louis was

themselves, who assumed to be kings of kings, and who, as Mr. Bliss has shown, really governed the princes of Europe with the authority of a suzerain; yet, until after the fall of Constantinople, none of them ever struck gold coins. It certainly seems odd that in his search for the fundamental principles of money Mr. MacLeod should have voyaged vacantly through this strange history, and amid these startling solecisms of coinage, only to anchor his conclusions in the pious deductions of the good, but simple, Oresme.

If he had observed that in the materials of history furnished to the modern world by the scribes of Rome, something had evidently got lost, for example, the Treaty of Seltz, between Charlemagne and Nicephorus, defining the boundaries, powers, and prerogatives reserved by the Basileus, or conceded to the Western "emperor"; if he had noticed that from the chessboard of European politics, one of the real kings of kings had dropped out of sight; if he had remarked that, until it was destroyed, the Byzantine Empire was the pivot upon which turned the entire history of Europe,—he might have been challenged by Mr. Bryce, but he would have at least offered some reasonable explanation of the strange neglect or renunciation of the coinage of gold by the Western princes of Christendom. But, filled with the vast ambition of uniting the names of Oresme, Copernicus, and Gresham as sponsors of a feeble generalisation—which applies no more to money than it does to cabbages, and sheds no light whatever on monetary questions—Mr. MacLeod saw nothing of the great problem of

found a few years since beneath a church in the Isle of Man, weight 68 grains. This weight and that of two others, 132 and 77 grains alone, make them suspected. No proofs of their genuineness have ever been offered, and I doubt if such proofs exist. Cartier, Guerard, and De Vienne all agree in the belief that neither Charlemagne nor Louis circulated any gold coins of their own minting and are very doubtful about their having struck any gold coins at all. In 1369, the canon of Dunmore was accused of forging both gold and silver coins. For other instances of the kind, consult my *History of Monetary Systems*, p. 226, and elsewhere. From Louis Debonnaire, 814-40, to Frederick II., 1215-50, there is not even a forged gold coin of any Christian prince.

history to which we have adverted, and has offered us no solution of it.[1]

Neither has he perceived that immediately after the fall of the Byzantine Empire all the princes of Europe at once hastened to strike gold coins. Here is a list of the principal ones:—

Earliest Gold Coinages of the Western Christian Princes.

Year.	Place.	Remarks.
1225	Naples	Augustals (doblas) of Frederick II., 82 English grs. fine.
1225	Portugal	Sancho I., ducats, 54½ grs. gross.
1226	France	Louis IX., pavillons d'or (De Saulcy, *Documents*, I., 115-25).
1250	France	Agnels or dinars of Louis IX., 63⅛ grs.
1252	Florence	Florins or ducats, 56 grs. fine.
1252	Genoa	Genovinas.
1252	Rome	Senatorial coin of Raimond Capizucci (Cinagli, p. 15).
1257	England	Maravedis of Henry III., 43 grs. fine.
1263	Leon	Ducats of Alfonso, 54½ grs. fine.
1265	Flanders	Mantelets d'or (De Saulcy, I., 31).
1276	Venice	Sequins or ducats, 55¾ grs. fine.
1300	Bohemia	Ducats of Venceslas II. (Bohemia and Poland), 54¼ grs., 0·958 fine.
1312	Castile	Doblas of 100 pesetas. Alfonso XI.
1316	Avignon	Sequins of Pope John XXII., 54½ grs. fine.
1325	Germany	Louis IV., ducats.
1336	Arragon	Pedro IV., florines.
1339	Holland	Ducats of Holland and Hainault.
1340	Guelderland	Duke Rainhold, ducats.
1342	Lubeck	Feb. 18. Patent from the Emperor Louis IV. Florins or ducats, 67¼ to the Lubeck mark.
1344	England	Edward III., nobles at 6s. 8d.
1356	Holland	Count William V., ducats.
1357	Flanders	Count Louis II., ducats.
1371	Scotland	Robert II., "andrews," 38 grs., Henry, *Hist. Brit.*, X., 269.
1372	Nuremburg	Patent from the Emperor of Germany, ducats of 53 grains.

[1] The so-called law of Oresme, Copernicus, and Gresham, was laid down nearly three centuries earlier than Gresham, by the Sieurs Biccio and Musciato François.—Villani, *Hist. Florence*, Lib. VIII. Ch. 55. It will also be found in the *Maxims* of Theognis, and the *Frogs* of Aristophanes.—*Hist. Mon. Systems*, first ed., p. 355.

It is not true, as Mr. MacLeod insinuates, that until the twelfth century, when, as he supposes, the French kings began to issue gold coins, there reigned a monetary calm, because there was no question of a second metal to disturb it; nor is it true that France endeavoured to maintain "bimetallism" from 1113 to 1874. The French kings issued no gold coins until after the fall of Constantinople, —not, indeed, until the reign of Louis IX. But although they issued no gold coins with their own stamp, they permitted the circulation of gold coins with the stamp of the Basileus, and, in point of fact, the circulation was equally filled with Byzantine gold coins and French silver coins. The monetary calm which existed was, therefore, not due to the absence of a second metal. On the contrary, it was due to its presence; it was due to what would now be called the "bimetallic" system established by Cæsar, and maintained with more or less difficulty by Augustus, Constantine, Justinian, and the other sovereign-pontiffs of Rome down to 1204. In short, from the origin to the downfall of the Roman Empire, there was, so far as the ratio is concerned, but one law and one system of coinage.

After the fall of the Empire, and until the period of the Dutch Revolution, the monetary systems of Europe (for now there were many systems) fell into the greatest disorder. Every prince and prelate of Christendom hastened to strike gold and silver, and many of them tin, copper and lead coins; some even issued leather notes. These they valued at will; and with little respect to their value in other States. They degraded and debased the coins; they sometimes issued them surreptitiously; they altered their legal function; they changed the ratio between the precious metals; they bought with one weight and sold with another; they exacted monetagium, seigniorage and brassage; they levied fines of a half, a third, a fifth, on all discoveries of the precious metals; they taxed quicksilver, which is indispensable to the prosecution of gold and silver metallurgy; they controlled the imports and exports of the precious metals; they restricted their employment in the arts; in short, they resorted to every known device to regulate or else to extort profit from the great materials of coinage. The tracts of Oresme and Copernicus were attempts to remedy some of these abuses. So also were the monetary tracts of Francisco Aretio, John Aquila, Albert Brunus, John Bodinus, Franciscus Curtius, Nicolaus Everardus, Henning Goden, Martin Garrati, Henry Hornmann, Elbertus Leoninus, Baron Malestroict, Jacob Menochius, Charles Molinaeus Bilibald Pirckheymer, John Raynaud, Antonio Rubaeus, Ludovicus Romanus, Marianus and Bartholomeus Socinus, Diaz Covarruvias, John Caephalus, and many others, which neither Messrs. Wolowski nor MacLeod appears to have seen, and which contain somewhat the same sort of material that is to be found in Oresme and Copernicus—namely, local arguments against the policy of corrupting the coinage for the profit of the prince—a subject which has no longer any interest except to the numismatist and historian. These are the sources to which Mr. MacLeod resorts for monetary principles, which he declares to be immutable, and would apply to present circumstances. In point of fact, they are long since dead, and have no relation whatever to present circumstances. The monetary system of Charles the Wise which Oresme discussed, the system of Sigismund the Great and the Prussian coinage which Copernicus discussed, the system of Edward VI. to which Gresham alluded, and the various systems which were discussed by the numerous other writers cited above, —all had this in common : they belonged to a period when there was no single control of the monetary systems; when there was no individual or free coinage to restrain the princes of Europe from tampering with money, and when such tamperings were the readiest resource of a needy finance.

The question as to whether the combined governmental power of Europe could or could not maintain a fixed parity between coins of the precious metals, was never before these writers. What they discussed were the coinage laws of their day—that is to say, the confused and warring coinages of the Renaissance, after the Roman regulation of money was broken down, and before the "responsible" classes removed the coinage from the control of princes who too often abused that essential prerogative of government.

The existing coinage laws, those in whose reform the present generation is interested, are of a totally different character. These arose out of the Dutch Revolution of 1572, and the institution of individual (or so-called " free ") coinage, which was never heard of before, and was enacted then for the first time in Europe. Before any one is in a position to offer any useful observations to the world on the subject of monetary systems, or to claim that he has discovered the great fundamental, or any other principle of coinage, it is obviously necessary that he should have some knowledge of these circumstances.

In 1524, Charles V., emperor of Germany, who perhaps hoped to maintain the same control over the monetary systems of the " empire " that the defunct Basileus (by monopolising the coinage of gold) had formerly exercised, issued an edict from Esslingen, by which he raised his gold coins from 10 (a frontier ratio) to $11\frac{3}{4}$ times the value of silver coins containing the same quantity of fine metal. In 1546 he again raised the value of his gold coins, this time to $13\frac{1}{3}$ times their weight in silver. To exemplify the unjust and mischievous character of these monetary ordinances, they reduced the silver ducaton to two-thirds of its former value, by substituting for its equivalent a debased ducat, first of 37 and afterwards of 35 grains fine, in place of the old one of 54 grains fine. Such a violent and sudden alteration in the value of money amongst a commercial people produced the widest distress and commotion. However, the prestige of the "empire" was still very great, and it was not until the abdication of Charles and the accession of Philip the Bigot, that the smothered discontent of the Hollanders, which, though piously capped with religion, had a large substratum of money and trade for its base, broke forth. The Confederation of Beggars was formed in 1566, the Revolution was proclaimed in 1572, pasteboard money was issued in 1574, and individual or "free" coinage was soon afterwards permitted by the Republic. In 1666 (18 Charles II., cap. 5) this institution was adopted in England. In France it followed close upon the heels of the Fronde. Before the close of the seventeenth century it was adopted in other important States. "Free" coinage entirely changed the monetary systems of the Western world. Not only this: by freely admitting metal to coinage, and interposing no efficient obstacles to the melting of coins into metal, it confused the subject of money, which is essentially a legal mechanism and institution, with that of metals, which belongs essentially to mining and the mechanical and chemical arts. During the ascendency of the Roman power the whole volume of money, through his control of the coinage of gold and the maintenance of a fixed ratio, was regulated by the Basileus; during the Renaissance there was no single control; and the volume of money was continually disturbed by the arbitrary acts of a hundred jealous and warring princes. Since the Dutch Revolution, and especially since the English law of 1666, the control has been left to the chance of mining discoveries, the demands for the arts, and the vagaries of doctrinaires who, like Locke and Harris, at one period sang the praises of silver, and, like Liverpool and De Parieu, at others chanted those of gold.

The real question at issue is not whether gold or silver is a better material out of which to make coins, but whether the entire volume of metallic money in each State of the Western world shall continue to be diminished by forbidding the coinage of full legal-tender silver, and failing to provide a sufficiency of equally acceptable money. That the demonetisation of silver was brought about by utilising the fear that to continue its coinage would endanger the stability of the Measure of Value, there cannot be the slightest doubt. But what has been the result? Prices have never been so unstable before; speculation, except in gold mines, has been extinguished; commerce, manufactures, agriculture, every branch of industry, has been prostrated; and the men whose ignorant advice has brought these disasters upon Christendom, are seeking to extenuate their colossal crime by explaining that all these results are due to the bounty of Nature—to what, in their misleading terminology, they are pleased to call "overproduction". Many of those who expected to gain mostly by this revolution of money, have, in fact, been the chief losers. Bank after bank, company after company, security after security has failed, and gone into the hands of liquidators and receivers; and after twenty years of suffering, we scarcely yet see the end.

III. It is designed to show the progress of Private Coinage from the time when it was assumed and permitted by the revolting caliphs of Moslem Spain and Egypt to the enactment of 18 Charles II., cap. 5. The appropriation by the goldsmith class of the royal prerogative has been accomplished in so stealthy a manner that scarcely a trace of it appears in historical works, and none at all in works devoted to political economy,—a glaring proof, if any were needed, of the prejudice and one-sidedness which have hitherto animated the teachers of that science. Of all the elements of political economy, money is the chiefest; of all the institutes of money, the right to create it is the most important; yet not a word concerning the origin, necessity, rise, fall, and loss of this once sacred right by the State, is to be found in any of the Economists. What appears in this chapter on the subject, as well as what he has written elsewhere, is the result of the author's unassisted researches. The legislation of Charles II. on the coinage of gold and silver money was indeed no secret, but its supernal significance had never before been recognised or pointed out. As for the legislation of Holland, Spain, and the Moslem States on this subject, the writer is chiefly indebted to the numismatists.

Certain vestiges exist in the laws relating to the precious metals and money, which prove that dominion over these subjects was formerly exercised exclusively by the State; for example, the custom of Treasure Trove, which is very ancient, the granting of gold and silver mines to the discoverer, and the granting of the right to a miner to pursue his vein through any man's property, both of which institutes are of Roman origin, and are still enforced in many parts of the world; the doctrine, custom, and prerogative of Mines Royal, which was assumed by the independent princes of Europe in the thirteenth century; besides many other provisions of law. So late as the year 1870 a clause appeared in the Mint Code of Great Britain, which was evidently saved by accident from the wreck of the ancient Statutes, and which the ingenious framers of this new Code would have probably destroyed had they perceived its significance. It reads as follows: "The Treasury may from time to time issue to the Master of the Mint, out of the growing produce of the Consolidated Fund, such sums as may enable him to purchase bullion, in order to provide supplies of *coin for the public service*".[1] This is a clear admission of the principle that money is a public, a societary instrument, and that supplies of coin are a matter of public concern, which may not be left to the discretion of individuals. Political economy, from the money-lender's standpoint, pleads for "free" money and "free" banking, in order that its patrons may monopolise the supplies of one and employ the other as an auction mart for the sale of their own credit. Political economy, from the public standpoint—which is the standpoint not only of the present work, but of all that the author has ever written,—replies that "free" money is as inconceivable as free law, or

[1] 33 Vict., ch. 10.

free policemen, or free prisons for usurers, or free gibbets for traitors. When Madame Roland adverted to the crimes that had been committed in the name of Freedom, she probably never dreamed of the greatest crime of all,—the "Crime against Mankind," as Pliny called it,—the crime of private coinage.

This subject is pursued historically in my other works. Suffice it to say in this place, that private or "free" coinage began in the Moslem States of Egypt and Spain after they had respectively renounced the authority of the Caliph, or Emir-el-Moumenin; that it was carried into India by the Moslem invaders and plunderers of that unhappy country; that it was practised successively by the Portuguese, Dutch and English adventurers in the East Indies; and, finally, that it was introduced into Europe by the Dutch during their revolt against the authority of Spain, and as one of a means to annoy and injure that power. The Spanish Mint Act of 1591 appears to have been designed as a counter move to the legislation of the Netherlands. It was repealed in 1603, but more fully re-enacted in 1608, which year may be definitively regarded as the birth time of Private Coinage in Europe.[1]

The law of 1608 permitted the Viceroys of Spain in America to coin money for private account, without limit, provided such coin was struck from bullion which had paid the King's Fifth, or tax on production. In 1620 the Spanish law provided that in addition to the Fifth (Quinto) there should be paid a seigniorage to the mints, amounting to three reals per mark. The seigniorage and quinto together amounted to 25 per cent. *ad valorem.* Was it to encourage the evasion of these imposts, and attract into the coffers of the London goldsmiths the metal upon which such imposts would have been levied, that Charles encouraged, rewarded, and distinguished the pirate Morgan, interdicted the coinage of silver at Boston, Massachusetts, and surrendered to the London goldsmiths the royal

[1] *Hist. Mon. Sys.*, first ed., p. 452.

prerogative of money? Whatever its object, it had far more mischievous results than were dreamed of at the time. Charles bargained away a measure of value, upon which must depend for countless generations the share of all public burdens and the distribution of all wealth. Under this legislation the royal prerogative was placed in abeyance; and, beyond its power to determine the ratio (between gold and silver), the State practically lost its control of money. In 1816 the Crown was persuaded to suspend the exercise of its power over the ratio. In this manner was silver demonetised in England. By the operation of an obscure and unnoticed clause in the Mint Act of 1870, so much of the power as the Crown retained to terminate such suspension and demonetisation was removed; and the last remnant of a prerogative whose exercise is essential to the autonomy of the State was innocently surrendered to private hands. Practically, since 1816 the measure of value for the vast transactions of the British Empire has not been Money, which may be limited by law and counted by tale, but Metal, which cannot thus be regulated, and which therefore has been resigned practically to the control of a class whose chief interest in the State has been to render it subservient to their own private advantage.

What has been the result? From the day when the royal voluptuary resigned a prerogative which, more than any other one, pleads for the continuance of kingly rule, to the present time, the commercial community has been subjected to alternate epochs of monetary contraction and expansion, in which much of what it accumulates at one period is insidiously filched from it at another. The reader has only to glance at the author's previous works to be convinced of the entire truth of this observation. The suspensions of banks of issue therein shown involved losses to the noteholders and others, amounting to more than the value of all the gold and silver money in the world several times over. Not only this: the surrender of

HISTORY OF MONETARY MECHANISMS.   83

the prerogative of coinage has tended to estrange the Crown from the people, whose disappointment has manifested itself in many painful symptoms. No man who takes pride in the glorious past of this Mother of States, and who would preserve that past from obliteration, should refrain from referring to these dangers, or pointing the way to avoid them in future. More than this: such dangers menace not the peace of England alone; they affect the entire commercial world.

The plain facts are these: Two centuries ago the King of England plundered the goldsmiths in London of all their ready money. Either for the reasons already mentioned herein, or to compensate them for his ~~father's~~ [uncle's] injustice, his ~~son~~ substantially sold and surrendered to the goldsmiths the State prerogative of coinage. Owing to England's commercial supremacy (due to the energy of her people, not to the intrigues of goldsmiths or money-lenders), this made the latter the sole arbiters of the measure of value, not merely of England, but of the Western world. These tremendous powers have been wielded with such inadequate perception of the equities and consequences they involved, with such lack of scientific or financial skill, and in so narrow and selfish a spirit, that its arbiters have repeatedly plunged the commercial world into bankruptcy, and confiscated or inequitably redistributed its accumulated earnings, either for their own benefit or else to save themselves from the effects of their own blundering.

From this selfishness, ill-management, blundering, and recklessness, from the evidence which they have given before governmental commissions on this subject, both in this country and in others, from the countless books and pamphlets in which they have contradicted each other both as to fact and opinion on the subject of money, as well as from many other evidences, it has become quite obvious that this class, which includes the managers of certain banks of issue, are less competent to understand and regulate the measure of value than are the representatives of the people, whose patriotism, conservatism, and societary instinct furnish a far more reliable basis for the stability of money, than the doctrines, the prejudices, or the selfishness of a new plutocracy.

Even amongst themselves this class has been unable to agree with regard to the diagnosis of monetary troubles, or the proper remedies to apply. Chaos in legislation has bred chaos in doctrine. All that has been perceived clearly is that, since the era of private coinage and private banks of issue not entirely controlled by the State, the industrial and commercial world has suffered repeated reverses, for which no indemnity has been offered, and no practical remedy discovered. But the synchronism of these events has itself disclosed the source of the trouble, and indicated the correct treatment to be applied in future. That treatment is the resumption by the State of its ancient prerogative of money. Upon referring to the author's historical works, which give an account of the monetary systems of various States, the reader will observe that private coinage has been forbidden as to silver in all the States of Europe and America except Mexico; and that as to gold it is a dead letter in most of them, because nearly all the available stock of this metal has become concentrated in three of the principal States, namely, Great Britain, France, and Germany, there being little or none of it held elsewhere except as mere funds or "reserves". The movement to couch the world's indebtedness in only one of the two metals which had previously answered for the basis of its monetary systems, has served its purpose; but it has had other results than those anticipated by its promoters; it has already terminated the Private Coinage of silver; it now promises to put an end also to the Private Coinage of gold.

The States which in 1873 were duped into doubling their indebtedness, have outlived their resentment, and become reconciled to a loss which has enabled them to dispense for the future with that mischief of Private Coinage, which alone rendered such loss possible. Most of them now exercise, for the first time in centuries, a more or less complete control over their own monetary systems; and the sense of relief and security which has followed the change, has communicated itself to other States, and stimulated a popular demand for the entire interdict of Private Coinage. The Trans-Mississippi Commercial Congress, which assembled at St. Louis, November 26-30, 1894, demanded that "all issues of paper money should be by the General Government" of the United States. The logical outcome of this resolution is, that all issues of metallic money should (also) be by the General Government; and such outcome will doubtless find expression in the "platforms" of many future conventions. In effect, the demand is that the State, which is now identical with the Crown, shall resume its ancient prerogative; for the State alone can stop the alternate melting down, shipping to and fro, and recoinages of metal, which lie at the base of monetary disturbances. The contention henceforth may be not whether the symbols of money shall be made of one metal or of two metals, but that the State and not the money-changers shall control its issues.

IV. It will now be shown how Private Coinage has developed into Private Money, and how the latter has resulted in the monopolisation of gold.

The inevitable result of Private Coinage has been Metallism, or the confusion of metal with money and money with metal. This confusion is not to be observed in any European treatises on money written before the Private Coinage Acts of the sixteenth century; after that date it will be found in-all of them. The moment that metals were permitted by Governments to be turned by private individuals into coins and coins into metals, without loss or expense, from that moment coins ceased to have a limit, they ceased to be a precise or equitable measure of value, they ceased to be money. Their place was usurped by metal, to which there is no limit, and which never can equitably perform the function of money. From the point of view of metal, bimetallism, or the proposition to make coins of two metals, is without apology or vindication. It is the merest sophistry, and as such John Locke, himself a Metallist, ran it fairly to earth two centuries ago. Its only justification is from the point of view that any money made and proclaimed by the State is good money, no matter what it is made of. The reservoir argument of Jevons is as weak as the water with which he imagines his reservoirs to be filled. The answer to it is that the irregular production of the chosen metal, when one alone is chosen, can be, as it has been, remedied by means of Government notes. Therefore, unlike water, it needs no double reservoirs with connecting pipes. From Locke's academical "monometallism" to Harris's academical "unit" was but a step. If money was metal, it could only effectively measure by weight. The unit of that weight was therefore necessarily the weight of a sovereign, or a dollar, or a franc,—in a word, so and so many grains. In short, the sovereign, or dollar, or franc, became the unit of weight. So argued Joseph Harris (1757), and so repeated Robert Morris (1782), Thomas Jefferson (1782), the Grand Committee of Congress (1785), the members of the Board of Treasury (1786), Alexander Hamilton (1791), and Lord Liverpool (1798), in his Letter to the King, published under date of 7th May, 1805. All of these eminent persons employed the same erroneous and misleading term. That it should have slipped into the United States Coinage Act of 1792 was inevitable, but its presence there adds neither to its propriety nor legitimacy. Laws are human institutes which prescribe a rule of action over human affairs. They have no more power to make metal identical with money than they have to create a stock company out of a rail fence. The natural sequence to Private Coinage (Act Charles II.), academical monometallism (Locke), academical unit (Harris), practical monometallism (English Act, 1816), practical unit (American Act of 1793), and universal monometallism (Acts of numerous States, 1867-73), was the monopolisation of gold metal, which seems to have been virtually achieved in 1894, as the following evidences appear to testify.

At the present moment there are substantially but three States where gold coins are in circulation as money. These are England, France, and Germany. In England the circulation of gold coins is common. With some unimportant exceptions, the paper currency consists of Bank of England notes, which are legal tenders except from the Bank, and are not issued under £5 sterling.

In Scotland notes are issued down to £1, and there is but little gold in circulation. The same may be said of Ireland and Wales. The whole sum of gold coins and of gold bullion waiting for coinage in England has been variously estimated of late by Mr. Goschen and other authorities at from £65,000,000 to £80,000,000 sterling, of which in September, 1894, about £56,000,000 was in the banks, and the remainder passing from hand to hand. In France at the same time there was about £90,000,000 sterling in the banks, and less than £10,000,000 passing from hand to hand. A portion (amount not known) of the gold in the Bank of France is reserved as a war fund. In Germany there was about £40,000,000 in the banks, £6,000,000 or £8,000,000 in the war fund at Spandau, and a few millions in circulation, say £55,000,000 all told. The details of the entire money of Germany, gold, silver, and paper, will be found in my *History of Monetary Systems*, page 386, of the English edition. At the same date Austro-Germany had £13,500,000 in bank, and none in circulation. Gold is at a premium in both silver and paper. There is supposed to be an Austrian war fund of gold, which some people have estimated as high as £16,500,000, but which probably does not equal one-third of that sum. Forty millions for all the gold in Austria would be a high estimate. The Russian banks claimed to hold £100,000,000 gold, including a war fund of unknown dimensions. But there is reason to believe that a portion of this sum is alternately deposited in London and Paris; and therefore that such portion, which a few years ago amounted to £26,000,000, is included in the gold credited to those States. In Russia gold bears a high premium, and none is in circulation.

In the United States, in September, 1894, there was of gold coin and bullion awaiting coinage, in the Treasury, in the New York banks, in the country banks, and circulating in the mining States of the trans-Mississippi, altogether about £46,333,000. There is little or none in circulation east of the Mississippi. Fifty millions sterling would be a fair estimate for all the gold in the country. This sum has since been increased by borrowing from a cosmopolitan Syndicate; but as the increment came from other countries, it does not swell the total. Mr. Carlisle thinks there is £120,000,000 buried in hoards. I cannot imagine what means he has of ascertaining how much gold people have been so imprudent and wasteful as to bury in the ground or stow away in cupboards, and therefore am obliged to conclude that this is a mere conjecture on his part, based on the silly figures of production with which he is supplied by ignorant or designing people, and his inability to account for the disappearance of the gold except by assuming it to be hoarded. It is far easier to assume that the production tables furnished to him are mere flights of the imagination. But some people are fond of the marvellous, and it is useless to reason with them.

Whether there is or there is not £120,000,000 in hoards, this is certain, that it might as well be in the mines for all the good it does. If the panic of 1893 failed to bring it out; if cotton at $4\frac{1}{2}$ cents the pound, and wheat at 50 cents the bushel, failed to bring it out, I can imagine no temptation strong enough to induce it to again take part in the circulation. It is as effectually buried as though it never had been mined at all. There has been as yet no premium on gold in the United States, because the people are accustomed to paper notes and do not want gold, and because the few who have applied to the Treasury for gold have always been paid gold. These last consist entirely of the class who are managing the gold corner. They will never press for enough to force the Treasury to suspend gold payments. They are far too clever for that; but they will press it close enough to compel it to borrow from them again and again.

A recent London pamphleteer claims that the Italian banks and State Treasury had £17,500,000 sterling in gold; that the Bank of Spain holds £8,000,000; that Egypt holds £15,000,000 in her State Treasury; that the State banks of Argentina hold £7,500,000, and the Chinese Imperial Treasury £12,000,000, all in gold. This makes £60,000,000 sterling. I take the liberty to doubt some of these items. Italy has a heavy gold debt, but no gold coin. Her currency consists of paper, copper, and silver, with gold at a premium. As for her banks, if they have any gold at all, it is a comparatively small amount, held against deposits, not against notes, and has but a feeble and remote effect upon the currency. What little gold is in Spain is practically a war fund. The currency is of silver, to which the mints are closed. Gold is at a premium, and there is none in circulation. Egypt and Argentina are in the pockets of the financiers, and if there is any gold deposited in their banks, it belongs to the financiers, and is already counted in the gold of France, England, and Germany, where the syndicates of cosmopolitan financiers reside. It would be fair to estimate the free gold coin of these States at £7,500,000, all of which is probably held as reserve funds.

The £12,000,000 of gold in the Chinese Treasury is mythical. China was glad enough in 1894 to borrow money at 7 per cent., and to mortgage her customs revenues for its payment. There is no gold money in China. There is no silver money, except a few millions in the hands of foreigners and the hongs of the treaty ports. Her currency is of bronze, and a very good currency it has doubtless been in its day; but that day is evidently past.

A new æra is dawning. On May 10, 1895, M. Honataux invited the Haute Banque to meet him at the French Foreign Office, to consider what European system of money should be imposed upon China, in return for the loans of £150,000,000 or £180,000,000, which, with the aid of certain European powers, are to be placed upon the markets by instalments. The adoption of any system which will identify the money of China with that of Europe will change the destinies and influence of the Flowery Kingdom.

From that moment she will draw heavily upon Europe for silver.

In Holland, Belgium, Switzerland, Scandinavia, and Roumania, there is, altogether, about £20,000,000 in gold, and in remote parts of the world, like Australia, the Cape, the Levant, etc., about £25,000,000 more. Let us now recapitulate.

The world's stock of gold coins and bullion waiting for coinage is: In the United Kingdom, £72,500,000; in France, £100,000,000; in Germany, £55,000,000; in Austria-Hungary, £40,000,000; in Russia, £100,000,000; in the United States of America, £50,000,000; in Netherlands, Switzerland, Scandinavia, and Roumania, £20,000,000; in Australia, the Cape, the Levant, etc., £25,000,000; in free gold in Italy, Spain, etc., say £7,500,000; making a grand total of £470,000,000.

This, then, is the world's stock of gold coin and gold bullion available for coinage, namely, £470,000,000, of which about £150,000,000 is reserved as war funds, upon which no notes are issued and probably no credits granted.

In order to engross the gold of the world it is only necessary to own or control about £300,000,000, say $1,500,000,000. To control this amount of first-class Government bonds, a margin of 5 per cent. would be sufficient; to control this amount of gold metal, a margin of 5 per cent. is ample; but for the sake of being unquestionably within the mark, let us make allowance for a margin of 10 per cent., that is to say, £30,000,000 or $150,000,000. Can anybody doubt that such a margin is available, or that the door is not wide open to the formation of a gold syndicate, secure in its operation and certain of ample profits in lending, withdrawing, and shipping gold to and fro, in depressing and enhancing the prices of commodities and labour, in precipitating panics, and in relieving them upon usurious terms? I think not.

The ease and security which invite the formation of cosmopolitan Gold Syndicates are, however, only negative evidences of their existence. I now proceed to more positive ones.

A few years ago a great Syndicate lent £16,000,000 to Italy, wherewith to resume payments in gold coin. The whole of that sum has since been withdrawn from Italy, and her payments are being made in silver, copper, and paper, whilst gold is at a premium. A similar Syndicate afterwards lent £40,000,000 to Austria for a similar purpose. This gold is already beginning to disappear. The currency is of silver coin and paper notes, while gold is at a premium.

A similar Syndicate lent gold to Japan for a like purpose, to ensure which an official was sent from England to open a mint in Japan and coin gold for circulation. In 1893 but nine-sixteenths of this gold remained; and by this time, 1895, nearly the whole of it has disappeared. The currency is of silver coins and paper notes, while gold since 1893 has been at a high premium.

A similar Syndicate recently lent the United States of America about £25,000,000—$125,000,000—upon several issues of gold bonds. Half of this has left the country; the operation is being repeated, and the Treasury is making abject terms with men who have had the insolence to inform the representatives of the public press that the operations of the Syndicate with the Treasury are none of their business.

A similar Syndicate recently lent £2,000,000 to Chile at 93½, with which to resume gold payments. For this loan she pledged her nitrate beds. The public took the loan off the hands of the Syndicate at par by subscribing for it four times over. Gold coin payments were to have been resumed in Chile this very month (July, 1895); and to render them effective, silver was coined at the so-called "market ratio" to gold, *viz.*, about 32 for 1. Both the gold and silver coins have already disappeared; and a telegram from Santiago, dated 7th July, 1895, says that the conversion law is a total failure, the banks having advanced their rate of discount to 10 per cent., a panic has seized the public, and business is practically paralysed. The fatuous President of this petty Republic, following the fatuous lead of the President of a far greater Republic, is insisting upon the formation of a Ministry favourable to the forcible carrying out of this suicidal policy.

These illustrations might be greatly extended, but I fear to invite fatigue. I claim that the ability of these Syndicates to lend such large sums of gold to the States mentioned is of itself proof that they virtually control the available supplies of that metal. If we add to this their ability, after lending it, to draw it away to the centres of their operations, namely, Paris, London, and Frankfort, then the evidence becomes greatly strengthened.

A crowning proof is afforded by their contracts with the United States Treasury. The combined imports and exports of the merchandise of that country amount to about $1,500,000,000 per annum, to say nothing of the imports and exports of bonds, shares, and other securities. This immense trade results in balances which have to be temporarily settled with gold. During the fiscal year, 1894-5, the adverse securities balance probably amounted to several hundred millions. To induce the United States Government to enter into another gold loan, a Gold Syndicate virtually contracted to satisfy this balance with their bills on London—in other words, to hold back the shipments of gold to Europe for a period of eight months, during which time, in order to keep their promise good, they must sell bills of exchange at a lower rate than that at which gold metal can be bought and transmitted to London, or else use some means to discourage such shipments. This contract they have thus far fulfilled. Unless the stock of gold money in Europe was under control, such a feat would have been hazardous and impracticable.

Had the various States held the command of such stock, the borrowings of the Syndicate to pay these bills in London would have created a sharp demand for gold, and enhanced the bank rates of discount. No such demand or enhancement took place. The evidence is, therefore, complete—the Gold Syndicates evidently command the stock of gold, and to command it is to corner it, for both expressions virtually mean the same thing.

The heaping up of gold in the three great European States where these gigantic combinations have their centres of operation; the comparative paucity of the stock, and ease with which it can be engrossed by the Haute Banque; the loans to Italy, Austria, Japan, the United States, Chile, and other powers; the ability to withdraw the gold thus lent, and again heap it up in European treasuries; the contract to control the foreign exchanges of the United States for two-thirds of a year; and the successful performance of this novel and gigantic undertaking—these are proofs as convincing as any that can reasonably be demanded of the existence and operations of such combinations as I have indicated.

With regard to new supplies from the mines, it is to be observed, first, that these supplies, of which rough conjectures are furnished by the Director of the United States Mint (if they are compared with the movement of new gold to the mints and with the commercial statistics), have been greatly exaggerated; second, that the mines of one country are often owned in others; and, third, that of the entire product of all the mines from 75 to 80 per cent. goes into the arts, and a portion of the balance is used to make good the wear and tear of coins.

If there yet remain any doubts that gold is cornered and controlled by Syndicates or Gold Trusts, you have only to take up some newspaper, and observe the anxiety with which the shipment of a single million or two is regarded. Yet those pallid dupes, who tremble with apprehension at what is, from their point of view, so trivial a circumstance, will be certain to assure you in another column of the same paper that it will bring ruin upon the country to abrogate this ruinous system of finance.[1]

[1] Speech at Washington, C.H., July, 1895.

CHAPTER VII.

THE LAW OF MONEY.

The Greek law—The Roman law—The Common law—Philip le Bel—Decision under English law—Corn rents—The Code Napoleon—The Court of Cassation—Decisions of the United States Supreme Court—Metallic theory—Black Laws of James III. of Scotland—Special Contract Law of 1878—Disastrous effects of this legislation—Imperative demand for its repeal—The Law of Nations relative to money.

THE law of money in the European or Western world is derived primarily from that of the Greek States, as epitomised by Aristotle and exemplified by Plato. Its later source is the law of the Roman Commonwealth, as axiomised by Paulus in the *Digest*. The substance of it is, that that is money which the State declares to be money.

This principle of the Civil law was incorporated in the Common law of the various States which rose upon the ruins of the Empire. In a process against the Count de Nevers for defacing his coin, the Procureur-General held that the Crown alone had the right to alter the coins, not for its own profit, but for the advantage, or the defence, of the State.[1]

Both the Civil and Common law were carefully consulted on this subject in the celebrated case known as that of "Mixt Moneys in Ireland," which was tried at Trin., 2 Jac. I., 1604. This case is referred to by the learned Sir Wm. Blackstone, but evidently only in reference to its least important aspect, namely that of borrowed money. In fact,

[1] Hallam, *Mid. Ages*, p. 148.

it involved much more important principles than those relating to loans upon interest.[1]

In order to pay off the royal army which was maintained for several years in Ireland to suppress the rebellion of Tyrone, Queen Elizabeth coined, in the Tower of London, a quantity of base pieces, with the royal arms and other marks of authority upon them, and sent them to Ireland. By proclamation of May 24th, 1600, these coins were made legal-tender in Ireland, for the payment of all debts and dues; and it was rendered an offence against the law to refuse them. By the same proclamation all other coins in Ireland were decried, annulled and ordered to be sent to the mints, where they were reduced to bullion.

During the month of April previously (1599), one Brett, of Drogheda, Ireland, bought certain wares of one Gilbert of London, England, for one hundred pounds sterling, "current and lawful money of England," and gave his bond therefor, the same being payable in Dublin at a certain day later than that of the Queen's new coinage and proclamation.

On the day appointed, Brett tendered at the proper place in Dublin £100 of the new Irish coins in payment of his debt, when Gilbert refused to receive them, and sued Brett before the Privy Council. On account of the importance of the case to the State, as a precedent, Sir George Carew, Lord Deputy and Treasurer to the King, requested the Chief Justices to consider it, and lay their decision before the Council.[2]

After examining the subject very thoroughly, the Justices decided in 1604 (the second year of James I.), that Brett had made a good tender. The following is a brief of

---

[1] *Blackstone's Com.*, I., 275.

[2] By some authorities this decision is attributed to Sir Matthew Hale. He is also regarded as having been the author of *A Short Treatise touching Sheriffs' Accounts*, in which the subject of money is treated with some learning. However, the attribution is wrong and the authorship of *Sheriffs' Accounts* is doubtful.

their decision, which will be found at length in *Davies' Reports*, and the *State Trials*.[1]

I. Money is a public measure (mensura publica, saith Bodin) intended to obviate the inconvenience and inequity of barter; and every commonwealth has adopted a monetary system which is peculiarly its own. There can be no society without exchanges, no system of exchanges without equity, and no equity of exchanges without money. (Aristotle, Paulus, Bodin, and Budelius.)

II. The sovereign, or those specifically licensed by him, has the sole lawful authority to create the money of his dominions, and it is treason for any others to do so. To render money lawful, six attributes are requisite in the pieces. These are (1) Ponderosity; (2) Fineness, or quality; (3) Impression, or type; (4) Denomination, or legal value; (5) Mark of authority of the sovereign; (6) Proclamation. When the sovereign declares a piece of money to be, for example, a penny, groat, or shilling, *that makes it so.* Several cases, both in the Civil and Common Law, are cited in support of this principle.

III. The sovereign has the right and authority to increase or diminish, to raise or lower moneys, to enhance or depreciate their legal value, to decry them, and to reduce them to bullion, or other raw material; in which condition they may be prohibited to be used as money. Various instances are cited of the exercise of this authority, by the sovereigns of England. It is evident from these cited cases, that the sovereign's prerogative enables him to alter the coins and value them at pleasure. This is a power which the State reserves to itself for its own safety and welfare. (Paulus, Budelius, and Molinaeus.)[2]

---

[1] *Les Reports des Cases et Matters, en Ley, resolves et adjudges en les Courts del Rey en Ireland* per Sir John Davies, *Chivaler*. London, quarto, 1674. The same case is also reported in *State Trials*, Vol. II., p. 114, ed. 1809.

[2] Carolus Molinaeus, *De Mutatione Monetae*, Cap. 100. Was it fear of this doctrine, or because of the profits to be derived from the bullion-trade with Holland, or some other reason, that induced the London goldsmiths in 1666 to introduce and urge the bill of that year, permitting Private Coinage?

IV. Decides the meaning of "sterling".

V. Every coin has intrinsic and extrinsic qualities. The intrinsic qualities consist of weight and fineness; the extrinsic, of denomination and value. (See Aristotle, Seneca, Budelius, Molinaeus, and Baldus.) The intrinsic qualities are conferred by nature; the extrinsic by the sovereign or the State. These qualities it can confer by seal and proclamation, and no matter how base the coins thus authorised, the power of the State is sufficient to confer upon them legal value.

VI. Proofs of the legality of coins minted in the Tower.

VII. The term "current" refers to the time of payment, and not to that when the contract is made—a very important distinction (29 Ed. I.; 6 and 7 Ed. VI.; in Dyer, 81b and 82b).

VIII. All other coins in Ireland but those minted as aforesaid, having been decried, annulled and reduced to the condition of bullion, it follows, that these coins remain the only money in which payment can lawfully be demanded of the defendant.

Apart from the prerogative of the State to degrade or debase coins, the arrivals of silver from America at this period were so vast, as compared with the stock on hand, that a general rise of prices took place, to avert the consequences of which, in certain directions, it had been provided by the 18th Elizabeth (1575), that a third of the rent of all college leases should be reserved in corn, to be paid either in kind, or according to the current prices of the nearest public market. "The money arising from this corn-rent, though originally but a third of the whole, is, in the present times (1775), according to Dr. Blackstone, commonly near double of what arises from the other two-thirds."[1] In France, during the seventeenth century, the Marquis Tavannes proposed to substitute iron metal for silver money for fear the latter would lose its value![2]

The Code Napoleon (1803) provides in effect that debts

---

[1] Adam Smith, Vol. I., Chap. V., p. 34.   [2] Brantome, *Mémoires*, IV., 29.

of money are payable, sum for sum, in the money of the day of payment, but that contracts for bullion must be paid in kind. Book II., Tit. III., art. 587 : " Where the usufruct comprises things which cannot be used without being consumed, such as money, grain, and liquids, the usufructuary has the right to use them, subject to the obligation to restore a like quantity and quality (of such things), or else the value or equivalent of the same at the expiration of the usufruct ".

Book III., Tit. X., art. 1895: "Debts are payable in the denominations of money mentioned in the contract. Whether there has been an increase or diminution of money previous to the time of payment (of a loan), the debtor must return the numerical sum lent, but is only bound to return such sum in the money current at the time of payment ".

These articles are followed by others of an entirely different bearing, and stamped with all the marks of an after-thought.

Book III., Tit. X., art. 1896 : "The principle laid down in the preceding article does not operate where the loan has been made in (crude or uncoined) bullion ".

Book III., Tit. X., art. 1897: "If it be bullion which has been lent, whatever may be the increase or diminution of its price, the debtor must always return the same quantity and quality, and must return that alone ".

Seven years before this Code was promulgated, the money of France consisted of 147,000 millions of genuine and counterfeit assignats, which had gradually become worthless and were finally demonetised, 1st July, 1796. Articles 1896 and 1897 of the Code Napoleon could hardly have escaped the lynx eyes of financiers (perhaps they suggested them), and may have not been without influence in shaping that celebrated " Letter to the King " of England, which Lord Liverpool signed on 7th May, 1805. The position of the moneyed classes may not unreasonably be summarised as follows :—

"Arts. 1896 and 1897, of the Code Napoleon, which make a distinction between debts of money and bullion, are the law not only of France, but also of those numerous States and Colonies which are subject to the influence of Napoleon's conquests. Owing to British jealousy and the abhorrence of any institutes bearing the name of Napoleon, it will hardly be adopted in England. However, the same end can be accomplished by closing the British mints to the private coinage of silver (at any ratio to gold fixed by the State) while keeping them open to the private coinage of gold; provided, of course, that the weight and fineness of the gold coins are preserved unalterably. For this last regulation, full dependence can be placed upon the conservative British character. The present moment is a propitious one for suspending the private coinage of silver. The money of England now (1805) consists of inconvertible bank notes. To close the mints to silver would therefore occasion no inconvenience and invoke no hostility. Let us therefore support Lord Liverpool."

Notwithstanding the suspicious solicitude for lenders of bullion, which is implied in the needless repetition of the "principle" contained in arts. 1896 and 1897, it is clear that arts. 587 and 1895, especially the latter, were intended to embody and assert the paramountship of the Civil and Common Law rule, that debts in denominations of money current at the period of the making of the debts, are dischargeable in like denominations of money current at the time of payment. Same in the Italian Code, art. 1821.

This rule was recognised and applied in a case which came up before the "Tribunal de Cassation," or French Court of Appeals, in 1856, when it was decided, in conformity with the Code Napoleon, that debts for money were dischargeable in the money of the day of payment, no matter of what material such money consisted.

In the Supreme Court of Pennsylvania, in 1864, it was decided that ground-rents, payable in "lawful money," were payable in the money of the day, which, in point of fact, was treasury notes, or "greenbacks". (Brightly's *Digest*, ed. 1877, II., 1751.) About the same time (1864), the State of California passed an Act providing that debts, within the State, were payable only in gold coins of the United States. This practically nullified the United States law of 25th February, 1862, which made the treasury notes issued under such Act (greenbacks) payable for all debts public and private, except customs-duties, and interest on the public debt. No man, therefore, was bound to obey the California law; and its observance within the State (for it was observed) was due entirely to local public opinion, and a general desire to keep only gold coins in circulation in a gold-mining State.

In the Supreme Court of the United States at Washington, the highest Court of Appeal in America, it was held in 1868 that legal-tender treasury notes (greenbacks) were a good tender for "gold and silver coin". (Bronson *v.* Rodes, 7 *Wallace Reports;* Justice Miller's dissenting opinion.)

In the same Court in 1869 it was held that greenbacks were a valid tender for "dollars". (Hepburn *v.* Griswold, 8 *Wallace Reports;* Justices Miller, Swayne and Davis' dissenting opinion.)

These opinions amply sustain the principle of the Civil and Common, the Napoleonic and Italian laws, and the English and French decisions.

The opposite principle, that one which arises from the belief that money is only so much metal stamped by the State, and owes its value solely to the material of which coins are made, is to be traced back to the Black Acts of James III. of Scotland, Act 23, A.D. 1467, the following account of which is given in Henry's *History of Great Britain*, 2nd. ed., Vol. X., p. 267: "Both the creditor and the debtor, the buyer and the seller, the borrower and the lender, the lord and the tenant, spiritual and temporal, be observant to the desire and the intents of them that were in the time of making the contracts and payment to be made in the same substance that was intended at the time of the making of the contracts". Dr. Henry observes that "there is sufficient evidence still remaining, that though several laws were made of the same tenor with that above, none of them could be executed".

It will scarcely be credited that this mediæval legislation was actually incorporated in the statutes of the United States of America, in 1878; yet such is nevertheless the fact. Dr. Henry has shown the reason why this law could not be executed four centuries ago; which was that the inadequate supplies of the precious metals, compared with the demands of commerce, continually raised the value of the former, and compelled the State to lessen the metallic contents of the coins. The law of 1467 increased the burden of the indebted, until they could not bear the weight put upon them. The debtor who borrowed £100 was called upon to pay £125, or £150, in order to extinguish his debt; and this, in many cases, he absolutely refused to do. A somewhat similar scarcity of the precious metal (gold) is occurring in America at the present time, though from different causes. The State has demonetised silver, while so large a proportion (about three-fourths) of the new supplies of gold is absorbed in the arts, and so small a proportion is coined, and remains in the form of money, that gold coin has largely increased in purchasing power; and debtors, in order to discharge their obligations, are obliged to sell nearly half as much again of the products of their labour, as were equivalent to their debts "at the time of the making of the contracts".

The most disastrous results have followed this legislation, and already a powerful party has vehemently demanded its repeal. Unless this is conceded, it will scarcely be denied that widespread dissatisfaction will ensue, and the great Republic of the West may discover, when it is too late, that the revival of mediæval legislation and contempt of historical experience and legal precedents is not one of the roads to progress. The expressions "dollars or units" (1792), "bimetallic money" (1878), "intrinsic value" and "bimetallism" (1893), besides many others, which occur in the Acts of the United States, all of which involve the admission of monetary theories, and which are either derived from an imperfect knowledge of the subject, or else were suggested by interested persons, also await revision.

The law of money would be incomplete without some reference to those principles relating to the subject which have engaged the attention of writers on the laws of nations. They may be conveniently summarised as follows:—

I. The issuance of money is a supreme national prerogative.

II. Cases in which foreigners are not subject to the local law of money.

III. A State may, without limit, lower the value of foreign money, or forbid its circulation entirely.

IV. States are not justified in imitating foreign moneys.

V. The value of coins is derived not from the metal of which they are composed, but from the stamp upon them. This admits them to the circulation, and enables them to form part of the Measure of Value.

VI. Governments are bound to fulfil the engagements of their predecessors, and where they affect foreigners, even to paying in a special sort of money.

These principles appear in the following form in the *Droit des Gens*, by C. F. de Martens, Paris, 1864, sect. 110, Vol. I., p. 298:—

No Government can afford to occupy itself in attempts to prevent all the evils which may menace its internal affairs; on the other hand, the integrity of a State demands the erection of institutes to protect the well-being and promote the convenience of its subjects. Foremost among these institutes is one, which, though it relates especially to commerce, yet has a much wider range of influence; this is money.

Every independent State has the right[1] to create

---

[1] And it is its duty to exercise this right.

money and regulate its value. In this respect, though a violation of equity should be avoided, yet the foreigner must be prepared to accept in payment that sort of money which the subjects of the State are obliged to receive.[1]

It cannot be denied that the State has the power to create money, for example, of paper, without any obligation to exchange it for metallic money; and the foreigner has no right to complain if he suffers from this as much as the citizen. Nevertheless, if the State has recourse to such a monetary system as would absolve it from satisfying its creditors, the violation of equity which results may authorise a foreign State to take the part of its own subjects in the matter, and to employ, with that object, should reprisal be found useless, all the methods which the privileges of war authorise in national conflicts.[2]

Although in reference to debts which the State may contract with individuals, the foreigner has the right to be placed on the same footing as the citizens,[3] and has no right to be preferred over them, yet where such superior right is secured by treaty,[4] or where financial measures grossly violate the rules of equity, a foreign power may justly champion the complaints of its injured subjects and have recourse to such prohibitive acts or reprisals as will secure its subjects from the injustice or vexation of such measures.[5]

No State is obliged to admit into its circulation the coins or paper money of another State. It may either entirely forbid their circulation, or admit them to such

---

[1] Treaty between England and Russia, 1766, art. 5.

[2] On the transactions which took place in Sweden after the death of Charles XII. in 1718 and in France under the Regency of 1719, consult Busch, *Weithandel*, pp. 229 and 276, and the Bill of Echasseriaux, in France, 1795.

[3] Burgoign, *Tableaux de l'Espagne*, Tom. II., p. 32.

[4] Peace of 1763 between Prussia and Saxony, arts. 7 and 72 in Martens' *Recueil*, Tom. I., pp. 75, 77, and 146; Peace of Luneville, *Recueil*, Tom. VII., p. 538; Peace of Vienna (1809), art. 9, in *New Recueil*, Tom. I., p. 210.

[5] Treaties of 1798, 1800.

circulation, after altering their value.[1] On these points, which are often important to the rights of individuals, the supreme right of the State is nowhere questioned in Europe.

We can scarcely admit in theory the right of a nation to mint money in close imitation to that of another friendly nation without the permission of the latter, although there exist many examples of such procedure.[2]

Although under present circumstances (the Germanic Confederation of 1815-56, and the Mint Convention called for 1857), the States which formed the old Empire possess less practical freedom than previously, as regards the right to coin money,[3] yet both toward their neighbours, as well as toward more remote States, their attitude is theoretically that of independent sovereignty. Further arrangements on this subject are now pending in Germany.

In a commentary on M. de Martens from the pen of Senhor Pinheiro-Ferreira, the latter holds with De Martens that in the case of State debts contracted with individuals, foreigners have no rights superior to those of citizens; and that where the State acts unjustly toward both, the injustice which the citizen is obliged to endure does not deprive the foreigner of the right to complain. He adds that, while the citizen cannot complain of the injustice of his own State, the stranger, who has taken no part in it, should not be placed on the same footing. Senhor Pinheiro-Ferreira appears to think that he is here at issue with M. de Martens; but as the latter expressly stated that "where financial measures grossly violate the rules of equity a foreign power may justly champion the complaints of its injured subjects," etc., there appears to be no essential difference on this point between them.

---

[1] Rousett, *Recueil*, Tom. X., p. 56; Moser, *Versuch*, Tom. VIII., pp. 15-43.

[2] The author here probably alludes to the Prussian banco thalers of 1766, imitating the Maria Theresas.

[3] Putter, *Institutiones Juris publici Germanici*, Lib. VIII., C. 2.

Senhor Pinheiro-Ferreira continues as follows: "It will be observed that we here allude to injustice towards the foreigner to the prejudice of his natural or acquired rights, and not to those which are merely the consequences of *bond fide* contracts between him and the State. But when the latter pays in money inferior to that stipulated in such contracts, it will not be sufficient if the State treats him no worse than it does its own citizens. Because the citizens submit to be wronged is no good reason why the foreigner should also submit. On the other hand, if in making payment the State takes advantage of its own laws, of which the foreigner was or could have been cognisant at the time when the contract was made, he will be obliged to submit to the laws, however onerous or unjust they may be. He must be assumed to have known them; and the presumption is that he made due allowance for their operation, by exacting a higher interest or greater profits; and if not, he must bear the penalty of his imprudence."

Another commentator—M. Charles Vergé—observes that Pinheiro-Ferreira's remarks find some exemplification in the action of the Neapolitan Government previous to the unification of Italy. In levying a seigniorage of 9 per cent. on coins of his own mintage, the king deemed it necessary at the same time to reduce by proclamation the value of the French coins which circulated in the kingdom, from $5\frac{1}{4}$ to 6 francs (silver) as the equivalent of the Neapolitan piastre (silver), a reduction of 13 per cent., an act which induced M. Vergé to deny that a State has the right at its pleasure to regulate the value of foreign money circulating in its dominions. But here the commentator's French patriotism has evidently led him astray; for if a State is sovereign in reference to its own money, it is unquestionably sovereign in reference to any other money which it may admit into its circulation; unless, of course, it is restrained by treaty stipulations to the contrary.

Our commentator goes on to observe that a change in

the form of an indebted government, or in the reigning dynasty, or in the person of the sovereign, does not alter in any respect the obligation of debt contracted in the name of the State by representatives duly authorised. Neither (continues he) does a change in the constitution of the State absolve a nation from the responsibility of its debts. The new government is bound to fulfil the engagements contracted by its predecessors.[1]

M. Vergé concludes as follows: " M. Martens questions the right of a State to mint money in close imitation to that of another friendly nation without the permission of the latter. Although there can be no doubt about the correctness of this position, Senhor Pinheiro-Ferreira asks how can it be theoretically refuted that France (for example) should have the right to pay England in coined money struck of the same weight and of the same alloy as the money in which England has paid France. It appears to us impossible to consecrate as principles those facts or hypotheses which only belong to struggles for empire and wars of succession. Money has circulation and value not merely on account of the metal which it contains, but also on account of the national imprint which it has received." [2]

The pending monetary measures alluded to by M.

---

[1] Grotius, *De Jure Belli et Pacis*, Lib. II., Cap. IX., sect. 8, notes 1 to 3; Puffendorf, *De Jure Nat. et Gentium*, Lib. VIII., C. XII., sects. 1, 2, 3; Vattel, *Les Droits des Gens*, edit. Guillamin, Lib. I., C. X., sect. 108, and the note of M. Prodier-Fodéré, I., 39; Wheaton, *Éléments du Droit International*, Tom. I., p. 39; Heffter, *Le Droit International*, tr. by M. Bergson, sect. 24. *Per contra*, see proceedings and policy of Ferdinand VI. of Spain, in *Money and Civilization*, 1st ed., pp. 111-12.

[2] The United States Act of Nov. 1, 1893, says: "It is hereby declared to be the policy of the United States to continue the use of both *gold and silver* as standard money". Neither gold nor silver ever were money (except among savages and thieves), nor are they money, nor can they be money again, because in civilised communities there can be no money without denominations. The Act of Feb. 28, 1878, sect. 1, contains a Special Contract clause overthrowing money. These tricky clauses have already cost that nation some hundreds of millions of money. They may yet endanger its autonomy.

Martens, who probably wrote in 1856, have since been realised in Germany, by the treaty of January 24, 1857, which went into effect on the 1st of the following May, between Austria and the other States of Germany, and which was to expire at the end of 1878.

AUTHORITIES ON LAW OF MONEY.—*Journal du Palais*, CVI. (year 1856), Part II., p. 267; CVIII., 202; CIX., 51; CXI., 1029; CXIX., 92; CXXIV., 1222; Bavard, *Traité de Droit Commercial*, III., 329; Bédarride, *De la lettre de change* Tom. II., No. 384; Locré, *Legislation de la France*, Tom. XVIII., p. 66; Massé, *Le Droit Commercial*, 2ᵉ ed., Tom. I., No. 611; *Annuaire de Legislation Étrangère;* Carli, *Dell' origine e del comercio della Moneta, e dell' instituzione delle zecche d' Italia, dalla decadenza dell' Imperio sino al secolo decimosettimo;* Aguilera y Velasco, *Codigo Civil Italiano*, art. 1821 (Lib. III., Tit. XVII., C. 1). For numerous decisions in Pennsylvania and elsewhere, see Brightly's *Digest of Decisions*, 1754 to 1877, Vol. II., p. 1751.

CHAPTER VIII.

THE UNIT OF MONEY IS ALL MONEY.

Origin of the word " money "—Its employment with reference to any period before B.C. 273 an anachronism—Money, or *nomisma*, meant originally the whole numbers of money—This was its classical meaning—During the Empire and the Dark Ages money came to mean one or more coins—This is the meaning attached to it in the laws of modern nations, because these laws originated in the Dark Ages—During the Renaissance it meant the whole quantity, not numbers, of money—This is the meaning sometimes attached to it by the Economists, because their systems date from the Renaissance—Incongruous nature of this definition—In speaking with precision, money can only mean all the numbers of money of a given country—Teleologically, the unit of money is all money.

MONEY, as a generic term for the common means of payment, the medium of exchange, the common denominator or measure of value, the expression of price, the sum of ponderable symbols, the mechanism in the numerical fractions of which either law or custom makes taxes, fines, debts, services, or exchanges, payable, was first used—that is, the *word* was first used—towards the middle of the third century before our æra.[1]

What we now call money was named by the ancient Hindoos *ayas*, meaning All, or the Whole, a term evidently derived from Ies, the name of the sun-god, whose image was probably stamped on their coins. Mr. Gaston L. Feuardent, the eminent numismatist, assured me that the

---

[1] From these circumstances it follows that the use of the term " money " with reference to any period previous to the date referred to is an anachronism. Such an instance occurs in the English translation of Genesis, when Abraham is said to have paid for Sarah's grave " four hundred shekels of silver, current *money* with the merchant " (Gen. xxiii. 9, 13, 16).

Tarantines, who stamped a similar effigy, that of Iassus or Taras, on their coins, used a similar term, and that this custom fell to the Romans of the earlier portion of the Commonwealth, whose principal coin was called the *ace*. Money was called by the republican Greeks *nomisma*, from *nomos;* and by the Romans of the later Commonwealth *numerato*, from the Greek *nomos* and *nomisma*.

The origin of *moneta* is given elsewhere. It appears probable that this term was at first used only in a collective sense, meaning all money, or the numerical sum of the entire coinage. This was certainly the meaning originally attached to *nomisma*, and *numerato*, which were the predecessors of the word *moneta*. This meaning of money—namely, all money, or the whole sum or numbers of money within a given legal jurisdiction or a given country—will herein be distinguished as the Classical.

Later on, that is to say, during the Roman hierarchical æra, the term "money" was applied to any considerable portion of the coinage, and still later to smaller portions; but not yet to a single coin.

During that lingering decay of the social fabric which characterised the Hierarchy, every combination, both of things and ideas, gradually resolved itself into its original elements. This means of warding off impending dissolution, Nature offers not only to composite things and ideas, but also to words. Isolation affords a refuge from which social existence may again emerge. The shattered trunk of a tree may survive after its branches and fruit are destroyed.

The Roman Hierarchy split into two, four, and many fragments, each of which was called a kingdom. In the course of time these kingdoms became divided into countships or dukedoms, and the latter subdivided into still smaller realms. Every institution which was composed of a plurality of men or things fell to pieces in a similar way. The Comitia and Senate perished, the tribunals of justice disappeared, the trade corporations or *collegii* vanished, the use of annuities and life tables was forgotten, the census fell into oblivion, even the organisation of armies ceased ; and counts and kings alike decided their quarrels by single combat.

Everything of a joint ownership, as a public road, an aqueduct, or a water-ditch, everything of a composite structure, from a sailing ship down to a piece of paper, every art which depended upon the association of labour, from the representation of a drama down to the blowing of glass, was lost.

The same course of disintegration attended the history of institutions, of ideas, of thoughts. The world, the commonwealth, the republic, the nation, the social state, the people, public opinion, commerce, credit, society—all these were ideas or institutions known to the Greeks and Romans in the widest sense. Says Pliny the Elder, " I do not suppose that the land is actually wanting, or that the earth has not the form of a globe ; but that on each side the uninhabitable parts have not been discovered ".[1] In the Dark Ages which succeeded the Augustan æra, the world dwindled to little beyond the compass of Southern and Western Europe ; the commonwealth was the duke's courtyard ; and as for the social state, public opinion, commerce and credit, these things died out entirely.

Words followed a similar process of decomposition. Their meanings gradually contracted, so that from embracing composite and collective ideas, they came to have only simple and single ones. They degenerated from forcible to weak ; from grand to petty. Many of the words were lost altogether. During the Renaissance which

---

[1] Pliny also quotes Eratosthenes and Hipparchus, both of whom knew, not only that the earth was a sphere, they had even computed its circumference ; the former at 252,000 stadii, the latter at 277,000. The rotundity of the earth had long previously been proved by Thales, 636 B.C. It was also familiar to Pythagoras, 540-10 B.C. ; Herodotus, 484-08 B.C. ; Aristarchus of Samos, 280 B.C. ; Posidonius, 150-35 B.C. ; Strabo, 60 B.C. -21 A.D. ; Ptolemy, A.D. 117-44, and many others of the Greek philosophers and astronomers.

followed the Dark Ages, a few of them revived, to puzzle the modern philologist with their successive diminuendo and crescendo gamuts of meanings. Among these words was money.

The descent of the word "money" from its original meaning of the whole numbers of the medium of exchange, or the whole coinage, to the feudal meaning of a single coin, piece, or fraction of the measure of value, is clearly traceable in words still extant.[1] There was a time, indeed, when its use expired altogether, and *species* in one country, *argent* in another, took its place.[2]

It was at this period, when every one of its constituent parts was on the point of dissolution, that the social fabric of Europe suddenly revived. Mahomet arose in Asia; the route to the Orient was reopened; the restorative of commerce was offered to a continent where manufactures had become unknown and agriculture was on the verge of extinction; and organised society—at first in Italy, afterwards elsewhere—began to evolve itself anew out of the moribund and disintegrating social elements known to us as Feudalism. Then followed the Fall of Byzantium, the extinction of the Hierarchy, the reconstruction of kingdoms, of states, of armies, and of legal tribunals; and the rediscovery of old truths and inventions, such as the rotundity of the earth,[3] sailing ships, glass and paper,

---

[1] Consult the use of the words *nomisma* in Aristotle and Plato; *moneta* in Cicero and Pliny; *moneta* in the *Essays on Money*, edited by Budelius; and *moneta* in Du Cange's copious *Glossary*.

[2] There is a parallelism in the decay and subsequent revival of the conception of money and the arts of music and poetry. During the Dark Ages the ancient art of music was lost, and poetry, which in the classical ages went by numbers, now went by accent. This was common to modern Greek and all the languages which sprang from or passed through the Dark Ages.—Leake's *Topography of Athens*, lxxxiii. London, 1821, 8vo.

[3] About A.D. 813-33, Almamon, Caliph of Bagdad, caused a degree of the meridian to be measured. During the twelfth century Ben Mahomed Edrisi presented to the heretical Roger II. of Sicily a silver globe representing the earth. The apocryphal Sir John Mandeville (1337), who probably stole from Hayton, Odoric, and Boldensale, and they from the Saracens,

together with some new ones, as gunpowder and printing on felted paper. Finally came a resuscitation of old words, among them "money"; but money shorn of its ancient meaning, money no longer meaning the whole of the measure of value, money meaning only what it meant previous to its entire verbal disuse—a fraction of such measure, a single coin. The plural of this word, meaning a number of coins, a term no longer in common use, was "moneys".

From this Renascent Age sprang the Law Merchant of England and America and the laws of other modern States. In these laws money is still alluded to as a single coin. The "unit of value," says the United States of America Act of 12th February, 1873, section 14, "shall be a one-dollar piece"; and this is further described in the same law as a piece of coined metal weighing so many grains.

From the time when the discovery of America had added the plunder of a new continent to the, as yet, meagre resources of Europe, down to the sixteenth or seventeenth centuries, the jurisconsults and writers who were conversant with the Roman civil law, for example those cited by Budelius and the English justices, evinced an acquaintance with the ancient meaning of money : but since that period, and especially in English works, the custom has been to use the word "money" in two senses : first, that of a number of coins; second, that of the whole quantity, not number of pieces, of the coinage. This last named meaning which the word "money" acquired after its entire disuse during the Dark Ages, and its subsequent resuscitation, is traceable back to the period of the Renaissance; and in order to

says that ships may sail around the earth, and he believes that they had already done so. During the early part of the fifteenth century, Olou-beg, successor to Tamerlane, made a measurement of the earth, based on its assumed sphericity—(Voltaire, *General History*, I., 32; II., 2, 45). A planisphere, or map of the world, showing the Cape of Good Hope, was delineated in the convent of Murano at Venice in 1459, thirty-seven years before Vasco de Gama's voyage.

distinguish it from the other meanings, it has been herein called the Mercantile.

So long as money was made exclusively of metal coins, no difficulty presented itself in reasoning from the Renascent meaning of money; and since it was during this period that the foundations of the present science of political economy were laid,[1] it was the Mercantile meaning that money acquired in the works of Joseph Harris and Adam Smith, and those who followed them. Paper money, beyond the phase of deposit receipts, was scarcely in use when the earlier of these Economists wrote; and as for those of a later date, though many have attacked and weakened the great Scotch sophist, none have had the genius or good fortune to overthrow him in popular estimation.

But since the æra of the Economists—since the time of Smith—money has come to be largely made of both metal and paper; and as it is physically impossible to express in one sum the total numbers of gold, silver, copper, and paper pieces, or fractions of money,[2] the silver and copper pieces, formerly full legal tenders, have been demonetised, or partly demonetised, and have been conveniently omitted from definition and argument;[3] whilst the fiction has been invented, that all paper constituents of money involve fulfillable promises, written or implied, to be exchanged for

---

[1] John Botero's works were published about 1590; Petty's, 1682-98; Montesquieu's, 1748; Joseph Harris's *Treatise on Money*, in 1757.

[2] The numbers of two or more unlike things cannot be added together into a sum of either one of them. A pound of fish and a pound of flesh cannot make two pounds of either fish or flesh. A dollar coin cannot be added to a paper dollar and make a sum of two coin dollars, or two paper ones.

[3] For example, in answer to the self-proposed question, "What is a pound?" (meaning a pound sterling) Sir Robert Peel, in 1844, said 123·275 grains of gold $\frac{11}{12}$ths fine. In this definition the silver, copper, and paper pounds which circulated at the time are left out of view. Sir Robert stated what a gold pound of that day was; but not what either one of the other pounds was or had been, or what any of them might be. His answer is, therefore, incomplete.

gold coins of like denomination. When these subterfuges have been overthrown, the economical sophisms built upon the Mercantile sense of money have resisted demolition by hiding themselves behind the ambiguous term "currency".

Thus we have three distinct meanings for money:—

1. The Classical: The Whole Numbers of money; the whole number of pieces or fractions of like denomination and function which the law requires or permits to be used for payments—no matter of what material they are composed.[1]

2. The Feudal: A Coin; plural, moneys or "species," meaning several or many coins.

3. The Mercantile: The whole quantity of Metal—gold or silver—of which full legal-tender coins are made, plus the quantity of such metal available for coinage under individual or private coinage laws.

With a view to determine the bearing which these varied meanings of money would have in practice, let it be supposed that the question were asked, "Of what does the measure of value in the United States consist?" The answers would be as follows:—

The Classical answer: There are many pieces of gold, silver, nickel, copper, and paper—no matter of what weight or size—legally called dollars. The sum of their numbers is the measure of value.

The Feudal answer: A gold coin legally named a dollar, weighing so many grains. Any one coin of this description is the measure of value.

The Mercantile answer: So many known tons of gold

---

[1] This meaning appears to be recognised, though somewhat indirectly, in the following sentence from John Locke's *Essay on Money*: "For the value of money in general is the quantity of all the money in the world, in proportion to all the trade; but the value of money in any one country is the present quantity of the current money in that country, in proportion to the present trade". Says Hume: "It is not difficult to perceive that it is the total quantity of money in circulation in any country which determines what portion of that quantity shall exchange for a certain portion of the goods or commodities of that country".

coined into so many million pieces, each of so many grains, legally called dollars—plus so many unknown tons of uncoined gold bullion ready to be coined for private individuals into similar pieces, free of seigniorage. The sum of this quantity is the measure of value.

It is evident that no succinct, no practical discussion of money can be conducted until a choice is made between these three different meanings of the term. For example, Mr. John Stuart Mill, the most eminent of modern economists, holds in one place that "the value of money varies inversely as its quantity". This rule is true of money when money implies numbers; but it is not true of money when money implies quantity of metal. The proof of this appears in a previous paragraph of Mr. Mill's work, where he holds that the total sum of money—no matter howsoever great or small it may be—will always have the same value.[1] This rule, apparently so contradictory of the other, is true of money when money implies numbers; but it is not true of money when money implies quantity of metal.

Bearing in mind Mr. Mill's great penetration and logical faculty, it is evident that he has fallen into this ambiguity through the subtle error of employing the term money in two different senses.

To avoid a similar mistake, and until a rightful meaning of the term is acquired by the reader through familiarity with the nature and function of money, the sense in which it is used in this treatise will be plainly expressed or implied in each instance.

When its nature is well understood it will be perceived that money is a Collective Unit or Mechanism; and that it is impossible to give it a precise or specific name unless such name has the meaning that it is believed belonged to *nomisma*—namely, All Money, or the whole sum of numbers of money in a given country, or within a given legal jurisdiction.

[1] Mill's *Political Economy*, III., viii., § 3, p. 300—evidently from Adam Smith, Book I., Chap. XI., Part III., p. 178.

When used with reference to all the world, money means—and must of necessity mean—all the money in the world. Therefore, teleologically, money, or, what is the same thing, the "unit" of money, is all money; and the term should not be used in any other sense.

So long as the various countries of the world employ different monetary systems, and each system consists of different kinds of moneys—that is to say, moneys having different legal attributes, as is the case now—it becomes necessary herein, unless new and strange terms are introduced, to employ the word money to mean sometimes all the money in the world, sometimes all the money of a given country, and sometimes all the money of one class—as metallic money, numerical money, etc.; whilst the word moneys will have to be used to mean sometimes two or more systems of money, at others two or more classes of money. The intelligence of the reader will doubtless guide him to the sense in which this, at present ambiguous, term is employed in the various parts of this work.

The use of the word money in the sense of a single piece or fraction of money has been avoided as far as possible; but in some places it was found inconvenient to do so without resort to tedious circumlocution. One striking fact asserts itself at the outset of this inquiry into the principles of money: if the "unit" of money is all money—and there can be no doubt that such is the fact—it follows that our knowledge of money, its composition, dimensions, distribution, operation, etc., must be derived from other sources than visual perception. We may, indeed, perceive a fraction of money, as a coin, a note, etc., but we cannot see all money. We must, therefore, consult the laws and customs of money for a knowledge of it; and since these laws and customs are exceedingly numerous and intricate, and are entwined with other laws and customs, and much affected by their operation, we find that money is something more than a mere mechanism—it is a legal device, it is an Institution. No individual can make it, or a duplicate of it, as one can a pint-pot or a yard-stick. It has to be established and maintained by society at large. Nor may this establishment be entirely arbitrary. It must be designed with respect to the other social and commercial arrangements already in existence, and liable to be affected by its operation.

The following letter from the author to a distinguished American writer on money is pertinent to the subject of the present chapter:—

"I notice that in the Congressional debates on the Silver Question, much use is made of the corrupt term 'unit of money,' which was introduced into the Mint Code by the same conspirators and by the same disgraceful means which they employed to abolish American silver dollars in the interest of their friends in Europe. Previous to that time, the term 'unit of money' was employed to mean merely unit of account, or the denomination in which sums of money were to be expressed, as dollars in America, 'pounds' in England, and francs in France. Now they have it to designate the measure of value. The structure and idioms of our language prove that money means the whole sum of money, and not merely one coin. 'Money is the measure of value,' 'Money is the unit of value,' 'Money is the medium of exchange,' 'Money is scarce, plentiful, tight, easy,' etc. In all these everyday expressions, money evidently means the whole sum of money, or, as in the last-named cases, the whole sum of money available. In no case does it mean merely one coin. Nobody, except these conspirators, holds that one coin is the measure of value; nor that one coin is the unit of value; nor that one coin is the medium of exchange; nor that one coin can be scarce, plentiful, tight, easy, etc.

"The defect of the law is that this whole sum is nowhere described, nowhere defined, nowhere limited, in the law. If one coin were money, we would know authoritatively what money is, for that coin, the gold dollar, is very carefully described in the law. If money consists of a sum of many coins or notes, we know not what it is; for the whole sum of coins and notes is unlimited and unknown. We cannot measure by the measure, because the measure is undefined; we cannot count by the 'unit,' because the unit is not described, but only an undetermined fraction of the unit; we cannot employ the medium of exchange with security, because the size of such medium is unascertainable. We can only know when money is scarce or plentiful, tight or easy, by a sort of rude approximation, by observing effects and results, which may or may not have been caused by such amplitude or scarceness. In a similar way we know, approximately, when the wind blows strongly or weakly; but without a wind-gauge, without a definite measure of some sort, we cannot tell exactly how strong or weak it is. Money, as at present constituted in the law, is like the unmeasured wind; its volume, its force, its pressure, cannot be determined.

"To show that money is not composed of one coin or note, appears to be like breaking a fly on a wheel, like blowing a cat from an Armstrong gun. Nobody doubts that the Thing which is the measure of value, the Thing which is used to measure value, the Thing in which Price is expressed, the Thing which, while it is in process of augmentation, or diminution, exerts a most powerful influence on the welfare of society, is *the whole sum of money;* not merely one coin or note. Yet this last is precisely what the law of 1873 says it is. Reason, analogy, experience, authority, custom, the obvious structure of language, all proclaim that the 'unit' of value is the whole sum of money; contrariwise, the conspirators' law says that 'the unit of value' is one dollar.

"Not only does the law say so, the Economists say so. They all begin by affirming the predicate that the value of money is in inverse ratio to its quantity, and they all wind up by concluding that such quantity means one coin.

None of them are free from this strange delusion. They all begin right; they all end wrong.

"This seems a bold opinion to pass upon such eminent logicians as Adam Smith and John Stuart Mill. Nevertheless, the justice of the opinion is susceptible of the plainest proof. These writers, indeed, all the Economists, hold that the value of money is in inverse ratio to its quantity.[1] Quantity here evidently implies numbers. Numbers mean more than one. But, overlooking this plain implication, the same authors afterward proceed to regard quantity as meaning one and one only. The laws of England, in perfect keeping with this defective reasoning, have regarded money as consisting of one single coin. Following English example, the American law of 1873 describes a dollar coin as the 'unit of value'. A unit means one. Yet directly after declaring the unit to consist of one, this same law provides for the coinage of illimitable other units of like weight and fineness, and declares each of them to be units like the first one, and to have precisely the same legal functions. How can they have the same functions, if the rule be sound, as undoubtedly it is, that the value—and this means, of necessity, the measuring function—of money is in inverse ratio to its quantity? According to the rule, the moment dollar number Two is added to dollar number One, the value of One is lowered one-half. How, then, can they both be units? It might as well be claimed that when one is divided into two parts, each part of one is a unit. On the contrary, such parts or halves are fractions, and instead of each piece of metal authorised, when coined, to be paid as a dollar, being called a unit, it should properly be called a fraction.

"But a fraction of what? A portion of that plural number, that Whole Number of pieces of money which Smith and Mill and all mankind mean by the term

---

[1] Yet Lord Farrer, before the Agricultural Commission of 1894, said that the "unit" of value was a bit of gold! So is a watch a bit of gold, but nobody has yet proposed to sell gold watches by weight.

'quantity,' when it is said that the value of money is in inverse ratio to its quantity.

"The politico-economical rule, therefore, needs to be amended, to render it explicit. It should read: *the value of money is in inverse ratio to its* NUMBERS. The progress of mankind often waits on the evolution of words from ambiguous to special meanings. In the rule of money, quantity does not, cannot, mean bulk, weight, or area; it means numbers, *nomos, numerato,* and it cannot mean anything else.

"If, as the statute of 1873 declares, the 'unit' of value in the United States is one dollar, then the entire history and principles of money will have to be rewritten; for nowhere in that history, and nowhere among those principles, is there any admission or recognition of the legal assumption that the 'unit' of value consists of one dollar, or one pound, or one franc, or one coin or note of any denomination. Both history and theory declare money to be a collective noun, and to consist of numerous coins or notes, or both together.

"The term 'currency' is frequently used as a synonym for money. It appears to have been devised in order to avoid the objection—based both on ignorance of history and contempt for logic—that money could not be money unless its symbols were composed of a commodity that would be just as valuable when reduced to raw material as it could be when fabricated into money and clothed by the law with the unique and potent function of legal-tender. Currency meant a paper money in contradistinction to a metallic one; or it meant a hybrid money, composed partly of paper notes and partly of coins. Whatever it meant in detail, it certainly in its largest sense meant money. Hence, in America, you have the legal office called 'Comptroller of the Currency'; and the expressions 'fractional currency,' 'regulating the currency,' etc. In all these cases it is undeniable that currency means the whole sum of money, not merely a part of it, much less a single coin or piece of paper.

"From these premises it follows that both money and currency mean the whole sum of money or currency; that the 'unit' of money is all money, and that the term, as smuggled into the law of 1873, and as used in current debates of Congress, is erroneous and misleading."

CHAPTER IX.

MONEYS CONTRASTED WITH OTHER MEASURES.

Differences between moneys and other measures, even when both are limited—1. Money is used to determine the value of numberless things at the same time; a yard-stick to determine the length of one thing at a time—2. Money determines a dynamical and variable relation; other measures, a statical and fixed one—3. Money determines a numerical and extrinsic relation; other measures determine quantitative or qualitative attributes—4. Money determines an equitable relation; other measures determine quantities which have no connection with equity—5. Moneys have a tendency to instantly amalgamate, and two or more moneys will merge into one money of the combined volume of both, which is not the case with other measures.

IT was shown in a previous chapter that money, as it is at present constituted in the laws of the several States of the world, differed from all other measures in the respect that its dimensions were not specifically nor precisely limited, defined, nor fixed in the law; whilst the measures of length, weight, volume, area, etc., are actually thus limited, defined, and fixed. Owing to this lack of limitation and fixity, the whole sum of money, which serves for the measure of value, is liable to be altered from time to time by various uncontrollable and uncertain events; thus exposing the important relation of Price to sudden and violent fluctuations.

In addition to this difference—which only applies to money as it now stands in the law—there yet remain other differences between money and other measures. These differences apply to all moneys, whether limited or not, and it is deemed useful to notice them in this place.

1. A money is used to determine a numerical relation

between itself and *all* other things, including other moneys, simultaneously. Contrariwise, a yard-stick is used to determine a numerical relation between itself and *one* other thing at a time. The former is a complex measure; the latter a unital or simple measure. Money cannot measure one thing without at the same time measuring all things; a yard-stick may measure one thing without measuring any other. The length of one object does not depend upon the length of other objects; the price of one object does depend upon the price of other objects.

2. Money is used to determine a kinetic and variable relation; other measures, to determine a statical and fixed one. Value varies with time and place; it also varies with the frequency of exchanges in time. Hence value is a variable relation, and it is this variable relation which money has to determine; whilst that which a yard-stick determines is an invariable and fixed relation. The determination of a yard-stick will last for ever, whilst a determination of money in price is only valid for a given time and place.

3. A measure of value can only be useful in the social state; a measure of length may be useful in the isolated state. This arises from the fact that length is an inherent and intrinsic attribute of matter; it is inseparably connected with it, and has no tendency to vary; whilst value is extrinsic and relative, and continually tends to vary. Length can be determined by comparison; whilst value can only be definitively measured by sale or exchange.

4. From the social function of money arises its relation to intellect and equity. There can be no such thing as an equitable or inequitable length; there may be an equitable and inequitable price. Length does not vary with the intellectual attainments, the knowledge, information, opportunities, virtues, and power of men; value does. When these advantages and attributes are unequal, the determination of value by means of money cannot be equitable; one party is certain to obtain an undue advan-

tage over the other. When they are equal, value becomes an equitable relation. Whether the determination of value be equitable or inequitable, its measure should be constant; for in the case of an otherwise equitable exchange an inconstant measure will make it inequitable; and in the case of an inequitable one an inconstant measure will only add one inequity to another, as is the case now with all exchanges.

5. Length and every other attribute of matter which is susceptible of numerical expression vary *directly* with numbers. Value is a numerical relation which varies inversely with numbers. Hence two yard-sticks cannot at the same time and collectively measure one relation of length; whilst two moneys may at the same time, that is to say collectively, measure one relation of value. Two moneys used collectively become instantly merged into one another, and thus become one money; two yard-sticks cannot be merged into one another. They cannot be made one. They will always remain two. Therefore they cannot be used collectively to perform the same office; as two moneys can.

6. The most important difference between money and other measures arises from the fact that the latter are only used for comparison, whilst the former is used for exchange. When cloth is measured by means of a yard-stick, the latter is not given in exchange for the cloth: when cloth is measured by means of money, one is exchanged for the other. The whole principle of the measurement is different. In using the yard-stick, the cloth is not measured by some unlike substance, but by an attribute of itself: in using money for valuing cloth, the cloth is measured against all other commodities. Now, what attribute of money is it that measures the relation of cloth to all other commodities and to all kinds of services? Is it cost of production? Clearly not: because experiment has proved that overvalued coins, irredeemable paper notes, or even a fixed sum of credits, are capable of

correctly measuring value.[1] Is it effort? For the same reason, no. Paper money which costs but little effort to produce will measure value as accurately as that gold for which we labour so strenuously and commit so many crimes. It is numbers, and numbers only. There is no natural common denominator for the varied services and commodities which make up the exchanges of a civilised community. Hence men have invented an artificial one, which must necessarily be arithmetical. It consists of an absolutely or relatively fixed Set of Numbers, represented by palpable and ponderable symbols suitable for transfer from hand to hand. That set of symbols is money: and so far as theory goes, so far as science is concerned, it makes no difference of what material these symbols are made,—whether of gold, silver, paper, or porcelain. The choice of such material belongs not to the Science but to the Politics of money,—a distinction that was not always observed by the critics who reviewed the earlier edition of this work. I am not here advocating paper money, or any other sort of money: I am endeavouring to explain what money is, what it does, and how it does it,—neither of them such simple matters as is commonly supposed.

[1] "The Italians and some other nations . . . have banks both publick and private, wherein they do assign their credits from one to another daily, for very great sums, with ease and satisfaction, *by writing only* . . . and by the said means they have little other use of money . . . more than for their ordinary expenses."—Thomas Mun, *England's Treasure by Forraign Trade*, 1664, Chap. IV.

CHAPTER X.

LIMITATION IS THE ESSENCE OF MONEYS.

Resemblances between money and other measures—All measures of precision are of artificial dimensions—To become a precise measure money must also be of artificial dimensions—All other measures are susceptible of exact numerical expression—To become a just measure money must be defined numerically—The efficiency of all measures, money included, depends upon the exactness of their limits, not the substance of which they may be composed—The limits of other measures are not left to be determined by supply or demand, nor should be those of money.

IT has been shown in previous chapters in what respects money differs from other measures; it will now be shown wherein it resembles or should resemble them. By measures, of course, is meant measures of precision.

1. All measures of precision are of artificial limits. Nature affords none. No natural productions are of an invariable length, volume, magnitude, area, or weight. There is a system of weights set forth very minutely in the pages of Manu, a Hindoo lawgiver of great antiquity. The basis of this system is a specified kind of mustard-seed. In order to ascertain the basis of this system, several modern investigators have each of them weighed many thousand mustard-seeds, and deduced an average weight from these numbers; yet no two of their results agree more than approximately.[1] Even the basis of the French metrical system, which is the ten-millionth part of a quarter of the meridian actually measured on the earth's surface, has been found to be variable. A measure of precision is the symbol of Justice. Nature has left this

[1] For the details of these experiments consult Wilson's *Ariana Antiqua*. The results are given in my *History of Money*, chapter on "India".

capstone of her sublime edifice to be completed by man. It is humiliating to observe how he has blundered the task.

If money were a measure of precision, its limits would also have to be artificial and fixed: and as in most States at present they are not artificial and fixed, but left to be determined by chance or private design, money is not in such States at present a measure of precision, although equity demands that it should be one.

2. All measures of precision are exactly numerical, that is to say, they are susceptible of exact numerical expression. A measure which is not capable of being exactly and numerically expressed is not a measure of precision. Money, as it now stands in the law of most States, cannot be thus expressed; for no one can tell exactly, nor even approximately, what the whole sum or limit of it is in any such State, nor in all States combined. It is, therefore, not a measure of precision; yet justice demands that it should be one.

Suns, moons, day's-journeys, posts, bow-shots, stone's-throws, and paces are measures of length; armfuls, loads, and cargoes are measures of volume; and a hide is a measure of area. These measures cannot be expressed exactly; they are not measures of precision; and none but savage, half-civilised, or unprogressive communities rely upon them for measures. Money, as it stands at present, cannot be expressed exactly; it is not a measure of precision; and is therefore not suitable for the requirements of intellectual, civilised, or progressive communities.

3. A measure of length, etc., need not be composed of a rare commodity. Nor need money be. The efficiency of a measure does not depend upon the rarity of the substance of which it is made, but upon the exactness of its limits; and this is as much the case with moneys as with other measures.[1]

[1] " By limiting the quantity of paper money its value in exchange is as great as an equal denomination of coin or of bullion in that coin."—

LIMITATION IS THE ESSENCE OF MONEYS. 129

4. The limits of other measures are not left to be determined by either supply or demand; neither should the limits of money; but, as the law now stands in most States, these limits are left to be formed by insatiable demand on the one side, and fluctuating and unforeseeable supply on the other. Unless money is of minor importance to society than yard-sticks or pint-pots, it would seem that it should be described and limited by law with at least equal precision.

5. The essence of a measure of any kind is limitation—indeed, this is the meaning of the term itself; and the more exact these limits are susceptible of being defined in the law, the more efficacious the measure becomes. This is the case with money. Indeed, the very essence of money is limitation; and such is the origin of the word *nomisma*. The more exact the limits of the volume of money are defined in the law of each State, the more equitable will it become in its operation upon prices and the dealings between man and man.

Ricardo. "The mere limitation of the quantity of paper made legal-tender is quite sufficient to preserve its value on a par with the value of gold, *or to raise it higher.*"—McCulloch. Both as quoted by Weston, pp. 40-41.

CHAPTER XI.

LIMITATION: A PREROGATIVE OF STATE.

The limitation of the monetary measure was anciently a prerogative of State—Its surrender by the State in the sixteenth century—Since that period money has been in a chaotic condition—The "automatic system" is no system at all—Neither individuals nor corporations can regulate money—The State alone can do this—Nor may the State do it arbitrarily—Circumstances and considerations that should control State action on the subject.

DURING the Roman Republic the limits of the monetary measure were imposed by the Senate; during the Empire they were fixed by the "sacred" coinages of the sovereign-pontiff; after the fall of the Empire they fell under the power of the various States and feudatories which rose upon its ruins. The princes and prelates who governed these States often abused their power, and in the sixteenth century, during the exploitation of the East and West Indies, the limitation of money in one European State after another was surrendered by the Crown and unwisely abandoned to chance and to the intrigues of moneylenders. This chaotic condition of money has since been termed by those who unjustly profit by it and by their sycophants and apologists, "the automatic system".

It is neither a system nor is it automatic. So far as the State is concerned, it consists in leaving the supplies of money to depend upon the following circumstances: (1) The chances of mining discovery; (2) The opening and working of mines; (3) The productivity of mines; (4) The ownership and transfer of mines: it being clear that when they are owned by aliens, as is the case to-day with many of the mines in America and South Africa, their product is no more available for the native mints than is any other metal owned abroad; (5) The demand for the precious metals in the arts; (6) The demand for such metals for export; (7) The wear and tear of coins, a circumstance that depends as much upon the emissions and denominations of paper money as upon the emissions and sizes of coins; (8) The loss of coins by accident and hoarding; (9) The mint laws; (10) The intrigues of the money-lending class, which now includes not merely millionaires, but sometimes ambassadors and ministers of State, and in a few instances reigning sovereigns, in their private capacity, and the members of their families.

This is not a system: it is a lottery, employed by money-lenders who play the game with loaded dice. There is nothing automatic about it. An automatic device is self-moving, or self-regulated. It has already been shown that Nature has left the device of money, in common with all other measures, to be regulated or completed by man; and that no measure can be completed, no measure can be self-regulated, no measure can be equitable, without being limited. Therefore without limits a measure cannot be "automatic".

Such limits can only be effectively imposed and regulated by society. If there are men in such society who are unwilling, or who affect to be unwilling, to submit their fortunes to its sense of equity, they should be invited to leave it and seek some other communion. Experience has abundantly proved that neither individuals nor private corporations are competent to preserve a limit to money. The moneyed class have been permitted to trifle with this most momentous subject for two or three centuries, and during that period have never even approached limitation or stability in the regulation of the monetary measure. It is not only contrary to their narrow and mistaken view of self-interest, it is quite beyond their power. Neither individuals nor corporations can regulate mining, nor the consumption of metals in the arts, nor the imports, nor the exports, of the precious metals, nor the number of coins that may be struck from them. Indeed, they are powerless to regulate their own issues of paper money. Whenever such issues have been left to private or corporative regulation, they have been so utterly mismanaged that, one after another, all the States of the world have been obliged to put a stop to the privilege. A glance at my *History of Monetary Systems*, Appendix B of the English, or Chapter XVII. of the American, edition, will serve to recall the frightful abuses and disasters that have followed this indulgence. The State alone is competent to limit money.

Nor may the State impose such limitation arbitrarily. Down to the present time the voice of the rich and powerful has been alone heard on this subject. Is a Treasury officer to be appointed? He is drawn from a bank. Is a Monetary Commission organised? It is officered by recruits from the mint. Is testimony on the subject to be presented to the Legislature? It is sought from the mouths of usurers and their followers. The people have never been consulted: they have only been duped. But the utter failure and collapse of class finance, and the peril from the machinations of fund-holders, which now threatens the very existence of States, have brought about a great change of opinion on the part of that vast Middle Class, which stands between the fund-holders and the masses. In future, the Middle Class will have something to say concerning the regulation of money; and it may be confidently predicted that their action in the matter will be such as will both satisfy the demands of justice and preserve the civil order.

The practical circumstances which should govern the regulation of money are the existing level of prices, the extent and rate of the growth of population and trade, the extension of credit, the velocity of money, and the danger from counterfeiting. But above all other considerations, there is one which the legislator must never lose sight of, for if the others are permitted to subvert that one, they will surely mislead him, and his work will fail and perish. That one is our sole warrant for stamping the name of God upon the current coin : it is Justice.

CHAPTER XII.

UNIVERSAL MONEY A CHIMERA.

This project was born with the legislation which permitted private coinage—Its progress down to the present time—Its agency in elevating and enriching the moneyed class—Their advantages threatened by the growing use of government paper money—Universal money is a scheme to enable these advantages to be retained by the money-lenders—Its impracticable character—Universal money impossible without universal government—Evils and dangers of national metallism—These are now local—With universal metallism they would become general—It threatens the autonomy of the State—It tends to degrade Europe to the level of India—Absolute measures of value—The basis of "universal money" is the cupidity of the money-lenders.

THERE are many signs which point to a desire on the part of the fund-holding class to bring about the establishment of a common money of the world: a money that shall pass current and have the same legal attributes in, at least, all commercial States. The various monetary unions of Germany, notably that of 1857, the Latin monetary union of 1865, the demonetisation of silver in all the principal States of Europe and America in 1867-73, the tricky re-wording of the Mint Codes, the repeal of the Bland and Sherman Acts, and many other proceedings and acts of legislation, all point in this direction. Prominent statesmen in France, Germany, and other States have lent themselves to the project of universal money; and it has been so persistently urged upon the public that the time has come when its practicability, advantages, and dangers (if there are any) should be considered, and that, too, in a broad sense, scanning the entire field of monetary experiment, and especially discussing the bearing of the measure upon the affairs of Great Britain and the United States.

The proposal is not limited to gold as the material of full legal-tender money; it embraces a common international ratio of value between gold and silver, so as to bring the latter also into use as material for full legal-tender money; it likewise contemplates the readjustment of the half-eagle, the sovereign, the twenty-five franc gold piece of France, and the twenty mark gold piece of Germany, so that each will contain exactly the same quantity of fine gold as the other, and thus become of so-called equal value. There are numerous organisations in Europe entirely devoted to the accomplishment of this latter portion of the scheme; and they have already done much to bring about a uniformity of coinages among the various States of the Continent.

Before the royal prerogative of coinage was surrendered substantially to the moneyed class, as was done in England by the Act of 1666 (18 Charles II., c. 5), a common money of the world hardly suggested itself to writers on the subject of money: immediately after the adoption of that Act, it occurred to everybody. In a word, like "unit of value," "metallism," and many other misleading terms applied to money, it had its origin in that Act, and was part of its prolific progeny.

With so-called "free coinage" established in all the principal States of the world, and nobody alive to the fact that free coinage is itself a monstrous absurdity, and teleologically means the total subversion of the measuring function of money, the advantages of a common money of the world lay upon the surface. The fledglings of finance have almost everywhere signified their approbation of the measure. The "influential" classes of Europe and North America may be said to have already agreed upon it. The gold coins of nearly all the principal States and many of the smaller ones are now struck from even sub-divisions of the French kilogram: those of England and the United

States being the two principal exceptions. Judging from appearances, it cannot be long before these States will also agree to adjust their gold coins to the same weights. When this is done there will be but two more steps towards realising the aspiration for a common money of the world. One must be the legalisation by each State of the gold coins of all the others, so long as they are struck strictly upon this basis of weight, and provided that they do not bear any objectionable devices or inscriptions. In the event of such legislation, a sovereign, a half-eagle, a twenty-five franc, or a twenty mark piece, will apparently mean the same thing, and have the same legal power to pay debts or to purchase commodities or services. The other step must be the adoption of a common ratio of value between gold and silver. In such case we shall have a money of the world. Then will disappear the vexatious commissions of the exchange broker, the losses now endured in transmitting coins from one country to another, that is, from countries where they are, to countries where they are not, legal-tender, and the troublesome arithmetical calculations which annoy the uneducated merchant and confuse the inexperienced traveller.

Were there no other considerations affecting this matter, it is clear that a common money would prove to be an unmixed advantage to the commercial world; but such is far from being the case. Money is an historical institution, and forms one of the foundations of State. The right to coin money and regulate its value has not only been deemed essential to the autonomy of nations, it has been jealously guarded by the judiciary, defended by acts of war, and (in remote times) even clothed with a sacerdotal character, in order to prevent coinage by parties other than the State; as well for other reasons and purposes. In favouring the establishment of an universal money a new æra is proposed to be inaugurated in the arrangements of the world. Before going any further in so grave a matter, prudence counsels us to carefully examine the trials and experience of the past. These may either fortify us in pursuing the project of a common money, or they may induce us to retrace our steps. The subject is so important, and so many powerful agencies are already engaged in shaping it for the proposed action, that it should at once occupy a prominent place in the discussions of legislators. The fact that the partial adoption of a common money has had the tendency to equalise the price of commodities and services, and to level the social conditions and rate of progress in the various countries that have used coins of like weights, for example, in the various States of the German Zollverein, and more recently in those of the Latin Union, develops another consideration, which the proposed monetary "reformers" have not sufficiently borne in mind. The varying proportions of paper money which the intelligence, virtue, credit, physical circumstances, and habits of different peoples enable them to safely use in connection with coins, are another circumstance from which due consideration seems to have been withheld. These and other objections to an international measure of value may disappear upon examination; but they certainly suggest the necessity of making such examination.

This has been done at sufficient length in another work (*The Politics of Money*), and it will only be necessary in the present one to allude to one of the objections therein set forth to this scheme.

That objection is, that a common money of the world will subvert the State. The money-lenders have already subverted the Crown. They have deprived it of its most important prerogatives; their present scheme will subvert the State. Their immediate object is to rid themselves of what is left of the power of the State over the Measure of Value. This remnant of power relates to paper money. The money-lenders already have absolute control of the mines and the mints; they now desire to control the public credit. A common metallic money is the first step. The abolition of Government paper money and the amalgamation of the banks of issue will be the next steps. The control of money will then mean Universal Empire, and the States that now exist will only be known to antiquarian research.

Two centuries ago the money-lending class was comparatively poor and humble. Bankers and goldsmiths waited upon their noble patrons in person, and obsequiously solicited their favours; to-day, though numerically a limited class, they probably own more than half the garnered wealth of the civilised world; they are the creditors of the nobility and the State; they drag the entire community by the heels, and their retainers fill every department of Government, every avenue of profit, and every source of influence.

The issue of Government paper money, that is to say, of money which cannot be melted down or refused, the growth of railways, steamship lines and telegraphs, and many other circumstances, in one State or another, now threaten to limit the opportunities of this avid class. Could the various principal States of the world be united in one general system of money, these opportunities might be greatly extended; and instead of being limited, as now, to certain States, and to the power of alternately inflating and contracting the currency of a single country at a time, the money-lenders would be endowed with the power to operate upon all at once. It is barely possible that they have not thought this quite out, and that little more than a sort of commercial instinct now actuates them; but it is an instinct that has rarely been at fault, and certainly is not at fault in this matter.

An universal money, without universal government, is impracticable; the original bases of the existing systems, that is to say, metallic moneys coupled with individual coinage, if they ever had any usefulness, have outgrown it; they have resulted in an increased and alarming instability of prices; they fail to measure value equitably; they perpetuate many feudal and other social conditions which belong to the past, and do not harmonise with the present; they degrade European progress to the level of Oriental inertia; they threaten to substitute Brahminism for Christianity; they obstruct national development; they induce fitfulness of national growth; they promote poverty by preventing a just diffusion of wealth; they encourage foreign influence and intrigue; they promote tyrannies of capital; they necessitate oppressive taxation; they defeat land reform; they debase public morals; they waste monetary experience; they encourage imprudent trading; they promote unprofitable mining; they are expensive to establish and maintain; they tempt counterfeiting and other crimes; and they have only failed to subvert the State already, because the State has invariably modified these systems by adding to them a fixed or relatively fixed proportion of paper notes; these forming the only essentially national elements of the currency.

Were the systems of money which are now established in the various States of Europe and America thrown into one system, the local disadvantages and evils adverted to would become universal ones. At the present time some of them are endured by one State, some by another. Upon the adoption of an universal money they would all be endured by every State. That equalisation of economical conditions and relations in one State as compared with others, employing like metallic money, with so-called "free coinage," which, in fact, has long gone on at a slow rate, would, in such case, soon proceed at a rapid one. During less than a century of "free coinage" in India, the ryot's wage, which, at the beginning of that period, was but one-tenth of the English labourer's wage, has now grown to be one-fourth as much. This is a good thing for the ryot, but is it a good thing for Europe?

As a moralist I rejoice in this improvement of the ryot's condition; in such an alleviation of his grievous burdens; as an Anglo-Saxon I would inquire into its effect upon Western labour, Western agriculture, Western commerce,

Western capital, and Western civilisation. Europe and America possess certain advantages, such as geographical position, climate, coal and iron reserves, a sturdy and intelligent population, mechanical skill, aptitude for the sea, fondness for commercial adventure, and a vast sum of capital seeking employment. Are they prepared to relinquish these advantages, by adopting, in common with other States, a system of money which might tend to level all economical conditions? These advantages have cost our race many centuries of effort, they have embroiled us in hundreds of wars, they are the fruits of endless sacrifices;—are we prepared to surrender them to a monetary theory which has never been tried; of whose bearings its very authors are ignorant, a mere dream of the schools, a phantasm of the Economists, a logical consequence proceeding from a false premiss, the abortive spawn of a Coinage Bill, wrung by usurers from the ignorance, the prodigality, or the necessities of Charles II.? I believe not.

One of the arguments in favour of an universal or international money is the singular one that it would form an absolute measure of value, and enable us to compare the prices of one age or country with another. It is not with the view to compare the wealth of communities, of classes, of generations, that the agitators for International Money would upset the laws of nations; it is to subject the commercial world to a system of barter, the mechanism of which they have already secured for their own exclusive use. It is not the Economists who are demanding this control of the financial world; it is the plutocrats. All that an Economist stands to win by advocating it is a college professorship, a bit of red ribbon, the vain parade of certain alphabetical characters at the end of his name. The plutocrats hope to win the earth: for nothing short of this seems sufficient to gratify their cupidity.

If any commodity can be made to serve as an equitable

measure of value, which, in the nature of things, is impossible; *if* that commodity were *par excellence* gold, which it is not; *if* the supplies of gold from the mines to the mints were so regulated by Nature as never to disturb the equity of the measure of value, which is not the case; *if* there was no danger that men or syndicates would obtain control of such supplies, and so be enabled to alter the measure of value at pleasure, which is not the case; *if* universal peace were established and no wars could occur to derange the equitable international distribution of gold, which is not the case; *if* gold alone, or gold plus the same proportion of instruments of credit, such as promissory notes, bills of exchange and bank cheques, were used for money in every State, which is not the case; *if* every State were of such an equal area, or possessed such railways, telegraphs, etc., that the rapidity of the circulation of money would be the same in all, which is not the case; and *if* at least a hundred other circumstances were precisely what they are not and cannot be, then this chimerical scheme might be worth a more extended discussion in this place; which, as the case stands, it is not.

CHAPTER XIII.

CAUSES AND ANALYSIS OF A RATE OF INTEREST.

Causes of a rate of interest—Temporary supply of money—Rate of profit in trade—Rate of profit in production—Rate at which animals, plants, and minerals increase—Rate at which the means of subsistence increase—Subsistence ultimately governs the rate of interest—Subsistence also governs the growth of population ; so that population and the rate of interest are related—When to the rate of interest, arising from increase of subsistence, there are added allowances for risk, taxes, and the cost of superintending loans, the market rate of interest follows—Present tendency of the market rate—Ignorance of American ministers of finance—Usury laws.

1. THE rate of interest for money is due, immediately, to the temporary or local supply of, as compared with the temporary or local demand for money, as a commercial loan. In case no recent change has occurred in the supply of or demand for money, the rate of interest depends upon :—

2. The net rate of profit in trade. When this is high, the merchant, in order to maintain or extend his business, can afford to pay a high rate of interest for money. When it is low he can only afford to pay a low rate. The net rate of profit in trade—and trade aside—the rate of interest—depends upon :—

3. The rate of profit in production, as in agriculture, the fisheries, mining, manufactures, and the means of transportation. The profit in production might be affected temporarily or locally by the supply compared with the demand for products ; but in the long run it must depend upon :—

4. The rate at which animals and plants increase and minerals are produced under the hand of man; in other words, the rate at which the means of human subsistence increase.

This, then, is the ultimate cause of a rate of interest: the rate at which the means of subsistence increase. Other things being equal, were this rate to double, the net[1] rate of interest would double; and were the rate of the increase of subsistence to diminish one-half, the net rate of interest would diminish one-half. In countries where such net rate of interest is high, the market rate of interest for the safest class of investments of money is high, and *vice versâ*. Thus the leading savings banks of California, than which there are probably no safer institutions of the kind in the world, were able so recently as thirty years ago to allow their depositors from twelve to fifteen per cent. per annum for money; and even at the present time, after the substantial exhaustion of the very productive placer mines of that country, these banks are able to allow five cent. To afford this, they must, of course, earn six or eight per cent.

During the decline of the Roman Empire throughout the Dark Ages, the disturbed condition of Europe so greatly diminished the rate of increase of the means of subsistence as to cause a continuous decline of the population, which in turn caused a decline of production. During the decline, the net rate of interest must have continually fallen, whilst the gross or market rate, from increased risk, continually rose. The decline of population and production was arrested by the reopening of commerce with the Orient, when civilisation changed from a moribund, or else a stationary condition, to one of growth, by the establishment of a sea route to India and the discovery of America. Henceforth the net rate of interest steadily

---

[1] The net, as distinguished from the market rate of interest, which latter includes allowances for risks, taxes, and the cost of superintendence of loans, will be explained farther on.

rose, whilst the market rate steadily fell. From this notable instance, and other similar though less notable ones, which might be adduced were it necessary, it follows that the growth of the means of subsistence governs the rate of the increase of population, and that this governs interest. That subsistence governs population is well attested by the laborious investigations of Malthus, Buckle, and others; but that it also governs interest has not, so far as I am aware, yet attracted the attention of either moralists or financiers.

That the rate of the increase or decrease of population in any vast area and during long periods of time, must conform very closely to the rate of the increase or decrease of the means of subsistence, may be regarded as having been satisfactorily demonstrated. That the net rate of interest upon capital closely obeys the same influence is an induction that, however novel, may be accepted with equal confidence.[1]

Having now determined that the ultimate cause of a rate of interest is the rate of the increase of the means of subsistence, and that such rate is, within very narrow limits, also identical with that of the increase of population, it remains to explain the difference between the net and market rate of interest for money.

In every loan of money the lender, in order to recoup

---

[1] The principle that interest is derived fundamentally from the growth of animals and plants in time was first broached by the author in 1865, in an Essay entitled *The Rate of Interest in Great Britain and Elsewhere*, published in the New York *Social Science Review* of that year. This principle was elaborated in his address on *Interest*, to the National Insurance Convention of the United States at New York, 1872, published in the *Proceedings* of that body, and again in his Essay on *Usury*, published in San Francisco, 1879. His fellow-townsman, Mr. Henry George, in his work on *Progress and Poverty*, has adopted the author's postulate with reference to the origin of interest, but has nowhere given him credit for it. As to the uses which have been made of this postulate, by associating it with wages and other foreign subjects, the author entirely dissents both from Mr. George's methods and conclusions.

CAUSES AND ANALYSIS OF A RATE OF INTEREST. 145

himself, must charge in the form of interest as much as he could earn—excluding all risks and expenses, by employing his money in trade or production. Let us suppose this to be, at the present time and throughout the entire commercial world, 2 per cent. per annum.

In addition to this, he must charge enough to cover the risk of the non-payment of the principal. In point of fact, this rate widely differs in various countries. For the sake of illustration, let it be supposed that throughout the commercial world the risk is equal, in the long run, to 2 per cent. per annum. Taxes, when levied upon money or loans of money—in addition to taxes upon production or trade (which latter form a part of the expenses of such production or trade)—have also to be recouped to the lender of money, and must be added to the net rate of interest. Let the item of taxes be supposed to amount on the average to a half of 1 per cent. per annum.

Finally, to recoup himself, the lender must charge sufficient to pay him for the cost of personally superintending the loan or transaction—such as seeking the borrower, examining his credentials or securities, ascertaining or enforcing his own rights at law, notarial expenses, etc. If this charge be fixed as equal on the average to, say, a half of 1 per cent. per annum on the sum of the loan, the average market rate of interest throughout the commercial world would be 5 per cent. per annum, as follows:—

	Per cent.
Net or unloaded rate of interest, due to rate of the increase of the means of subsistence, and agreeing substantially with the rate of the growth of population	2
Risk	2
Taxes on money or loans of money	½
Cost of superintendence of loan, legal and notarial expenses, etc.	½
Market or gross rate of interest	5

In some countries, as in England, where the risk and cost of superintendence are comparatively small, more than one-half of the average market rate of interest, which is about 2½ per cent., consists of the net rate, or that arising from the net profit of trade, equivalent to the increase of the means of subsistence. In others, as in Turkey, where the increase of the means of subsistence is substantially *nil*, and the cost of superintendence, perhaps, not much greater than elsewhere, the market rate is due almost entirely to risk and taxes, which in that country at the present time are both high and fluctuating. In the United States the increase of the means of subsistence is probably about 2¼ per cent., whilst risk, taxes on loans of money, and cost of superintendence combined, probably amount to about 1¾ per cent. more, making the average market rate about 4 per cent.

While temporary and local circumstances combine to greatly modify the market rate, it is of the highest importance to know of what elements this market rate consists, in order to be able to accord to each modifying circumstance its due degree of importance. For this reason the analysis of interest herein made, besides being otherwise necessary to the design of the present work, will, it is hoped, prove to be of immediate and practical use to all persons connected with monetary transactions.[1]

It may be affirmed with safety that generally throughout the commercial world the market rate of interest at the present time has a tendency to fall; and it is a knowledge of this fact on the part of money-lenders and capitalists that renders long loans under permanent and equitable governments, and upon good security, more desirable, and therefore more valuable, than short ones. Ignorance of this fact on the part of the finance ministers of the United

[1] The practical character of the author's essay on *Interest*, referred to on a previous page, is evinced by the fact that it has frequently been republished by insurance journals both in England and America, the *London Insurance Sun*, 1892, the *United States Review*, 1893, etc.

CAUSES AND ANALYSIS OF A RATE OF INTEREST. 147

States has cost that country since the Civil War nearly as much as the whole present sum of the public debt. How much it has cost in the equality of fortune and the welfare of its citizens it would be difficult to compute.

The present tendency of the rate of interest to fall has been greatly promoted by those obstacles to production and trade which have been occasioned by the adoption of Metallism in place of Money. When this is remedied, when the European and American States resume their abandoned Prerogative of Money, the net rate of interest will again advance. The great European capitalists are standing in the way of their own advantage. When they discover this fact, as they will sooner or later, and renounce their usurpation of the public mints, their incomes from investments will increase.

After proving that, teleologically, interest arises from the rate of the increase of animals and plants, and is therefore founded upon the provisions of nature for the development of organised life, it need hardly be said that usury laws, though doubtless often enacted with benevolent intentions, have the defect of being at variance with the laws of nature, and therefore cannot be maintained during æras of societary growth and progress.

CHAPTER XIV.

VELOCITY OF CIRCULATION.

Opinions of Locke, Thornton, Mill, and Fawcett—Elements of the calculation—Money used for paying labour—Money and credits used for commerce—Transportation—Finance—Real estate transactions—Money used for insurance—Savings—Taxes—Summary—Comparison with actual circulation and reserves—Deduced rate of velocity—Unwarranted conclusions of Mr. Horr and others—Coincidence of the sum of exchanges with that of money and credits, when reduced to a like velocity.

"THIS shows the necessity of some proportion of money to trade; but what proportion that is, is hard to determine, because it depends not barely on the quantity of money, but the quickness of its circulation." Thus wrote the illustrious John Locke in 1691.

"It is on the degree of the rapidity of the circulation, combined with the consideration of quantity, and not on the quantity alone, that the value of the circulating medium of any country depends." Thus repeated Henry Thornton during the early part of the Bank of England Suspension. More than half a century later, these valuable observations were rescued from oblivion by John Stuart Mill, who remarked "that the value of money is inversely as its quantity multiplied by what is called the rapidity of circulation ".—*Political Economy*, B. III., Ch. VIII., § 3.

Before Mr. Mill's work was published, I myself wrote in the *New Nation*, of July 23, 1864: "With improved means of doing business (including the use of credits), and with increased rapidity in transporting money and commodities, a lesser quantity of money than formerly may be used for the same amount of exchanges, because the same pieces of money will perform a greater number of offices ".

However, neither Locke, nor Thornton, nor Mill, nor any other writer, so far as I know, ever attempted to ascertain inductively what was actually the velocity of the circulation of money. With little more than the object of distinctly marking the phenomenon of velocity, I roughly accorded to the money of the United States the velocity of four times a year, or once a quarter. This was in 1864, before the establishment of the National Banking System, and when the currency had but recently consisted chiefly of State bank notes of comparatively slow and local circulation. In 1877 Mr. W. Fawcett (*Gold and Debt*, Chicago, 1877) accorded to the money of the United States a velocity of once a week. My own rough conjecture was based on the local character of the State bank notes, the backwardness of the railway and telegraph system, and the average duration of commercial credits at that time, modified by the payments for wages and some other considerations: Mr. Fawcett's was evidently based largely on the fact that the wages of labour are commonly paid by the week. It is now obvious to me that my own estimate was far too low, and Mr. Fawcett's somewhat too high; that the velocity at the time I wrote was less than once a month, and that at the time he wrote it was probably under once a fortnight; whilst at the present time—such has been the increase of railways, telegraphs, and commercial facilities, credits, and economies—the velocity of money has actually attained the high rate at which he estimated it some twenty years ago, namely, once a week.

The principal elements of the calculation which has been made herein, are the wages of labour, the transactions of commerce for money and credit, the receipts and payments for transportation, the transactions of finance for money and credit, the alleged sales of real estate, the receipts and payments of insurance companies in life, fire, marine, and other insurance, the revenues and expenditures of government, besides sundry other items, both for money and credit. To bring all these elements into correspondence with money, to reduce the credits employed in trade to the same rate or degree of velocity as money, has been a most difficult task; and the author is by no means confident that he has been able to accomplish it to the satisfaction of the reader.

With this understanding he ventures to submit to his indulgence the following rough calculation.

Labour.—The wages of navvies, miners, mechanics, railroad men, clerks, journalists, and other classes of stipendiaries, in the United States, are usually paid weekly. Such of these wages as are paid out at once soon find their way into banks of deposit, where they again become available for the wage-fund in the course of two or three days. But a large part of the wages are not paid out by the stipendiaries at once; they are expended gradually throughout the week; a portion is saved for rent, which is commonly paid by the month; a portion is laid by in savings banks, from whence it does not find its way back into the wage-fund for several weeks. Other classes of stipendiaries, as sailors, farm labourers, and domestic servants, are paid monthly, and their wages would probably require several weeks (sometimes months) to find their way back into the wage-fund. Weighing all these circumstances together, it is deemed a fair estimate to regard the whole body of wages as paid once a week, and that it requires a week for these wages to return to the wage-fund. The population of the United States is about seventy millions; the stipendiaries number about eighteen millions; their average wage is about ten dollars a week.[1] Hence it requires a currency of about 180 million dollars,

[1] In manufactures only the number of hands employed in 1890 was 4,712,000, and the wages paid 2585 millions, or about 550 dollars a year each.

with a weekly velocity, to pay them off and get the same money back in time to pay them again.

Commerce.—Statements have repeatedly been put forth by American statisticians and public men that the domestic commerce (sales of merchandise) in that country amounted to at least fifty times as much as its foreign commerce. The comparison is somewhat fallacious. The foreign " commerce " (imports and exports) shows the value of merchandise exchanged or valued once, at a given point, to wit, the custom-house. It is, in fact, rather the value of the product than of the commerce. If the value of the domestic commerce is deduced by these statisticians from the bank-clearings, which seems to be the case, it shows the value of (the same) merchandise exchanged and valued frequently and at various points. Were these exchanges reckoned but once, like the foreign exchanges, or were the foreign exchanges (of the same goods) reckoned as often as are the domestic ones, the disparity would be far less. The total value of the products of eighteen million labourers at ten dollars a week is about 9000 million dollars, which is only six times the value of the imports and exports combined; instead of fifty times as much, as claimed by these statisticians. This is a fair comparison, because it is product against product. If the "fifty times as much" is deduced from the bank-clearings, it involves a *petitio principii;* because the clearings include the cheques paid and received for foreign commerce, and these amount to, at least, 1500 million dollars. But this is a minor objection.

These exchanges of commerce are transacted partly by means of money and partly by credit, the latter chiefly in the form of promissory notes and bills of exchange. The loans and discounts of the 3755 "National" banks (exclusive of "State" and savings banks) in 1894 were about 2000 millions, of which about 370 millions were on demand and 1630 millions "on time"; the latter meaning usually about fifty or sixty days. Whilst these promissory notes are maturing they are not employed for payments, therefore as a matter of fact their velocity of circulation is once in two months, or about 8½ times less than that of money, as above assumed. Hence, to bring the promissory notes to the same rate of velocity as money, it is necessary to divide their sum by 8½. This brings the 1630 millions of time-bills down to the equivalent of about 200 millions cash, or legal-tender money.

The 370 millions of demand loans are difficult to deal with, because the period of their service is indeterminate, and it varies enormously with the fluctuations of credit. It is as though these 370 millions were bank capital and reserves, which were loaned to the stock and share market on call, and which in case of a severe run were called in at once. It is these loans that (when paid) largely make up the sum of cheques in the clearings. For practical purposes they may be regarded as equal, in good times, to twenty-eight day notes, or notes having one-fourth the efficiency of money. At this rate the 370 millions of demand loans would be equal in efficiency to about 90 millions of money. (See "Finance" below.) The loans of savings banks amounted to about 1000 millions, of which about 750 millions were on real estate and 250 millions on "other securities". If the latter be accorded an average velocity of 70 days, they would equal in efficiency about 25 millions of money. Let us say that the loans on real estate run on the average about fifty weeks, this would reduce the 750 millions of such loans to the efficiency of 15 millions of money. Now add 750 millions for the loans of "State" banks, equivalent to say 100 millions of money, and we have the following results: total credits, 3750 millions; equal to 430 millions of money with a weekly velocity. The amount of actual money which, in addition to this, is directly employed in wholesale exchanges of merchandise, excluding the expenditure of wages with shopkeepers already included, is left to conjecture. For the present I have ventured to estimate the actual money of wholesale commerce at 70 millions, with a weekly velocity: though not without great misgivings as to the correctness of the sum.

When we come to use the statistics afforded by the clearing-houses, it will perhaps be objected that the sums represented by the loans and discounts are duplicated in the cheques; and therefore that they are employed twice over. The argument is that borrowings (loans) and promissory notes (discounts) are merely deferred payments, which, when they are liquidated, find their expression in cheques. This is quite true, but we have endeavoured to avoid the duplication to which reference is made. The loans and discounts are used herein for the purpose of determining the relative sums of money and of credit employed in commerce: whilst the cheques are used to determine the relative magnitude of commerce and finance. This plan involves no duplication.

Transportation.—The principal agency of transportation in the United States is railways. Their annual gross earnings in 1893 amounted to about 1200 million dollars, of which about 840 millions were paid for improvements and expenses. Of the remaining 360 millions, there were paid for interest 238, dividends 94, and other purposes 28 millions. These revenues and expenditures were substantially in money, whose rate of velocity cannot have varied materially from that assumed for the wage-fund. Therefore 24 millions of money (used over say fifty times a year, or about once a week), would suffice to transact all the cash business of railways. As this sum includes the wages paid railway employés, already included under the head of Labour, we may reduce the requisite money for this purpose to 20 millions. The shipping of the United States in 1894 amounted to 4,700,000 tons, of which 3,200,000 tons were employed on the ocean; 1,200,000 on the lakes; and 300,000 on the rivers. About half each of the whole were of steam and sailing vessels. In my official report on shipping (Treasury Department, November 15, 1866, p. 4) the gross earnings from freight or carriage in the foreign, coastwise and river trades were estimated at 16⅔ to 20 dollars per ton per annum. The increased proportion of steam vessels employed since that time will warrant the use of the last figure for the whole tonnage.[1] This would bring the earnings of steam and sailing vessels to about 94 millions, say, together with other vessels, not included in the above tonnage, 100 millions a year. To these earnings cannot be accorded a velocity of more than once a month; so that it would only require 8⅓ millions of money to satisfy them; say, for round figures, 10 millions.

Finance.—The combined clearings of all the banks of the United States in 1892 were 60,000 millions; 1893, 58,000; and 1894, 45,000 million dollars. This falling off was due partly to the panic of 1893, and partly to the fact that, beginning with 1893, the clearing of stocks, formerly made through the banks, has been made in New York (as to many stocks) through the New York Stock Exchange Clearing-House. It is difficult to apportion the falling off in the exchanges to these various heads respectively; but it will probably not be far wrong to estimate the normal cheque business of these three years at 60,000 millions, because one of these years was exceptional and also because there are some cheques which are passed between persons doing business with the same bank, in which case they do not go into the clearing-house at all. Add to this assumed sum of cheque transactions one-fourth more for the cheques drawn in the small cities and towns in which there are no clearing-houses, and the total will amount to 75,000 millions, of which one-third was drawn in New York City. These 75,000 millions are the estimated sum of cheques drawn on (substantially) all the banks of the country. The question is: What proportion of these cheques was drawn

---

[1] Official returns relating to 25,000 tons of steamboats belonging to Louisville, Cairo, and Nashville in 1868, showed that their gross receipts were about 140 dollars per ton per annum.

to facilitate stock, share, and speculative transactions, and what proportion to facilitate commerce? I am not aware of the existence of any data which will enable this question to be decided satisfactorily. The number of brokers in New York and the average capital employed in their business, the average daily sales of shares, bonds, etc., and other data, have been examined and rejected as unsatisfactory. Finally, the reported clearings of the various bank clearing-houses have been adopted as a means of affording a rough guide to the solution of the problem. After much consideration they have been arranged and apportioned as follows:—

Face value of all cheques passed through the various bank clearing-houses in the United States during the calendar year 1894 (including the estimated face value of the cheques on clearing-house banks drawn in normal years, also of the cheques on clearing-house banks which do not pass through clearing-houses, also of cheques drawn on banks in cities without clearing-houses), together with an estimate of the portions drawn respectively for "commercial" and "financial" purposes. Sums in millions of dollars.

Classes of cheques drawn.	Commercial.	Financial.	Total.
New York City Clearing-House	10,000	15,000	25,000
Nine other principal clearing-house cities	5,000	10,000	15,000
All other clearing-house cities	5,000	...	5,000
Total reported clearing-house cities	20,000	25,000	45,000
Add one-third for the cheques on clearing-house banks drawn in normal years and for cheques on clearing-house banks, which do not pass through the clearing-house	10,000	5,000	15,000
Total estimated cheques in normal years	30,000	30,000	60,000
Add one-fourth for cheques on banks in cities having no clearing-houses	15,000	...	15,000
Total estimated annual sum of cheques in normal years	45,000	30,000	75,000

Note to Table.—The actual value of the sales of stocks, bonds, and shares, etc., in New York during the year 1894 is given by the *Financial Chronicle* at 1500 millions, and of the cotton, grain, etc., at another 1500 millions—total, 3000 millions. If these sums and the proportion of cheques above accorded to "financial" are even roughly correct, it would follow that the sum of cheques drawn in New York is five times as much as the value of the transactions effected.

The general result is that of the 75,000 million dollars of cheques annually drawn at the present time in the United States, about 45,000 are deemed to be applicable to "commerce" and 30,000 to "finance". In other words, "commerce" is 1½ times greater than "finance". The Stock Exchange or "finance" business in America is done without any further recourse to credit than is involved in the use of bank-cheques, overdrafts, and call-loans. In other words, settlements between brokers are made daily, instead of fortnightly, as in England. As to the monetary equivalents of the few hours' credit involved in the use of cheques by brokers and other financial houses, or in the employment of overdrafts, these are exceedingly difficult problems. To call-loans has been tentatively accorded an average duration of twenty-eight days, though I am inclined to regard this as too long. On the whole, if we grant to "finance" the same proportion of money and credits (after the latter are reduced to the velocity of money) as has been already granted to "commerce," we shall probably not be far wrong. This proportion is about one-seventh in cash to six-sevenths in credit instruments. (See table below.) It is quite likely that to a certain extent the sum thus deduced is identical with the sum previously deduced for short bank loans, or credits, and accounted for under the head of "commerce"; but I confess my inability to do any better at present with the meagre statistical materials on the subject.

Real Estate.—I have seen it stated somewhere that the sales of real estate in the United States amount to about 10,000 million dollars per annum. Many of them are made in part upon credit in the form of bonds and mortgages, but as the latter are arranged to be paid or satisfied at somewhat uniform intervals, it may fairly be assumed that as many fall due and are payable in one year as another; substantially, therefore, a sum equal to the whole amount of the annual sales is payable in money. With a weekly velocity the sum of 200 millions of money would suffice for the whole. This allowance is purposely made liberal because I am uncertain about the data.

Insurance.—Say 200 millions fire and marine, and 200 millions life, together 400 millions of premiums paid in annually and paid out (in losses, etc.) say once in three years, therefore locked up for about two years. Reduced to weekly velocity, say 10 million dollars.

Savings.—In 1893 and 1894 (average) the number of depositors in savings banks was about 4,800,000, and the sum of deposits about 1750 millions. From 1888 to 1893 these deposits increased at the rate of about 100 millions a year, say two millions a week. This has already been counted as part of the expenditures (savings) of labour. The years 1893 and 1894 (during and following the Panic of 1893) were exceptionally bad years, when a great number of stipendiaries were for a time thrown out of employment. In normal years the savings of labour would rise to more than double.

Taxes.—The combined annual revenues of the National, State, and local governments amount to about 1000 millions, of which about half is derived from an annual tax on real and personal property, and another half from customs, excise, and other sources. Many of the expenditures are made at long intervals, and the money does not probably circulate more than twice a year for the first mentioned half of the revenues, and four times a year for the second half. If reduced to a weekly velocity, it would require twenty millions for the first half and ten millions for the second, say thirty millions altogether. Much of this is included in the rents paid by stipendiaries and in their expenditures for subsistence, the prices of which also embrace part of the customs and excise taxes.

Estimate showing roughly the classes of payments made in the United States, the actual money used, when reduced to a weekly velocity of circulation, and the sum of credits employed, after the same are reduced to a like velocity. Sums in millions of dollars.

Classes of Payments.	Money.	Credits.
Labour	180	...
Commerce	70	430
Transportation	30	...
Finance	50	310
Real estate transfers	200	...
Insurance	10	...
Taxes	30	...
Sundries, say	150	...
Total	720	740

According to this table the money (coins and circulating notes) employed in payments amounts to 720 millions, with a velocity of once a week, and the credits (promissory notes, bills of exchange, and other credit instruments and credits) to 740 millions, with a like velocity of once a week.

We have now to ascertain as nearly as possible the sum of money actually circulating in the United States.

Table showing the circulating money of the United States, July 1, 1894. From the U. S. Finance Report. Sums in millions of dollars.

Classes of Money.	In the Treasury.	In banks and circulation.	Of which, in the Nat'l banks.	In other banks.
U. S. notes ("greenbacks")	80·1	266·6		
Silver notes (legal tenders), Acts of 1878 and 1886	10·2	327·0	120·5	65·0
Treasury notes of 1890	18·0	134·7		
"National" bank notes	6·6	200·2	18·6	
Gold coin and bullion	131·3	?		
Silver coin (dollars)	495·4	52·0	120·0	25·0
Subsidiary silver	17·7	58·5		
Gold certificates	...	66·3	66·3	...
Silver certificates of 1872	0·3	58·9	58·8	...
Gold coin in the Trans-Mississippi States, say	...	30·0	...	...
	759·6	1194·2	384·2	90·0
Deduct amounts in National and other Banks		474·2		
In circulation		720·0		

VELOCITY OF CIRCULATION.

Omitting the Treasury estimate of gold "in the hands of the people and in hoards," which neither the senator mentioned below nor myself believe to have any existence whatever, beyond the 30 millions credited above to the Trans-Mississippi States, Senator J. P. Jones of Nevada estimated the monetary issues of the entire country at 1100 millions. (Speech 1893, p. 129.) If we deduct from this sum the amount in banks, part of which is supposed to be held as security to "convert" the remainder, the actual circulation on 1st July, 1894, was only 720 millions, as shown in the table above.

It follows from these premises that Mr. Fawcett's estimate of the velocity of the circulation (of money only) twenty years ago is substantially correct for to-day, and that the whole sum of circulating money in the United States has at the present time a velocity of about once a week. It also appears that the vast sums of cheques, promissory notes, call-loans, credits, and bills of exchange in use, when reduced to the same rate of velocity, only amount to about as much again as the money; so that the practical outcome of this Inquiry is that these various forms of credit only serve to double the effective currency, in other words, to increase the efficiency of the actual money, by accelerating its velocity, to an average of twice a week, instead of once a week.

This conclusion is corroborated by another calculation. A century ago, say in 1795, the circulating money of the United States per capita was about half what it is now, whilst prices were about one-fourth. In other words, there is now twice as much money per capita, whilst prices are four times as high—a proof that the effectiveness of money has doubled. This doubling can only be due to the extension of credit, or, what is the same thing, the increased velocity of money occasioned by the larger use of instruments of credit, book accounts, railways, telegraphs and other devices and inventions.

Very liberal and unwarranted use has been made of the

observation that "95 per cent. of the business (now transacted by banks) is done without the use of money". Mr. Ralph said lately in the London *Statist* that "each £1 of deposits (in the English banks) consists as to 17s. of opinion or credit, and as to 3s. of coins". These proportions are 85 per cent. as to credit and 15 per cent. as to coins, in which last (I take it) is meant to be included all kinds of money. Mr. Ralph is utterly mistaken.

In a recent public debate on the subject of money an American ex-Congressman, Mr. R. G. Horr, argued from the increased use of banking and other facilities, that 100 dollars would do more (work) now than 2000 dollars would formerly (Debate, p. 377). This is a gross misconception. The employment of credits by banks relates entirely to commercial and financial transactions. They do not pay wages. They do not expend wages. They do not buy from the butcher, the baker, the grocer, nor the milkman. They do not pay taxes nor insurance. When they are employed as substitutes for money, credits do not supplant nineteen-twentieths of the circulation, as supposed by Mr. Horr and others, but only one-half of it; not 95 per cent., but only 50 per cent. Credits, whether in the form of cheques, promissory notes, or bills of exchange, rarely pass through more than two or three hands before they are extinguished. Cheques rarely pass through more than two hands; that of the payee and of the bank upon which they are drawn. Whilst money passes through an endless succession of hands, and continues in use when credits are dead. The efficiency of a dollar in money in the United States is probably equal to that of more than ten dollars in time-notes and credits. This inference is derived from the proportion of 720 millions of money to 7200 millions of miscellaneous credits. The whole volume of credits may be reduced (it has already more than once been reduced) to a considerable extent without materially affecting prices; whilst a similar reduction in the volume of money would bring about (indeed a far less reduction has actually brought about) a panic and a tremendous fall of prices.[1]

When these researches are examined from another point of view, they lead to very important conclusions. The currency, as before stated, consists of 720 millions of money and 740 millions of private credits used in the place of money, and having a like function and velocity. If these sums are added together they make 1460 millions, with a weekly velocity. Multiplied by 52, the number of weeks in a year, they would equal 74,880 millions, with a velocity of once a year. This sum so closely coincides with the total sum of exchanges in a year, as to render it all but certain that one is the measure of the other, that the two are co-relative; in short, that the total sum of circulating money and credits on the one hand, and the total sum of exchanges on the other, when all are reduced to a like velocity, must of necessity be equal. So that if the money (including credits) is reduced, prices must fall, in order to bring the sum of the exchanges within the reduced limits of money; and if the money is increased, prices must rise, in order that the sum of the exchanges may expand to the increased limits of money.

One word more. The object of these researches is neither to aggrandise the importance of money nor to belittle the usefulness of banks. It is to discover an obscure but supernally important truth. The object is not political; it is purely scientific. The banks need no defence. Their number, wealth, and respectability bespeak

[1] "The slower the circulation, the greater the quantity wanted in order to effect the same number of money payments."—Thornton's *Inquiry*, Phila. ed., 1807, p. 42. "Bills of exchange, on account of their slower circulation, must be larger in amount than the notes of which they would take the place."—*Ibid.*, 43. "It is on the degree of the rapidity of the circulation, combined with the consideration of quantity, and not on the quantity alone, that the value of the circulating medium of any country depends."—*Ibid.*, 260. "The effect produced by paper credit on the price of articles depends not merely on the quantity of paper (notes) in existence, but also on its currency, or, in other words, on the rapidity of its circulation."—*Ibid.*, 226.

their usefulness. They are the handmaidens of production, that is to say of labour, of commerce, and of finance. They deserve great consideration. So also do the great sources of wealth whose pecuniary affairs are entrusted to their keeping.[1]

Since writing the above I have seen in the *Economista* of Madrid, dated 20th July, 1895, an account of a paper recently read by M. Pierre des Essars, before the Statistical Society of Paris on the "Velocity of the Circulation of Money". While the distinguished lecturer recognises the existence of the phenomenon, he does not associate money with credit instruments, nor reduce the velocity of the circulation to any certain figure. He merely shows that in some countries money circulates more rapidly than in others; also that in the same country it circulates more rapidly in some years than in others. I have also seen an extract published in the New York *American Banker* from Mr. Willard Fisher's paper in the September *Journal of Political Economy*, Chicago. Mr. Fisher's researches have had for their object "the relative magnitudes of the cash and credit transactions of the country as a whole". My own researches have had for their object, first, to ascertain the sum of exchanges in time as measured in monetary denominations, and, second, the total sum of such denominations, whether of money or credits in use, after the same are reduced to a common velocity. Although the objects and method are both different, yet the results are of somewhat similar character. Mr. Fisher sums up the exchanges from all the "credit paper" (including bank cheques) received by the banks at 150,000 million dollars a year. He estimates "the active circulation of our country, outside of both Treasury and banks, at about 1000 millions";

---

[1] "The value of money will depend upon its quantity, together with the average number of times that each piece changes hands in the process."—Mill's *Polit. Econ.*, Book III., Chap. VIII., sec. 3. "The essential point is not how often the same money changes hands in a given time, but how often it changes hands in order to perform a given amount of traffic."—*Ibid.*

and assuming that on the average an equal sum of such "credit paper" and cash appear in all the exchanges, he accords to the estimated circulation a velocity of three times a week, in order to make it equal to the assumed sum of yearly exchanges. Thus 1000 dollars × 3 × 50 weeks = 150,000 million dollars cash, as against 150,000 million dollars "credit paper" per annum. Whilst I welcome Mr. Fisher's contribution to the solution of this vast problem as a distinctly scientific one, I can see nothing in his paper to induce me to alter a line of what has been written herein.

CHAPTER XV.

RELATION OF MONEY TO PRICES.

Given the level of prices and the sum of exchanges in time, the sum and velocity of the circulation are deducible—Prices have nothing to do with the material of money—Nor value with the names of coins—Blunder of striving to maintain metallic systems with private coinage—Voice of authority—Logic of events—Nearly every modern State has been obliged to abandon such systems—Example of Russia—False principles deduced from metallism—Different influences on prices and trade, of metallism and numerical money.

AT the present level of prices in the United States, when expressed in dollars, the annual sum of exchanges, including the wages paid to stipendiaries and all other kinds of payments, is about 75,000 million dollars. Now, assuming that, on the average, dollars circulate as rapidly as once a week, in other words, that every circulating dollar is paid away for value received exactly fifty-two times a year, how many dollars would be required to effect the total sum of exchanges? Answer 75,000,000,000 ÷ 52 = 1,442,307,692, dollars. Say, for round figures, 1440 millions. Suppose that half of these payments or exchanges were effected by means of credit instruments, such as promissory notes and bills of exchange, how many circulating dollars would be required to effect the remainder? Answer, 720 million circulating dollars.

It is evident if the dollars were fewer and the number of exchanges or payments were the same, that prices would have to fall. It is equally evident that if the dollars were more abundant and the exchanges were the same, prices would have to rise. So, with fewer dollars and stationary prices, the number of exchanges or activity of trade would have to diminish; and contrariwise, with more dollars and the same prices, "business" would increase. I shall revert to this phase of the subject farther on; but meanwhile, let me ask, what, in the name of sanity, have these purely arithmetical problems to do with the material of which the circulating dollars are made? Nothing. What have they to do with the hardness, or colour, or ductility, of such material? Nothing. What have they to do with the cost of producing or reproducing such material? Nothing whatever. Would it make any difference, in the relation of value, if, instead of the word "dollars," we used the word *nummi*, or any other word, in which to express money and prices? Not the slightest. Value is the relation between two or more commodities or services in exchange. Only when such value is expressed in money have the denominations of money anything to do with the matter.

Assuming that the President of the United States, the Secretary of the Treasury, and the numerous other persons, both official and non-official, who, at the present moment, are straining every means to establish a money of gold dollars, struck for individuals, and of a given weight and fineness, and are endeavouring to banish every other sort of money except such dollars and private bank-notes based on them,—I say, assuming that these gentlemen are sincere, and are acting, as they profess, in the public interest, how can their policy and conduct be reconciled with the nature of value and the function and operation of money, as shown in this volume? It cannot be reconciled. Either the reasoning of this book is faulty, or else these gentlemen do not sufficiently understand the nature of the subject about which they speak so positively, and are acting so rashly. Not only are their views incapable of being reconciled with those expressed herein; they contradict the reasoning of Aristotle, of Plato, of Paulus, of the English Justices, of Bishop Berkeley, of Mirabeau, of Bastiat, of Sesmit Doda, of Count Rosconi, of Justice Miller, and of a host of other philosophers and publicists, both ancient and modern, whose opinions on this subject are certainly entitled to respect, and may not be disregarded.

If we appeal from opinion to the logic of events it will be seen that, with the exception of Great Britain, France, and Germany, every State in the modern world, after having tried a metallic system with individual coinage, has abandoned it as impracticable and dangerous. In all these States public men have argued in vain to evade or overthrow the brief but emphatic views of the Greek philosophers concerning the nature of money. No statesman ever displayed more ability in pursuing this course than did Count Storch in reforming, as he termed it, the circulating money of Russia. This was during the early part of the present century. One has only to substitute "the President" for Storch and "dollars" for "roubles," to read in the past history of Russia the result of the present hopeless efforts of the United States. And just as the former is encouraged by the designing and applauded by the unsophisticated, so was Storch. The result was that he nearly wrecked the Empire; that his name is now almost an offence to utter; and that to this day the Russian administration knows nothing of the true principles of money, but meanders on helplessly, with a sort of stupid faith in paper roubles, which it issues without system, and has therefore unnecessarily permitted to depreciate in value. In a recent debate on the relation of money to prices, Mr. Roswell G. Horr said: "It is not abundance of money that makes business active; it is business that makes money active". This would be quite true of metal; but it is not true of money. When money is made of metal, and is free to be coined by individuals, or at the public mint on their request, and free to be melted down or exported—as is the case at present—it assumes a deceptive aspect. It is and it is not, metal; it is and it is not, money. It is money one moment and metal the next, or *vice versâ*. Hence the principles deducible from its action or influence are deceptive and misleading. Mr. Horr's deduction is drawn from metal and innocently applied to money; whereas, as shown by the arithmetical examples at the outset of this chapter, it has nothing whatever to do with money. It is as inevitable that an increasing money will "make business active," and that a diminishing money will make it inactive, as that two and two will make four.

Mr. Horr's mistake is a common one, and is to be imputed to the confusing operation of the idiotic Act of 1666. It is the confusion which this Bill has made between money and the material of which its symbols are composed, that is responsible for the whole present difference of opinion on this subject. Abolish the private (or, so-called "free") coinage of gold, and it would end at once.

When money consists of numbers (limited by a set, or volume, of concrete symbols), it is the sum of denominations, or volume, of money, in circulation which determines the parity of exchange, or level of the prices of services and commodities. When money consists of metal (as it does with private coinage), it is the level of prices which determines the quantity of metal that will remain in circulation. The reason for this difference is that metal can be increased by mining or diminished by melting or exporting, which is not the case with numerical money. With the latter, there is no tendency either toward diminution or increase. Other things being equal, prices will exactly conform to its volume, and this conformity and harmony would continue even were the volume of money altered or did the demands of exchange vary. No such conformity occurs with metal, or, what is the same thing, metallic money coupled with private coinage. With such money, when exchanges of services or commodities become less frequent than before, a portion of it becomes superfluous, and it has a tendency to seek exportation or the arts, from which it returns with difficulty should exchanges become more active or frequent. Hence (with such metallic money) there follows a continual, though intermittent or spasmodic, demand for new metal, which as continually goes through the same senseless career of production, coinage, melting, absorption in the arts, and renewed demand upon the mines.

An arithmetical machine could be constructed, which, with a given volume and velocity of money, and a given sum and velocity of exchanges, together with some other arithmetical elements, would grind out the resulting rate of wages for all classes of stipendiaries; and the price, at any one time and place, of any product of their labour. But no machine, that the mind of man can invent, would enable him to determine beforehand (even approximately) the prices of wages, or products, in grains, or ounces, of gold or silver, metal. In the former case, all the elements of the problem are arithmetical, and so would be the character of the quotient. In the latter, all the elements are not arithmetical, and no arithmetical result, no determinate prices, would follow. In a purely numerical money there is a known "unit," which consists of the whole sum of such money, a sum that cannot be diminished by melting or exportation, nor increased by fresh exertions of capital, or labour. In a metallic money with private coinage, there is no known "unit"; because there is no fixed volume, or sum of denominations. A problem of prices in such a money can never be solved, because it cannot be stated.

In attempting to practically utilise the principle of these problems by applying it to the volume of money and rate of wages in a given State or country, it must be remembered that there are, in fact, other arithmetical variants to the problem. However, those mentioned are among the principal ones, and they are regarded as sufficient to demonstrate that the relation (Price) which appears in the exchange of commodities or services on the one hand, and the volume of money on the other, is purely arithmetical; that, as to Money, it relates to the whole number of dollars or other denominations of money in circulation, plus actual credits reduced to a like denomination and velocity, and that it has nothing whatever to do with the material, whether gold, silver, copper, or paper, out of which such dollars may be made, nor the weight nor fineness of such dollars. Such a demonstration with reference to ounces of metal or any other numbers not defined and limited, would be impossible. Prices can be deduced from numbers, but not from metal, or the cost of producing metal. A metallic money whose numbers or sum of denominations is not limited, is a measure of value which is both indeterminable, uncertain and inequitable, and it cannot fail to offer an obstacle to the preservation of social order and the prosperity of the State.

CHAPTER XVI.

INCREASING AND DIMINISHING MONEYS.

The fallacy that value flows from labour—Dr. Smith and Bastiat—Error of supposing that the currency of a State cannot be artificially increased—Historical examples to the contrary—Milan—Spanish America—The United States during the Civil War—Crescendo and diminuendo moneys.

BASTIAT has a very felicitous remark concerning Adam Smith's erroneous premiss, in which value is made to flow from labour. "Adam Smith would not have gained his great and just renown had he not written his magnificent chapters on education, on the clergy, and on public services, and if he had, in treating of wealth, confined himself within the limits of his own definition. Happily, by his inconsistency, he freed himself from the fetters which his premises imposed upon him. This always happens. A man of genius, who sets out with a false principle, never escapes inconsistency. Without this, he would get deeper and deeper into error; and, far from appearing a man of genius, would show himself no longer a man of sense."[1]

Smith's erroneous derivation of value is not his only mistake: his chapters on money bristle with mistakes, not merely of doctrine, but also of fact. In Book II., Chap. I. (Vol. I., p. 230), he advances the principle that the money of a country cannot be increased. To illustrate this principle, he supposes a country with a circulation of one million sterling, in coins, this sum "filling the channels of circula-

---

[1] Bastiat, *Har. Polit. Econ.*, p. 147.

tion". Some time afterwards its banks issue a million sterling of circulating notes, keeping back two hundred thousand pounds in coin as a reserve. He contends that the result will be that eight hundred thousand pounds in coin will be exported, until the circulation diminishes to the original million, which will now consist entirely of notes. "Eight hundred thousand pounds must overflow." . . . "Gold and silver, to the amount of eight hundred thousand pounds, will be sent abroad, and the channel of home circulation will remain filled with a million of paper, instead of the million of those metals which filled it before." Four pages further on he admits that, whereas the circulation of Scotland, in 1707, was only about £410,000 silver coins, and about £490,000 gold coins, total about £1,000,000, yet, that by the middle of the century, in consequence of the introduction of paper issues, it rose to £2,000,000, of which the coin did not amount to more than half a million. Here is evident inconsistency: yet, two pages further on, Dr. Smith reiterates his "principle" in these words: "The whole paper money of every kind, which can easily circulate in any country, never can exceed the value of the gold and silver, of which it supplies the place, or which (the commerce being supposed the same) would circulate there if there was no paper money".

Thus the principle is not attempted to be sustained by evidence, but by reiteration. It forms part of Dr. Smith's theory of money, without which—and none knew it better than himself—the theory would fall to pieces upon the least approach of argument. His principle is, in fact, not a principle at all; it is a corollary of the hypothesis that the value of money is always, and must be, necessarily due to the economical cost of its production. In a previous work, I made the following remarks on this subject:—

"It is a corollary of the metallic theory of money that, if and when the precious metals are produced upon an economical basis, only sufficient of them will be sought for to make good their loss by attrition, accident, or demand for the arts. This corollary has been urged as a rule by Adam Smith and his followers; but the reason upon which the theory rests has been ignored, and the reason at bottom is more significant than the rule at top. The reason is, that the metal produced beyond those requirements, when added to the stock of money, causes each coin to fall in value as it increases in volume. Says Smith himself: ' As their mass increases, their value diminishes' (*Wealth of Nations*, I., xi., 3, 3, p. 178). Hence all new metal is produced at a continually increasing loss. Under such circumstances—that is to say, production upon an economical and coinage upon a metallic basis—there could neither be a fall nor a rise of prices; and all those societary relations which would develop under a rise of prices would remain fixed and stationary" (*Mon. and Civ.*, p. 74).

In another place I said: "If (or when) the value of gold and silver conformed to the current economical cost of their production, and individual or 'free' coinage was permitted, the gold and silver legal-tender coins, which happened to be in a country, could not be increased at pleasure by industrial means; because any addition to the coins would lower the value of the whole stock, including that of the materials of which they were made. If mining stood upon a similar footing (cost of production), this fall of the precious metals would arrest mining, and the arrest of mining would diminish the product of bullion, and lower the stock of coins to its previous limits. Thus money, so long as its value conforms to the cost of its production, repudiates its own office. Cost fixes the quantity of money, a fixed quantity of money fixes prices, and fixed prices invite barter and lessen the necessity of money. To a population with a tendency to increase in numbers, the only remedy for such a retrogressive state of affairs is foreign war, conquest, and slave mining; and, indeed, to such devices have all nations been driven who have founded their societary relations upon metallic money subject to such conditions. The civilisations of India, of

Egypt, of Greece, and of Rome, have all moved toward a vanishing point, the point where gold and silver mining ceased to be remunerative" (*Mon. and Civ.*, p. 194).

Dr. Smith's dogma, that money cannot increase, is not only contradicted by what he himself says with respect to the increased circulation of Scotland, it is inconsistent with what he admits (elsewhere) concerning the increase of the precious metals from America and their coinage into money, which caused a rise of several hundred per cent. in the prices of commodities and services throughout maritime Europe (see Chap. XVIII. hereof). It is also contradicted by the experience of every State in the world, in every generation since the *Wealth of Nations* was written. And these contradictions of fact not only relate to increases of currency from the influx of the precious metals, they also embrace increases of currency from the emission of paper notes, both convertible and inconvertible: although this is really of no importance; for, if the principle were correct, it would apply equally to any kind of money. But it is not correct. The rule laid down so confidently by Dr. Smith is without the least foundation in fact.

It would not have been deemed necessary to traverse it so emphatically were it not that this so-called principle of money is still believed in by many persons who rely upon the great and deserved authority of Dr. Smith to support the conclusion thus cheaply gained. In a recent public debate on the subject this oft-exploded rule was again brought forward; but only with the result of confirming the axiom that errors (and sophisms) die hard.

Take Milan for one instance out of a hundred, not because it has any especial significance, but simply for the reason that it relates to a period long anterior to the discovery of America, and therefore is not complicated with the circumstances which grew out of that great event. I quote:—

"In 1240 the Milanese, whose trade had been interrupted by the war, and had not yet resumed its accustomed flow, made an issue of paper notes, which Authur Young has termed 'the origin of all paper money that has since passed in Europe'. These paper notes appear to have been employed, until the resumption of its trade with Germany enabled the city to retire them, and substitute silver coins in their place. . . . During the period of the Milanese paper currency, the commerce of the city recovered so rapidly, and the receipts of bullion from Germany became so great, that, in 1260, Milan found it necessary, in order to comply with the requirements of its merchants, to put more than a hundred mints in operation" (*Mon. and Civ.*, p. 54). In this instance, the employment of paper money, instead of driving away the precious metals, attracted much more of them than had ever been in use before; a fact that runs precisely contrary to the rule laid down by the illustrious Scotch logician.

Numerous writers, among whom is to be included Dr. Smith himself, have shown that the metallic money of every State in Europe largely increased after the discovery of America. Mr. William Jacob proved quite conclusively that the world's stock of metallic money had previously, and throughout a very lengthy period, continually diminished. Thus there exist evidences of both increasing and diminishing moneys. It will not do merely to reply that the previous decrease occurred because commerce had declined, or that the subsequent increase occurred because commerce had revived. Those who make such a reply will be required to show that commerce was the cause and money the effect. This they cannot do. Mere assertion is not sufficient. If it is attempted to be shown that a revival of commerce brought forth the produce of the American mines, it will next be inquired if the same cause also led to the Conquest of America, the subjugation of the Indians, and the discovery and working of the mines! The whole course of events proves that the contrary was the case: that it was the produce of the mines which brought about the revival of commerce, and not a revival of commerce which occasioned the discovery and working of the mines, or the increase of money.

A similar course of events took place after the breaking out of the American Civil War of 1861. In consequence of the failure of numerous banks and of the purely local credit and local circulation of the surviving private or "State" bank notes, which formed the circulation of the country previous to that event, the currency became greatly contracted. In 1862 prices fell so low as to occasion a profound depression in trade and an unprecedented number of commercial bankruptcies. It was in that year that "greenbacks," or, properly speaking, United States legal-tender treasury notes, were first issued. Almost at once and as if by magic, trade revived. With the continued issuance of these and other notes, trade reached in the course of a few years conditions more prosperous than had ever been known before. The circulation per capita of population was in 1861 but £2 14s. 10d.; in 1862 it rose to £4 4s.; and in 1864 to £5 14s., the highest point it ever reached. With the close of the war, the rehabilitation of the South, and the addition of several millions of population to employ the additional currency which had meanwhile been issued, the per capita circulation sank in 1865 to £4 19s. 7d., and it has continued, under the process of contraction and from the effects of anti-silver legislation, to fall ever since, so that at the present time the outstanding circulation (omitting the hoard of silver coins and other moneys in the treasury, and also omitting the reserves of the banks) amounts to little more than half as much as it did thirty years ago. This is an instance of expansion and contraction, of crescendo and diminuendo money, so recent and so marked, that it puts Dr. Smith's hypothetical corollary out of court altogether, and consigns it to where it properly belongs, namely, the regions of the imagination.

Having demonstrated that to be true, which Dr. Smith denied, namely, that the money of a State may be increased or diminished; having proved it in relation to Milan and the United States, as well as from the evidence concerning the Spanish American supplies of silver, which Dr. Smith himself adduces; I shall proceed in the next chapter to show the effects which are bound to follow from such alterations in money.

CHAPTER XVII.

EFFECTS OF EXPANSION AND CONTRACTION.

Consequences of increasing and decreasing moneys—Their influence upon trade, upon social and domestic relations, upon character, upon genius and invention, upon morality, upon crime, upon political affairs—Opinion of the Monetary Commission—Social consequences of contraction—Opinion of Mr. Tooke—Influence of expansion upon enterprise and art—Money and civilisation—The halcyon age of Europe.

IF all prices advanced or declined simultaneously, it would make no difference whether the currency was great or small, whether it was expanded or contracted; but as a fact, prices do not move together, and the change from a large to a small currency, or *vice versâ*, is by far the most important economical circumstance that can influence the affairs of a nation.

This phenomenon was first attentively examined by Hume, who has left us a graphic account of its effects. Though it escaped the penetration of Dr. Smith, it was observed by Mill, since whose time it has engaged the attention of numerous writers. The cause and the actual order of the advance or decline in the prices of various classes of commodities and services will be treated in the next chapter. Meanwhile it is desirable to trace the effects of expansion and contraction as a whole.

"In a period of increasing money, prices rise, the poor are provided with constant and profitable employment, the middling classes have the choice of a great variety of remunerative occupations, the wealthy possess numerous opportunities of investment and speculation, commerce is active, manufacturing is attended with profit, the farmer and the merchant can pay their bonds and notes with ease, mining is pushed forward with vigour, new railroads are planned and laid, new houses are built, the good qualities of mind and body possess a market value—honesty, virtue, persistence, enterprise, foresight, strength, agility, activity, boldness, caution, calculation—all these business characteristics are in demand; the nation prospers and surprises the world with its rapid progress, which is not merely apparent but real; everybody wears a smiling face; all are happy, and all contented. Why, then, ever end it? Why not keep it up? Why contract? Contraction is deduced from a defective theory. Why choose a bad theory, when a good one, much easier to enforce, is available for the common benefit?

"In a period of decreasing money, prices fall, the merchant sees his hard earnings melt before his eyes, the poor are thrown out of employment, and the few who are fortunate enough to find places are forced to accept beggarly wages, and are in constant risk of losing even that pittance, for there are plenty to step into their places; the middling classes are deprived of all resource, the wealthy can find no investment more attractive than trading on the necessities of the poor; commerce is languid and confined to the barest necessities of life; manufacturing is given up, or prosecuted with fear and trembling; the farmer, the merchant, the tradesman, the householder are forced to sell out at a sacrifice or to go through bankruptcy; mining is abandoned; rail-roading is stopped; no new dwellings are built; if rents do not increase, accommodation daily diminishes, and the poor are huddled together in close rooms and damp basements; foresight and calculation become worthless—it is a fight against a power that is irresistible—strength, enterprise, activity, boldness, caution, are all in vain; the miser wins in spite of all; crime abounds; the prisons are filled; the scaffold is busy; hunger, destitution, and misery sit brooding in despair; the nation crawls along, weak, pinched, ready to fall an easy prey to commotion from within and foes from without; every mind is clouded with gloom, every face is sad, every heart is bleeding, and every voice protests against the hard, stinging, unnecessary burden of the times, cursing the hour that brought him forth upon a world which nature has deceitfully clothed in eternal green, and lighted with an everlasting lamp." (New York *Mercury* editorial, June 20, 1869.)

"While the volume of money is decreasing, even though very slowly . . . those who have contracted to pay money find it constantly becoming more difficult to meet their engagements. The margins of securities melt rapidly away, and the confiscation by the creditor of the property on which they are based, becomes only a question of time. All productive enterprises are discouraged and stagnate, because the cost of producing commodities to-day will not be covered by the prices obtainable for them to-morrow. Exchanges become sluggish, because those who have money will not part with it for either property or services, beyond the requirements of actual current necessities; for the obvious reason that money alone is increasing in value. . . . This results in the withdrawal of money from the channels of circulation, and its deposit in great hoards, where it can exert no influence on prices. This hoarding of money, from the nature of things, must continue and increase, not only until the shrinkage of its (the general) volume has actually ceased, but until capitalists are entirely satisfied that . . . the lowest level of prices has been reached. It is this hoarding of money, when its volume shrinks, which causes a fall in prices greater than would be caused by the direct effect of a decrease in the stock of money. Money in shrinking volume becomes the paramount object of commerce, instead of its beneficent instrument. Instead of mobilising industry, it poisons and dries up its life currents. It is the fruitful source of political and social disturbance. It foments strife between labour and . . . capital; while, itself, hidden away in security, gorges on both. It rewards close-fisted lenders; and filches from and bankrupts enterprising borrowers. It circulates freely in the stock exchange, but avoids the labour exchange. It has, in all ages, been the worst enemy with which society has had to contend." (*Report U.S. Mon. Com.*, 1876, I., 53.)

"In every department of activity, from the subtle statecraft of Richelieu to the perfection of counterpoint by Palestrina, mankind evinced its capacity for radical improvement the moment its social shackles were removed, and effort and reward were permitted to bear some sort of an equitable relation to one another. It was an age of miracles. The land was cleared; marshes were drained; forests were felled; roads and bridges were constructed; palaces arose on all sides; and every art that could contribute to the comfort and happiness of society soared at once, through the busy mind of man, from discovery to perfection. Everything was thought of; everything attempted; everything done. From the North Pole to the South, from the Cabinet of Louis, where Colbert planned every enterprise that France afterwards completed, to the frozen tides of the Neva, where Peter originated every reform that Russia has since accomplished, there was to be observed an unceasing activity of action and of thought. Men lived by centuries instead of years; they saw more movement, more change, more progress, more growth, in one generation than had been seen before in one hundred. There was no 'depression of trade' in this Renascent period; 'over-production' was unheard of; the rich were prosperous; the poor were satisfied; everybody wore a smiling face—for prices were rising.

"Nor is this Renaissance to be attributed to the opening of commerce with America, for the aborigines produced nothing which could have tempted a voyage across the ocean, and, in point of fact, no new commerce existed, except commerce for the precious metals, until after the Renaissance of the North had occurred. The commercial development which Petty noticed in 1699, was noticed because it was new and strange. It had but little existence, for instance, in 1599. It was not the cause of the Northern Renaissance, but one of its effects. The development of the Mercantile Doctrine, and its treatment by the economical writers of the age as the basis of all true policy on the subject of trade, are a sufficient proof of the correctness of the position that the new commerce of the period grew out of the rise of prices. They thought—and at that period, when paper money was impracticable, they were right in thinking so—that it was essential to the prosperity of each country that it should secure as much as possible of the material for making money. And it may here be remarked that, much as this policy has been berated by modern writers, it is still actually pursued as a cardinal rule of action by all the great banking corporations of Europe, the Banks of England, France, Germany, and others. They evidently labour under no hallucinations on this subject, and still less so did the commercial writers of the ages of Elizabeth and Henri Quatre." (From *Money and Civilisation*.)

Tooke's *History of Prices* (Vol. VI., Appendix II., Part XXV., p. 409) contains a "Series of Conclusions deduced from the Whole Inquiry," in which, after showing that the stock of gold and silver in Europe had risen from 33 millions sterling in 1492 to 220 millions in 1640, or 600 per cent., whilst prices had risen only 200 per cent.,[1] Tooke concludes his investigation in these words: " We have the fullest warrant for concluding that any partial inconvenience that might ensue from the effect of the American supplies of the sixteenth century in raising prices was

[1] If Tooke's figures of the stock are correct, and the population increased from 40 to 80 millions, as shown in the work cited below, the increase per capita was 250 per cent. ; if the stock and the population shown in my *History of the Precious Metals*, first ed., p. 203, are correct, the increase per capita was 275 per cent. ; and if, with Dr. Smith, the prices of corn and other staples are taken as criteria, the increase was from 200 to 400 per cent.

compensated and repaid a hundred-fold by the activity, expansion, and vigour which they impressed, for more than one generation, upon every enterprise and every art which dignifies human life or increases human happiness ".

There is a sophism connected with the subject which deserves some mention in this place :

Says Professor Miller, of the economic department of the University of Chicago: "Simple justice demands that he (the debtor) should return (to the creditor) the same sacrifice (same amount of labour), and not the same amount of commodities ".

This sophism is based upon the delusion that labour is the measure of value, whereas, in fact, the measure employed to determine value is not labour, but money, which has nothing to do with labour, but is simply a set of numbers symbolised by coins and notes, which are made of metal and paper, and have at times, with equal success, been made of bricks, glass, porcelain, etc.

But even if there were no money, and if exchanges were conducted with barter, it would not be just, but, on the contrary, very unjust, to require from a debtor, a commodity whose fabrication involved just as much sacrifice or labour as the one he borrowed. If the debtor had the option of determining the commodity, he would naturally select some antiquated thing, some mediæval clock, or spinet, which cost a vast amount of labour, but had since become comparatively worthless, with which to pay his debt. If the creditor had the option, he would, on the contrary, select the latest product of invention, something that cost far less labour to produce than similar products did previously, such as steel rails, or printing paper. In the first case, the debtor would unjustly receive all the benefit conferred upon mankind, by the modern economy of labour in producing the most ancient commodity extant. In the second case, the creditor would unjustly "*receive all the benefit conferred upon mankind by improvements since*

the time the debt was created. The debtor in borrowing the capital took the risk from improvements; that is to say, every person engaged in production runs the risk of having the value of his capital diminished as the result of improvements; and it is manifestly just that he who runs the risk from improvements should, in proportion to his risk, receive the benefits which result from improvements. The creditor runs no risk from improvements, in fact, the loan is usually limited to one-half or two-thirds the value of the security, in order that he may escape the risk from improvements."
("Justice," in the *Chicago Inter-Ocean*, 8th July, 1895.)

CHAPTER XVIII.

THE PRECESSION OF PRICES.

Explanation of price—It cannot be expressed in a given coin or sum of coins independent of other coins—It varies directly with the whole numbers of money—Logically a doubling of money will instantly effect a doubling of all prices—In point of fact, this doubling occurs in time, and the time varies in various States and with different commodities—This variance subject to natural law—Such law called the Precession of Prices, or Movement of Prices in Time—Results of practical observations on the working of this law—Danger of employing a money without fixed limits—Other practical observations concerning moneys.

PRICE cannot be definitely expressed in a single coin or a sum of coins independent of other coins; because coins are legally interchangeable one for the other. When notes are legally interchangeable for coins and coins for notes, or when bullion, coins, and notes are all interchangeable, as is the case at present in the foremost States of the world, then price can only be expressed in the total sum of such composite money, or the definite fractions thereof.

"Price," said Montesquieu, "depends fundamentally upon the numerical proportion of commodities to symbols."[1] This is only a brief way of saying that value is a numerical ratio between commodities exchanged; and that price, which is its expression in money, varies with the numbers of money.

The variation of price is *directly* with the numbers of money; whilst the expression of the value of money in exchanges varies *inversely* with the numbers of exchanges. Thus, the more numbers of money or the fewer exchanges,

---

[1] Montesquieu's *Esprit des Lois*, XXII., 7.

the greater price; and the fewer numbers of money or the more exchanges, the lesser price.

The logical consequence of this rule is that, for example, a doubling of the sum of money will result in a doubling of price; and all the logicians, from Locke to McCulloch, have come upon this deduction and hastened to enlarge it.[1] But here they have done violence to Nature, whose movements are performed only in time; an element, of which logic has usually taken but little account. It is upon the movement of prices in time that the Precession of Prices depends.

It was asserted by David Hume, and admitted by Lord Overstone and John Stuart Mill, that whilst the volume of money might be increased or diminished instantly, the resulting movement of prices would only occur after an interval of time.[2] Mr. Mill appears to have supposed that this interval of time was only that which was sufficient " for the increased supply of money to reach all markets, or, according to the conventional metaphor, to permeate all the channels of circulation ".[3]

The partial regulation to which money was subjected in the United States during the Civil War drew the author's attention to this interesting subject, induced him to observe carefully the actual operation of money upon various classes of exchanges, and led to the discovery on his part of the natural law which he has termed the Precession of Prices.[4]

---

[1] McCulloch's *Political Economy*, 217, 401.

[2] Hume's Essays; Lord Overstone's *Thoughts on the Separation of the Departments of the Bank of England*, 1840; Mill's *Political Economy*, III., XIII., § 4, p. 333. Tooke, in his *History of Prices*, says something of the same kind.

[3] Mill, III., VIII., § 2, p. 299.

[4] At that time I did not know that this phenomenon had already attracted the observation of the illustrious Englishmen mentioned in the text. That neither of them followed it experimentally was, perhaps, due to the immense labour involved in the work under a composite system of money. Like many other laws relating to money, this one is only apparent under a regulated system.

The observations made were published in the New York *New Nation*, during the year 1864.

From these observations it appeared that in the United States, following an increase of money, and taking no account of the very brief time involved in geographically distributing the increase, it nevertheless required a period of several years for all prices to conform to the increase. During this time the prices of a certain few classes of commodities or services doubled, after which the prices of others doubled, and so on successively, until the doubling of all classes was completed. In other words, the doubling of prices was not simultaneous, but took the form of a precession, the order of which was somewhat as follows:—

1. Bullion. 2. Stocks and bonds. 3. Shares of incorporated companies. 4. "Staples," or crude and imperishable commodities. 5. Merchandise, including perishable commodities, crude articles of subsistence, etc. 6. Fabrics, such as machinery, manufactured food, articles for wear, etc. 7. Landed property, or real estate. 8. Skilled labour, or artisans' wages. 9. Unskilled labour, or the wages of labourers, soldiers, seamen, etc. 10. Professional services, or the emolument of authors, inventors, lawyers, engineers, clergymen, accountants, and other professional and clerical classes.

The interval between the doubling of the prices in these various classes of commodities or services was not uniform; in other words, supposing ten years to be the time required for the entire doubling of prices, and the classes of commodities and services to be ten in number, it would not follow that each successive year would add one to the classes with doubled prices. After once commencing to feel the effect of the increased sum of money, some classes doubled in price quicker than others. Leaving this irregularity out of view, and supposing that if during the upward movement of prices, say after the fifth year, the money of the country had been suddenly diminished to its original sum,[1] the Precession of Prices would have appeared as in the diagram below.

From this diagram it will be observed that at the sixtieth month the prices of some commodities are falling, while those of others are still rising, and that both movements arise from a single original impulse and its reversion; the falling commodities having passed through the rising period, and the rising commodities being yet within it. This is, in fact, what did occur, though not in the symmetrical order delineated.

Upon examining with attention the details of this induction, it was observed that the order of precession conformed to the marketability of, or ease of selling or exchanging, the various classes of commodities and services

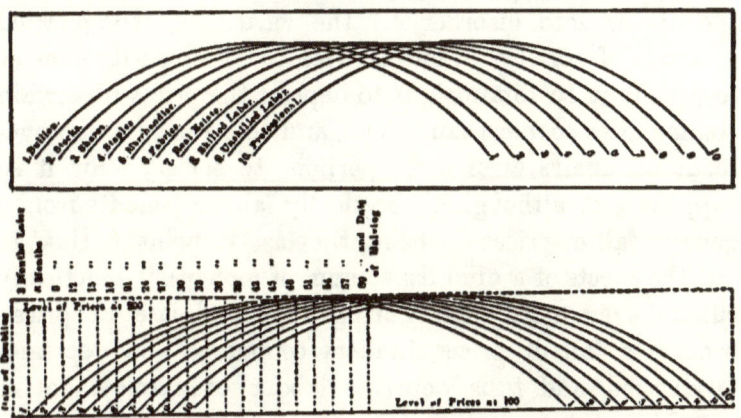

enumerated. Thus, bullion, belonging to Class 1, was more readily saleable than a Government bond belonging to Class 2, or a railway share belonging to Class 3, or a bale of cotton belonging to Class 4; whilst the latter was more marketable than a sack of flour belonging to Class 5, or a piece of cloth belonging to Class 6; and so on. All kinds of moveable commodities were more readily saleable than

[1] And assuming population and trade, and therefore the demand for money, to have remained unchanged.

land; whilst land commonly commanded a readier market than labour or professional services.

The operation of this principle reveals the danger of all empirical measures designed to expand or contract the money of a country, and the folly of exposing money, as it is now exposed, to the voluntary or chance expansions or contractions occasioned by war, intrigue, mining or commerce. Before meddling with money it is obviously necessary to determine the natural laws which govern its influence upon prices. From the observations made by the author it appears that to increase money, or permit it to increase, is not merely to enhance all prices simultaneously: it is to enhance the price of some things in point of time before others; it is to benefit certain classes of the community at the expense of the remainder; it is to derange and throw into disorder all the varied and complicated interests of society. Contrariwise, to diminish its sum, or to permit it to diminish, is to depress the prices of certain commodities sooner than others, and to occasion a derangement of affairs even more perilous to society; for it so happens that, although theoretically labour benefits from a general fall of prices (it being the last, in point of time, to feel the effects of a diminished sum of money), it practically suffers even more than during a general rise of prices, because a fall of prices hinders commerce and depresses production, and thus deprives labour of employment or tangible existence.[1]

Hence, the only kind of money which is demanded by the interests of the productive classes is that one which is

[1] During a fall of prices all enterprises are checked, among them gold and silver mining enterprises, or searches for the precious metals upon a commercial basis. So that so long as money is made of these metals, every accidental scarcity of them will promote greater and greater scarcity. Contrariwise, during a rise of prices, mining enterprises are stimulated, and plenty of metal thus begets renewed researches for more. With a commodity-money, it is always a dearth or a feast; and in these days of machinery and associated capital this fact has a significance which it never had before.

also demanded in the name of general equity—a money of a fixed sum; fixed either absolutely or relatively to population or production; but fixed.

The observations alluded to above brought to light other noteworthy peculiarities in the movement of prices, *viz.*—(1) That whilst war, harvests, production, speculation, and the other principal influences, other than money, which affect prices, may affect the prices of many things, they do not and cannot either separately or collectively affect the prices of all things; (2) that whenever they enhance prices in one direction they depress them in others, and *vice versâ;* and (3) that no cause or influence can enhance or depress the prices of all things, either simultaneously or in the order of the Precession of Prices, except an increase or diminution in the whole Sum of Money.[1]

With reference to the periods of time set forth in the diagram, these must not be regarded as exact, without further and nicer experiments to determine them. In countries other than the United States the precession would occur at longer intervals.

When "staples" and "merchandise" were included in one class the following precession was observed to have occurred in the prices of their constituent sub-classes:

    (*a*) Cotton, iron, lead, copper, spelter, nails, cordage, linseed oil, common whale oil, fine wools.

    (*b*) Coffee, tea, cocoa, sugar, clover-seed, hops, timber, hemp, wood-ashes, coal, zinc, whalebone.

    (*c*) Flour, grain, rice, molasses, beef, pork, tallow, lard, hides, horn, ivory, india-rubber, cork, honey, bees' wax, bristles, candles, soap, tin, petroleum.

    (*d*) Coarse wools, sperm oil, naval bread, dried fish, leather, deal boards, salted butter, brimstone, hay, lime, laths.

---

[1] Tooke spent a lifetime in trying to refute these simple and almost self-evident principles, and he failed. Yet the fallacious doctrine that commercial depression may be caused by "general over-production" (a myth) is still taught.

CHAPTER XIX.

REVULSIONS OF PRICES.

Coins are made of gold and silver not because of the intrinsic qualities of these metals—The practice arose from the superior constancy of their quantity as compared with other substances, and during æras when artificial moneys of fixed quantity were politically impracticable—Historical examples—The precious metals were never permanently used for coins until the conquest of Spain by Rome—When the first effects of this conquest subsided, the precious metals were less used as materials for coins, until the Spanish conquest of America—The effects of the conquest of America and its great supplies of gold and silver to Europe upon prices have been sustained by means of convertible paper notes—This system incapable of further safe extension—Necessity for reform in money—Fluctuations of prices which have resulted from the failure of "convertible" note systems—Their disastrous and baneful effects.

SAYS Montesquieu, "That which is the common measure of all things should of all things be the least subject to change".[1] It has ever been the theme of ill-informed writers that money came to be made of gold and silver coins because gold and silver metals possessed certain intrinsic qualities, such as brilliancy, incorrodibility, portability, divisibility, reunitability, and the like. But these qualities did not prevent the Hindoos, the Chinese, the Greeks, nor the Romans of the Commonwealth from voluntarily putting these metals away and using in their stead other substances for coins or monetary symbols—substances the supply of which, like baked clay, copper, or iron, was less capriciously furnished by nature, and therefore more amenable to the control of man. Indeed, it cannot be shown that either gold or silver was per-

[1] *Esprit des Lois*, XXII., 3.

manently used for money in any country of the world prior to the conquest of Spain by the Romans. It was this event that brought to Rome a sufficient accumulation of the precious metals to assure a certain stability in their value, and it was this stability of value that determined their permanent adoption as the material of coins, and not the intrinsic qualities of the metals. Previous to this time the Athenians had, indeed, owing to their control over the productive silver mines of Laurium, employed a money consisting chiefly of silver coins; and the Macedonians had used for this purpose both gold and silver, which they derived from Alexander's plunder of Asia. But in neither of these cases can the monetisation of the precious metals be regarded as having lasted permanently. The mines of Laurium were closed long before the time of Pausanias, and were not re-opened until A.D. 1870.[1] Alexander's stock of the precious metals soon became dispersed; and from this time until the extinction of Greek liberty the material of the moneys of Greece was frequently changed.

Nor was the stability of value which, after the Roman conquest of Spain, led to the adoption of silver and gold coins, a permanent or unalterable attribute of the metals of which they were composed, but a purely adventitious one, derived from the immense quantity of such metals which the Romans had been enabled to collect, primarily by plunder, afterwards, and much more extensively, by means of mine-slavery. It is now but too well ascertained that the tragical fate which befel Aboriginal America in the fifteenth and sixteenth centuries had already overtaken many portions of Europe during the period B.C. 200—A.D. 300. In America, the Spaniards immolated in the mines some twenty or thirty millions of the native inhabitants; in Europe, the Romans had probably sacrificed fully as many.[2]

[1] *History of the Precious Metals*, and *History of Money*.
[2] Gibbon and Merivale estimate the population of the Roman Empire in Europe during the Augustan æra at sixty millions. At the period of the Hegira it was not over thirty millions.

The influence of these last-named historical events marks the limits in the two æras of comparative stability which have attended the value of gold and silver. The first æra commenced and ended with Roman conquest and slavery. The second æra commenced and ended with Spanish conquest and slavery. When the Roman Empire declined, the level of prices which its violent acquisition of the precious metals had established, was sustained as long as possible by means of over-valued coins, leather-moneys,[1] corn-moneys, and a great variety of similar devices. It was not until after the second æra of their comparative stability of value had commenced (this was after the conquest of America) that gold and silver coins, at or near their bullion value, were again used commonly and permanently for money.

When the Spanish-American Empire declined, the level of prices which its violent acquisitions of gold and silver had established was sustained by means of convertible, afterwards combined with inconvertible, paper money; and this practice has continued down to the present day.

The signs that this level can no longer be sustained are making themselves more and more apparent every day. Many of the so-called convertible systems of paper money have become in reality hopelessly inconvertible ones. This is certainly the case in Russia, Austria, Turkey, Brazil, Buenos Ayres, and some other countries; it is probably also the case in the United States, notwithstanding the pretensions of metallic resources periodically set forth by the Treasury.[2] The mechanical devices for accelerating

---

[1] In my *History of Monetary Systems* more than a dozen emissions of such moneys are shown to have been made in the various countries of Europe during the Middle Ages.

[2] The Government of the United States is now so strong and rich that, in the scramble of nations for the world's scant stock of the precious metals, it probably has the power to secure more than its due share. In other words, the great European Syndicates should no longer be permitted to monopolise the flow of the precious metals. With an independent

the efficiency of money have received no important addition since the general introduction of railways and telegraphs. The clearing-house system (which, by the way, is of long standing) does not appear to be capable of further extension. The annual supplies of the precious metals, to which a sporadic impetus was imparted by the accidental discovery of the Californian and Australian placers, are almost entirely absorbed in the arts. Even the product of Africa will not help the case.

Those whose blind faith in the stable value of gold and silver cannot be shaken by considerations which cover such great periods of history as the rise and fall of the Roman and Spanish-American Empires, or who may not be disposed to admit that the present decline in the supplies of gold and silver to the mints is final, need only to consult the fluctuations of price, in any commercial country during the past half-century. These will show that even the comparative stability in the value of the precious metals has varied to the extent of four or five times.

We need not go far to ascertain the causes of these fluctuations of prices. Although not sufficiently exact to furnish grounds for researches into the nature and function of money, the statistics on the subject serve well enough to exhibit the main cause of the fluctuations of prices.

Commencing in 1775 with $4·40 of money per capita of population, the United States, for example, had $6·25 in 1791; this decreased to $5·85 in 1792; increased to $7·40 in 1794; decreased to $4·60 in 1798; increased to $5·30 in 1800; decreased to $4·60 in 1803; increased to $5·30 in 1804; decreased to $5·20 in 1805; increased to $6·40 in 1808; decreased to $6·10 in 1811; increased to $8·80 in 1813; decreased to $8·00 in 1815; increased to $9·20 in

policy, the Treasury and Banks of the United States are capable of exercising an important influence upon this movement. It ill becomes the possessors of such power to permit the employment of the feeble and juggling tables of "coins in circulation," published by the Director of the Mint and Comptroller of the Currency.

1819; decreased to $9·00 in 1820; increased to $9·20 in 1825; decreased to $7·20 in 1830; increased to $14·00 in 1837; decreased to $12·50 in 1838; increased to $13·40 in 1839; decreased to $6·90 in 1843; increased to $11·10 in 1848; decreased to $10·50 in 1849; increased to $16·40 in 1855; decreased to $16·10 in 1856; increased to $16·70 in 1857; decreased to $14·00 in 1858; increased to $15·40 in 1859; decreased to $13·70 in 1861; increased to $28·50 in 1864, and, with some unimportant variations, it has decreased to about $11·00 at the present time.[1]

Surely no one will contend that the alternate periods of increasing and decreasing, or, as the present writer has termed them elsewhere,[2] of Crescendo and Diminuendo money, which these figures bespeak, have been beneficial to society: no one will claim that the undeserved changes of individual fortune which they produced, or that the many social distresses and disturbances which they occasioned, were desirable. On the other hand, that these revulsions were entirely preventable and avoidable can scarcely be doubted. They all sprang from money.

The adventitious gains and losses occasioned by these fluctuations in money have led to two very deplorable classes of results. First, they have subjected all mercantile transactions to extraordinary and unnecessary uncertainty; effaced the distinction which formerly existed between commercial adventure and stock-jobbery; and fostered a spirit of gambling and jockeying, so deeply rooted in the community that not all the pulpits in its midst have hitherto been able to check it. Second, they have tended to shorten credits; depreciate the commercial value of honesty, foresight, and skill; discourage commercial enterprise; and led to a baneful growth of irresponsible corporations and limited liability companies.

[1] *History of the Precious Metals*, pp. 216-17.
[2] In the *New York Economist*, in 1868; in the first edition of *Johnson's Encyclopædia*, article "Currency"; and in several other publications of the period 1864-1873.

If society has thriven and progressed in spite of these obstacles, it is because the productive resources which have furnished the basis of such progress have hitherto been sufficiently numerous and ample to overcome a bad system of money, and not that such a system has been without its effects upon the general welfare. But these resources are no longer numerous and ample. There are no more virgin lands or forests, no more free "cattle-ranges," no more unworked placer mines, etc. The New World is deflowered, and is fast settling down to the industrial conditions of the Old. Before South Africa is exploited, the present monetary systems will have to be abandoned.

In the Roman Commonwealth, which was provided with an artificial, permanent, and unalterable Measure of Value, the debtor had so little excuse, beyond his own lack of foresight or skill, for failing to meet his engagements, that the law, without working any noticeable hardship, accorded to the creditor a claim not only upon the former's property, but his person.

In modern States the measure of value is so uncertain and fluctuating that no man cares at to-day's prices to sell on long credit, or to rent or lease upon long terms. Bank loans, for the most part, are limited to a few weeks;[1] and long credits of any kind to private parties are regarded with so much apprehension that in many cases they are forbidden or defeated by law.[2]

If it be answered that whatever perturbations of prices have occurred, they were not due to the unstable value of

---

[1] In 1867, while Director of the Bureau of Statistics, I obtained a return from most of the National Banks, which showed that the average period of discounts was about fifty days—the first return of the sort ever obtained.

[2] Such is the operation of the Statutes of Limitation in America relative to mortgages, loans, leases, etc., by private persons, and such the operation of squatter laws and customs, and of bankruptcy acts. On the other hand, Government and corporative loans and leases for lengthy periods have been upheld in law. There is a contradiction in these two classes of practices.

the precious metals, but to the promotion of paper notes to the dignity and function of money, the reply is that but for such promotion the perturbations would have been still greater. The interests of society are so strongly opposed to unstable prices, that it resorts to every expedient for the purpose of keeping them steady; and it is only when an efflux of the precious metals—occasioned by peremptory demand elsewhere, or by fears of war—takes place, that paper money systems have ever obtained a footing against the prejudice which they had to encounter. Paper notes have often in derision been termed the " Money of Revolutions"; but they were never adopted by the revolutionists of any country until after the precious metals had fled away, and left such country exposed to more than the accustomed hazard of unstable prices.

CHAPTER XX.

REGULATION OF MONEYS.

Fluctuations of price which do not belong to the domain of science—Variations which do—Practical considerations for the regulation of money—Effect in the United States of an absolutely fixed sum—Influence of a fixed sum per capita of population—Actual movement of population and money during the past century—Had money been regulated instead of being left to commerce, chance, and political contention, the great panics of 1815, 1821, 1837, 1861, 1873, and 1893 might have been averted.

BESIDES those changes in the general level of prices which arise from changes in the whole sum of money, there is a subsidiary and partial movement of prices—a change in the prices of certain things, not of all things—which arises from war, legislation, speculation, foreign commerce, fashion, the chances of mining discovery, good and bad harvests, the progress of mechanical invention, "over-production," and other causes.[1]

These influences directly affect value, whilst money only affects price; these influences, whether separately or combined, may only affect the value of some things, they cannot affect that of all; whilst money cannot affect any, without affecting every one. With the fluctuations of value occasioned by the various causes above set forth, the Science of Money has no concern; they belong to the counting-house.

When money consists, as it does now, partly of gold, made freely into coins, by or for private individuals, and partly of notes, whether convertible or not, and its Sum is

---

[1] There can only be a permanent over-production of two commodities: improved lands and the precious metals.—See *History of the Precious Metals*, pp. 226, 275.

liable to be affected by the commercial or political supply and demand for gold metal, then the relation of the gold to other commodities, and consequently its value in commodities, becomes of a dual character. As coins, its value is determined by the numerical proportion which such coins bear to the sum of the exchanges of all commodities and services in time. As bullion, its value is due to the circumstances of its acquisition, the demand and supply of metal, etc.

This dual character of privately coined money, and the complex relations which flow from it, belong to the domain of madness. Science may try to reduce them to order; but the task will ever be a fruitless one.

Apart from these considerations, the relation of money to price must always be a general one. Money can promote a general rise of all prices; it can occasion a general fall of all prices; it can cause all prices generally to remain fixed at a given level; but upon the subsidiary movement of prices money has no influence whatever, save what influence arises from the phenomenon of Precession.

In making an effort to decide in what manner the Sum of money may best be regulated, we are met by the gravest difficulties; for money is not, like other measures, made to determine a relation of unvarying dimensions; it is designed to determine one whose dimensions tend continually to vary. Value, the relation to be determined, varies continually with the volume of exchanges, and these with the growth of population, the extension of commerce, and the march of invention.

In any given State, if money be regulated and limited to an Absolutely fixed sum, there would ensue a general fall of prices, because the sum of commodities and services to be exchanged therein within a given period—and whose value is to be expressed in money—is at present continually increasing.

If money in a given State were limited to a fixed sum Relative to Population, there would also ensue a fall of prices, although such fall would be far less great or rapid than in the case of an Absolutely fixed sum of money. The fall in the case of a Relatively (to population) fixed sum of money would be due to the fact that exchanges at the present time tend to increase somewhat faster than population.

If we consult the history of money in the United States (where the statistical materials are most abundant), and endeavour to learn if the whole sum of money has actually conformed to any other determinable quantity, we shall find that the determinable quantity to which it has conformed most nearly is that of population. This is not to say that it has kept pace with population, or only kept pace with it; but that the average rate of its augmentation appears to have borne a definite numerical relation to the augmentation of population. Thus the population of the United States has increased during the past century at the rate of about three per cent., or thirty per mille per annum compounded. The money of the United States, though not without frequent, injurious, and dangerous fluctuations, appears to have augmented on the average at the rate of about thirty-three per mille per annum.[1]

Another determinable quantity to which the actual increase of money appears to have conformed is the net rate of interest for money. This quantity is not so readily nor easily determinable as the increase of population; nevertheless, it is determinable. The net rate of interest means the average actual or market rate of interest, less risk, taxes, and the cost of the superintendence of loans. This rate in the United States has been about thirty-three per mille per annum. It is now about 2¼ per cent.

Without as yet assuming that these indications offer a practical solution to so difficult a problem, let it be supposed that the money of the United States, instead of being left, as it has been, to alternately expand or contract with the commercial movements of bullion, the paper emissions

---

[1] Consult the author's *History of Precious Metals*, pp. 214-17.

of private banks, the exigencies of governments, and the contentions of party, had been regulated so as to augment at the rate of thirty-three per mille per annum—then these results would have followed :—

1. The country would have had, all along, substantially the same average amount of money that it has had; only, instead of alternately increasing and diminishing, in some years to more than half the extent of its previous volume, it would have augmented steadily at the rate of $3\frac{1}{3}$ per cent. per annum.

2. The inflations, speculations, bankruptcies, and repudiations of 1814, 1819, 1829, 1837, 1857, 1862, 1873, and 1893, would not have occurred.

3. The contractions and stringencies of trade that characterised these æras would not have been occasioned.

4. Nor would it have been necessary to pass the stay-laws and bankruptcy Acts, nor tolerate the receiverships which were designed to relieve the distresses occasioned by these contractions, and into which innocent and honourable men were drawn, together with the designing and dishonourable.

Though the character of these advantages does not rank them among the most important which such regulation would have promoted, yet surely even these are worthy of attention. To secure to each class of persons in a State the uninterrupted and peaceful enjoyment of their industrial advantages, should certainly form an object of desire to statesmen. To discourage recklessness or dishonesty; to visit upon the labouring and indebted classes no unnecessary nor peculiar hardships; to incur no reproach of pecuniary turpitude ; to hold out no inducements to fraudulent bankrupts; to let no rascal through meshes of the law which are strong enough to bind the innocent,—these surely are ends which no progressive community can long afford to disregard or neglect.

F I N I S.

INDEX.

Abrasion of coins, 64.
Ace, the Roman archaic term for money, 52, 109.
Act of 1666, 49, 81, 167.
Alexander the Great, his plunder of the precious metals, 191.
America. *See* United States.
Argent, a term for money, 1.
Aristotle on money, 27, 40, 35, 95.
Assignats, 99.
Austria, money of, 90, 192.
"Automatic system," 130.
Ayas = all, 109.

Banks, their usefulness, 161.
Bank cheques, comparative use of, 158.
Bank deposits, impropriety of including them in money, 153.
Bank loans, shortness of, 152.
Bank of England, *Preface*.
Bank notes, general increase of, in nineteenth century, 6.
Bankruptcy laws, operation of, in Rome, 195; in United States, 200.
Barter, 2.
Baugs, 61.
Bimetallism, 75, 86.
Black Acts of James III., 101.
Brazil, 192.
Budelius cited, 113.
Bullion, influences of new supplies upon prices, 33, 187.
Buenos Ayres, inconvertible note system of, 192.
Burmah, 45.

California, nullification of United States monetary laws by, 101; high rates of interest in, 143.
Capital, growth of, affected by money, 185; rate of augmentation in United States, 146; rule to determine same in any country, 146.
Cash, or ready money, 152.

Chase, Chief Justice Salmon P., his definition of money, 36.
Cheques, bank, comparative use of, in various countries, 35.
China, monetary systems of, 55, 89.
Circulation, rapidity of the, 148, 162.
Classical conception of money, 115.
Clearing-houses, *Preface*, 155, 193; system of, not new, 193; incapable of further extension, 193.
Coinage is an attribute of sovereignty, 71, 135.
Code Napoleon, 100.
Coins, not a measure of value by themselves, 30.
Commerce, distinction between and stock-jobbery becoming effaced, 194.
Commercial crises, averted by paper notes; their æra coincident with closure of Spanish American mines, 192.
Commodity money, 188n.
Contractions of money injurious to trade and social progress, 178.
Convertible moneys, 192.
Convertible note system, danger of further extending, 192.
Corn money, 98, 192.
Corporations, baneful growth of, 194.
Credit and money, proportions of, 160.
Crescendo and diminuendo moneys, 194.
Crises, commercial, 194.
Currency, ambiguity of the term, 8, 121; used by Sir R. Peel, 36; by Chief-Justice S. P. Chase, 36.

Decay of monetary conceptions, 111, 115.
Decomposition and renascence of classical terms, 111-115.
Demonetisation of silver, 102.
Deposits, bank. *See* Bank deposits.
Discovery of America, influence of, 118.

INDEX.

Disintegration and resuscitation of monetary conceptions, 111.

Efficiency of money. *See* Circulation.
England. *See* United Kingdom.
England, Bank of. *See* Bank of England.
England, rate of interest in, 146.
Enterprise, its commercial value reduced, 194.
Equity, as established by value, 14; as affected by money, 189.
Europe, revival of mining in, 112.
European civilisation, decay and revival of, 112.
Evolution of words, 109.
Exchange is a social act, 1.
Exchanges in Great Britain, *Preface;* in the United States, 155.
Expansion and contraction, 177.

Feuardent, Gaston L., 109.
Feudal conception of money, 112.
Feudal origin of existing monetary systems, 112.
Foresight, its commercial value reduced, 194.
France, 59, 98, 99, 166.
Free or gratuitous coinage laws, 49, 81.
Function of money, the, is to measure value, 25.

Genesis, anachronism in, 109.
George, Henry, cited, 144n.
Gold. *See* Precious metals.
Gold and silver supplies, 6, 55; first permanently used for monetary symbols after Roman conquest of Spain, 191; value of, not due to cost of production, 15, 165. *See* Precious metals.
Gold never coined by any Christian prince except the Basileus until A.D. 1204, 72; table of earliest gold coinages, 74.
Grain money, 98, 192.
Grammar of money, 67.
Greece, ancient, monetary systems of, 27, 27n., 52, 190.
Greenback notes of the United States, 101, 175.

Hamilton, Alex., 86.
Harris, Joseph, cited, 86, 114.
Hegeler, Prof., 44.
History of money, materials for, 67, 95
Honesty, its commercial value, 194.

Hume, David, cited, 177, 185.
Hydraulic or placer mining, 191.

Ies, the origin of *ecus, unus,* and *one,* 52.
Illimitable money, illiterate suggestion of, 44.
Inconvertible moneys, 192.
Individual notes as money, 151.
International moneys, 134.
Interest, market rate of, to what due, 142; ultimate cause of, the rate of the growth of plants and animals, 143; this cause also affects the growth of population, 144; hence the rate of interest and population are directly related, 145; analysis of a rate of, 145; present tendency of the rate to fall, 146; usury laws at variance with nature, 147.
Ingot money, failure of, 61.
Italian code of law, 100.

James III., Black Acts of, 101.
Jefferson, Thomas, 86.
Jews, usury and the, 144.
Julius Paulus quoted on money, 27n.
Justice and money, 14, 127, 189.
Justinian, code of, on money, 27n.

Kinetic character of money, 124.

Labour, as affected by money, 182, 186; earnings of, 150.
Land, this and money alone liable to be permanently "over-produced," 197; long leases of, contrary to spirit of American laws, 195n.; sales of, their frequency in the United States, 195n.
Laurium, silver mines of, 64, 191.
Law, money an institute of, 67.
Laws of money, 95.
£ s. d., 67, 68, 69.
Leases. *See* Land.
Legal instrument, money a, 67.
Limitation, the essence of money, 127; it can only be imposed by the State, 130.
Limited moneys, 64, 197.
Limited companies, growth of, 194.
Liverpool, Lord, 86, 99.
Livius Drusus, 67.
Local circulation notes, 149.
Locke cited, 115, 148, 149.
Lost arts, revival of the, 112.
Lycurgus, 40, 62.

INDEX. 203

Mahomet, influence of, upon Europe, 112.
Mark of authority upon money, 57, 97.
Measure of value, or money, present illimitability of, 32.
Measures, when precise, are always artificial, 127; and numerical, 128; their efficiency does not necessarily depend upon the material of which made, 128; but upon their limits, 128; these limits fixed by human law, 128; essence of, is limitation, 129; this is the meaning of *nomos*, 129; function of, to number, 28; substantial immutability of, 29; such not the case with money as at present constituted, 123-6.
Mercantile system, influence upon monetary laws of the, 23, 24.
Metallism, 85, 138, 166, 171.
Milan, paper notes of, 173.
Mill, John Stuart, cited, 7, 148, 185.
Mines royal, 5, 57, 80.
Mining for the precious metals a losing industry, 52; why kept up, 53; revival of, in Europe, 191; experience in, of ancient world, 192.
Mint codes, alteration of, 80, 82.
Mixed moneys, case of the, 95.
Moneta, 38, 110.
Money-lenders, 138.
Money, origin of term, 38; original or classical meaning of, 110; feudal meaning of, 112; renascent and modern meaning of, 113; different senses in which used, 113; the thing money far more ancient than the term, 101; money an institution of law, 116; an equitable one, 188; an institution of State, 25, 97, 103; a national measure, *Preface*; of the world, a chimera, 134; of account, 149; palpably it is a collective unit or thing, 116; the whole of which cannot be seen at once, 117; its function is to measure value, 125; compared with other measures, 123; palpable characteristics of its fractions, 120; legal attributes of same, 121; advantages of stable moneys, 200.
Montesquieu quoted, 10, 11, 184, 190.

Napoleon, Code, 100.
"National" bank notes of the United States, 158.

Nations a law to themselves as to money, 97, 103.
Newton cited, 33*n*.
New World, deflowerment of, 195.
New York Clearing-House, 155.
Nomisma, the ancient Greek term for money, 37.
Nomos, the Greek word for law, numbers, measure, limits, etc., 37.
Nullification of monetary laws, 101.
Numbers, abstract nature of, 28.
Numerato, the Republican Roman term for money, 37, 121.
Numerical moneys of Greece and Rome, 8.
Numerical theory of money, 184.

Oriental commerce, reopening of, 112.
Over-production of land, money, and commodities, 197; fallacies concerning, 188.
Overstone, Lord, cited, 185*n*.

Pandects of Justinian, quoted, 95.
Panics, 194.
Paper money, 5; great expansion of, 6; at present forms most of the measure of value, 6; has lessened the perturbations of price, 196; derisively called "the money of revolutions," 196.
Paulus cited, 27*n*., 95, 97.
Peel, Sir Robert, his definition of a pound sterling incomplete, 114*n*.; his definition of money proves this, 36.
Plato, 95.
Plate-ships, arrivals of, their influence on prices, 33*n*.
Politics of money, 137.
Political economy, origin of present science of, 114.
Ponderata, 45.
Population, 191*n*.
Pound sterling, 114*n*.
Precession of prices, the, 184.
Precious metals, value of, not due to present cost, 53; they are at present greatly undervalued, 53; value of, not stable, 191; fluctuations in value of, 192; supplies of, 6; ebb and flow of, controlled by syndicates, *Preface*, 91. *See* Gold and Silver.
Prerogative of money, 103.
Price, is value expressed in money, 21; it cannot be expressed in a single coin or note independent of other coins or notes, 21; but

only in the total sum of money or its definite fractions, 21; it varies directly with the total numbers of money, 22; this variation effected only in time, 23.

Prices, how affected by money, 185; revulsions of, in the United States, 138, 164, 190.

Principles of money, *Preface*.

Private or "free" coinage, 49, 77, 81, 86.

Production as affected by money, *Preface*, 188.

Profit, the basis of interest, 142.

Quickeners of money, 35.

Rapidity of circulation, *q.v.*

Ratios, 77.

Recoinages of money, 108.

Regulated moneys, 197; absolutely fixed moneys, 198; moneys fixed relative to population, 199; moneys fixed relative to the rate of interest, 200.

Renascent meaning of money, 115.

Repudiations, 194.

Reserves in banks, 148.

Revival of European civilisation, 112.

Revulsions of prices, 190.

Rome, monetary systems of, 66, 74, 190, 195, 110; peculiar relations of debtor and creditor in, 195.

Rotundity of the earth, 111.

Russia, inconvertible notes of, 192.

Science of money, *Preface*.

Scotch banks, 87.

Seigniorage, 106.

Silver. *See* Precious metals.

Skill, its commercial value lowered, 194.

Smith, Adam, cited, 10, 21, 53, 114, 170, 174.

Sophisms of money, 160, 182, 188.

Sovereign, weight and fineness, 114*n*.

Spanish America, mines of, 193.

Species, a feudal term for money, 112.

Special contract laws of money, 99, 103.

Sphericity of the earth familiar to the ancients, 111.

Stability of value, the, once possessed by the precious metals led to their choice for monetary symbols, 191; not a permanent relation of these metals, 191.

Stability of money, 190, 200.

Standard measures, where preserved, 32.

State bank notes of America, 149.

State money, 85.

State sovereignty over money, 97.

Statutes of Limitation, operation of the, 195*n*.

Sterling, 98.

Stock-jobbery, 194.

Storch, Count, 166.

Subsidiary coins, 158.

Suspensions of coin payments in various States, 192.

Syndicates controlling money, 91.

Tavannes, 98.

Token coins, 158.

Tooke's *History of Prices* cited, 181, 185*n*., 189*n*.

Transport notes, 5.

Treasury notes, 158.

Treasure trove, 80.

Turkey, inconvertible note system of, 192; rate of interest in, 146; growth of capital in, 146.

Under-valuation of precious metals, 53.

United Kingdom, growth of capital in, 146; rate of interest in, 146.

United States fluctuations in its volume of money, 193; heterogeneity of its money, 158; statistics of money in, 158, 190; ignorance of its finance ministers, 146; the silver dollar, 86; rates of interest in, 146; growth of capital in, 146; monetary revulsions in, 190.

Unit of money, the, is all money, 109, 120.

"Unit of value," a myth, 51, 86; defined in the laws, 32, 113; political significance of the term, 35. *See* Money.

Universal money, 134.

Usury. *See* Interest.

Value, its nature, 7; it is not a thing, 7; the classical root of the term was *valeo*, or numerical power, 8; evolution and decay of this conception, 9; revival of the term with a different conception, that of an attribute, 9; this the view of the Economists, 9; fallacy of this conception, 9; its true meaning, that of a numerical power, ratio, or relation, rediscovered by Montesquieu, 10; elaborated by Bastiat, 10; it is a numerical ratio expressing a power of exchange, 10; to be measured most equitably by means of money, 15; it depends upon many uncertain influences, it is an equitable relation, 16; it is extremely variable, 16; it is not connected with cost of production, 16; it can be expressed with precision only in numbers, 16; it is a numerical relation, 17; it can only be precisely measured by an artificial unit, 17; that unit is the whole sum of money, 15; common error of substituting the term for "worth," or of using it as a noun substantive, 18.

Value of money, 16; under existing laws indeterminable, 31; not due to the material of moneys, 31; due to numbers, 31; an arithmetical relation, 41.

Velocity of money, 148, 162.

Volume of money, the, not specified in the laws, 32.

Walker, Francis, 26, 27.

World's stock of coins, 6; of gold coins, 90.

Demy 8vo. Cloth.   Price 15/- net.

HISTORY OF MONETARY SYSTEMS
IN
VARIOUS STATES.

By ALEX. DEL MAR.

A work upon which the Author has been engaged for many years, and which contains the latest and most elaborate collection of historical materials on this great subject.

The following List of Chapters affords some view of the immense scope of the work :—

Chap.
- I.—INDIA FROM THE EARLIEST TIMES.
- II.—ANCIENT PERSIA.
- III.—HEBREW MONEYS.
- IV.—ANCIENT GREECE.
- V.—ROME B.C. 369 TO A.D. 1204.
- VI.—THE SACRED CHARACTER OF GOLD.
- VII.—POUNDS, SHILLINGS, AND PENCE.
- VIII.—GOTHIC MONEYS.
- IX.—MOSLEM MONEYS A.D. 622-1492.
- X.—EARLY ENGLISH MONEYS.
- XI.—MONEYS OF THE HEPTARCHY.
- XII.—ANGLO-NORMAN MONEYS.
- XIII.—EARLY PLANTAGENET MONEYS.

Chap.
- XIV.—LATER PLANTAGENET MONEYS.
- XV.—THE COINAGE PREROGATIVE.
- XVI.—SAXONY AND SCANDINAVIA TO DATE.
- XVII.—THE NETHERLANDS TO DATE.
- XVIII.—GERMANY TO DATE.
- XIX.—ARGENTINE CONFEDERATION TO DATE.
- XX.—PRIVATE COINAGE.

App. A.—STATISTICS OF THE RATIO.
    B.—BANK SUSPENSIONS SINCE THE ERA OF PRIVATE COINAGE.
    C.—THE GOLD MOVEMENT OF 1865-73 AND THE EXISTING MONETARY SYSTEMS.

PRESS NOTICES.

"We follow Mr. Del Mar in his attack on the extravagant waste of public money, both in this country and in the United States, in coining gratis gold which bullion dealers melt down again periodically into bullion."—*Daily Chronicle.*

"Mr. Del Mar displays a commendable grasp of his subject, and enables his readers to see many episodes of the past from a new point of view."—*Morning Post.*

"Peculiarly worthy of attention from students of money problems."—*Free Review.*

"Will no doubt constitute for many years to come the standard work on the world's systems of interchange. It is impossible to speak in too high terms of praise of the erudition displayed by the author, without one trace of anything like pedantry. The book is as interesting as a good novel, and vastly more entertaining. One of the valuable and interesting contributions to the history of economics ; voluminous in its information ; exhaustive in detail."—*Journal of the Institute of Bankers.*

"A valuable and weighty volume on the history of currency in the various countries of the world."—*Pall Mall Gazette.*

"Apart from any views which an author may propound, as derived from his study of the facts on which these are based, it is always a grateful task to recognise ability, industry, and learning in the collection and statement of the facts themselves. In Mr. Del Mar's present work these qualities are conspicuously present, for none can open the book without seeing in every page evidences of the most laborious inquiry on fields of research and learning wide as the world itself. Every age and country, from Egypt centuries prior to Abraham's sojourn, the Brahminical records of India, the parchments of Greece, Judæa, Rome, and Arabia, down to the exploits of the Argentine Republic in our own day, have been explored and made to furnish their quota to this great museum of the facts of monetary history. . . . All being treated with a wealth of reference and allusion, with a breadth of knowledge and minuteness of detail, which can leave little to be desired. . . . Treating of a subject nearly as old as the hills, it is as interesting as a novel and immensely more profitable. . . . Mr. Del Mar's book will continue a monument of his learning and industry wherever monetary science is studied; deeply interesting and valuable to advocates of every shade of opinion or school of finance. Holding strong views on the evils caused by the demonetisation of silver, he fairly follows the promise of his preface, ' that he has not laid his historical works under contribution to support them,' but honestly ' seeks, by analysing the various experiments that have been made with this subtle instrument (money) to derive from them whatever light they may be able to throw upon the questions that vex us to-day.' "—*North British Economist.*

"We quite agree with the author that money is something more than the mere metal or paper of which it is composed."—*Manchester Guardian.*

"The literature of monetary science and history is undoubtedly enriched by this able and exhaustive work. . . . the bringing together of so vast a body of evidence on the world's experience in the matter of coinage is an invaluable service towards the elucidation of a problem on which men's minds are much exercised at the present time. . . ."—*The Scotsman.*

"Heine was said to have achieved an almost impossible literary feat when he was witty in German. Mr. Del Mar has completely succeeded in what may be, without doubt, considered yet more difficult in the writing way: he has given us a book having both charm and value upon the subject of money. Charm there indubitably is, as indeed there always will be, when a deep student of the ancient world gives us the result of his studies in the form of ' unassuming expression of knowledge that has been perfectly assimilated,' as Hamerton once said."—*London Senate.*

"As an authority on monetary systems this work deserves to rank high. It is in fact an encyclopædia on the subject, and no one who is making a study of this important matter can afford to be without it."—*New York Herald.*

"Those bewildered by the mass of literature issued on all hands supporting this or that currency scheme cannot do better than obtain Mr. Del Mar's work. We welcome it with peculiar pleasure."—*Bankers' Magazine.*

"A valuable work."—*Hamburg Börsenhalle.*

"After passing through the crucible of Mr. Del Mar's vigorous mind, this work has emerged without bearing any trace of partisan bias. . . . There can be little doubt that it will come to be regarded as a standard authority on the subject. . . . A deeply-interesting book."—*Bombay Gazette.*

"The latest solid work in which the gold and silver question is receiving common-sense treatment."—*Brooklyn Eagle.*

"Mr. Del Mar's reputation as a statistician and as a writer on monetary subjects makes this work a necessity at the present time to every person who wishes to know or wishes to teach the lessons of experience."—*New York World.*

www.ingramcontent.com/pod-product-compliance
Lightning Source LLC
Chambersburg PA
CBHW021810230426
43669CB00008B/696

9 783743 317376